To Marsha and
In friendsh
and affection!

Patrick Kay Bidelman

PARIAHS STAND UP!

PARIAHS STAND UP!
The Founding of the Liberal Feminist Movement in France, 1858-1889

Patrick Kay Bidelman

CONTRIBUTIONS IN WOMEN'S STUDIES, NUMBER 31

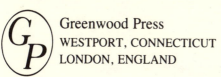

Greenwood Press
WESTPORT, CONNECTICUT
LONDON, ENGLAND

Library of Congress Cataloging in Publication Data

Bidelman, Patrick Kay.
  Pariahs stand up!

  (Contributions in women's studies, ISSN 0147-104X ;
no. 31)
    Bibliography: p.
    Includes index.
    1. Women—France—History—19th century. 2. Men—
France—History—19th century. 3. Feminism—France—
History—19th century. 4. Women—France—Societies and
clubs—History—19th century. 5. Women's rights—France
—History—19th century. 6. Liberalism—France—History
—19th century. 7. Women—Suffrage—France—History
—19th century. I. Title. II. Series: Contributions in
women's studies ; no. 31.
HQ1613.B5   305.4'2'0944   81-4222
ISBN 0-313-23006-4 (lib. bdg.)   AACR2

Library of Congress Catalog Card Number: 81-4222
ISBN: 0-313-23006-4
ISSN: 0147-104X

First published in 1982

Greenwood Press
A division of Congressional Information Service, Inc.
88 Post Road West, Westport, Connecticut 06881

Printed in the United States of America

10 9 8 7 6 5 4 3 2 1

TO MY MOM, PEG

CONTENTS

ACKNOWLEDGMENTS

Although this study bears only my name, it is as much a product of collective effort as of individual effort. Without the social, economic, and political support of many people, I doubt that this study would now be ready for release or possess whatever merit it may have. It is thus with a sense of excitement and joy that I express my gratitude to the many among the many who must necessarily remain unnamed and the few among the many who, although appearing only as names below, have encouraged me to think anew while enabling me to feel a part.

Bettina Aptheker, Donald Baker, George Beech, Corin Bennett, Donald Berthrong, Craig Bidelman, Todd Bidelman, Dick Bizot, Al Castel, Dale Clifford, George Colburn, Les Cohen, Dolores Dawson, Jane Decker, Grace Dienhart, Rachel Fuchs, Joyce Good, Jean Goris, Madame Léautey, Beth Lindquist, John Harrison, Steven Hause, Darlene Hine, Jim Johnson, Nancy Johnson, Elizabeth Jordan, Donald Lammers, Spencer LeGate, Steve Lodle, Bill Marion, Dorothy Mays, Ann Meyering, Michael Miller, Paul Miller, Claire Moses, Pierre Mourier, Tom Noble, Karen Offen, Michele Perrot, Brian Price, Lee Quinby, Carol Richer, Dave Rozelle, Jim Sargent, Ellen Skidmore, Chips Sowerwine, Kathy Sullivan, Richard Sullivan, Doris Swanson, Bill Sweet, Dena Targ, Harry Targ, Solange de Ternay, Jim Terry, Mary Katherine Wainwright, Liz Weston, and Steve Woods.

INTRODUCTION

> Man makes the laws to his advantage and we
> [women] are obliged to bow our heads in silence.
> Enough of resignation. Pariahs of society, stand
> up!
>
> Hubertine Auclert, 1879

North of Paris stands a monument that unwittingly represents the historic subordination of women in France. The Cathedral of Saint Denis towers above a working-class suburb, its twelfth-century Gothic façade casting an awkward shadow over a neighborhood that no longer toils in the name of God. Inside the cathedral, whose innovative design signaled a remarkable advance in uniting height and light, shadows of a different kind linger. Scattered about the interior are the tombs of French kings and queens, princes and princesses, who for over a thousand years had their mortal remains consigned to Saint Denis. Today the tombs are empty; revolutionaries destroyed their royal contents during the Reign of Terror. But the sarcophagi remain, mute witneses to an attitude seemingly as old as man himself. Carved into the stone coffin covers of former kings and princes sit lions, designating the masculine values of courage, power, and dominance. At the feet of queens and princesses lie dogs, symbolizing the feminine virtues of loyalty, humility, and obedience. Thus, in desecrating the bones of tyrants while leaving the sarcophagi largely intact, the New Order portended by the Great Revolution of 1789 joined hands with the Old in sanctioning one of humankind's oldest injustices, the subordination of women to men.

The Great Revolution also evoked one of the Western world's first protests against woman's subordination. Indeed, according to an early twentieth-century German feminist, "the European woman's rights movement was born in France; it is the child of the Revolution of 1789."[1] But, like the outburst of feminism that accompanied the later Revolution of 1848, the woman's rights protest of 1789 proved short lived. Consequently, whereas the legal, political, and socioeconomic position of men as a group improved unevenly but steadily during the nineteenth century, the relative status of women as a group declined. So wide did the sex-role gap become, in fact, that in 1879 Hubertine Auclert, the founder of French suffragism, urged her countrywomen to engage in a campaign of all out resistance. "Man makes the laws to his advantage and we are obliged to bow our heads in silence," she shouted. "Enough of resignation. Pariahs of society, stand up!"[2]

By then, however, Auclert and other French advocates of women's emancipation had behind them more than two decades of literary and organizational activism. Conducted over a long generation that began under the Second French Empire (1825-1870), stretched through the early years of the Third French Republic (1870-1940), and ended with the second French Congress for Women's Rights of 1889, this activism produced a feminist movement in which the question of how to emancipate women from *masculinisme* became inextricably linked to the question of how to emancipate France from monarcho-clericalism.[3] As with their counterparts in the United States, Australasia, and elsewhere in Europe, the founders of the French feminist movement employed the rationale of liberal individualism to demand opportunity reforms aimed at permitting women to compete fairly with men for basic well-being, wealth, and status. Such reforms included equal education, equal access to posts within the professional meritocracy, equal pay for equal work, and equal control over income and property. The founders also demanded moral reforms, such as eliminating the double standard for adultery, abolishing governmental regulation of prostitution, and allowing unwed mothers to file paternity suits. The rationale for these moral reforms lay both in the liberal emphasis on individual accountability, a trait thought by feminists to be singularly absent in too many men, and in the popular belief in women as the repositories of irreproachable virtue.

In the grand struggle against *masculinisme* these two dimensions of reform enabled the founders of the French feminist movement to see themselves as part of the transnational nineteenth-century quest for women's emancipation. Within France itself, however, the proponents of liberal feminism confronted a deep-rooted tradition of monarcho-clericalism which in their view upheld not only women's subordination to men but also the hierarchical subordination of most everyone to a few. Hence, although French feminism remained ideologically attached to liberal principles, its development as a movement involved a highly specific, even revolutionary, adaptation of those principles to a society that had yet to institutionalize liberal republican channels for change.

This adaptation assumed a form that can be called liberal-political feminism. Like the Marxist feminists who have posited a proletarian rising as the essential first step toward women's emancipation, the founders of the French feminist movement also accorded priority to a political precondition. Unlike the Marxists with their precondition of class abolition, though, the founders of the French feminist movement demanded first of all the establishment of a class-based, internally mobile, liberal republic. In their view, no improvement in woman's status could take place until representative government, stripped of all monarchical and clerical trappings, had made it possible for peaceful change to come from below. Once France had shed its feudal past and become an "equal opportunity" society, women could employ their special talents and capabilities to bring about its moral regeneration. As an adaptation of liberal aspirations to a specific configuration of national conditions, therefore, liberal-political feminism envisaged a progressive, two-stage transformation of French society: first, the new political order, a liberal republic open to reform from below; then, as women found scope for expressing their special qualities, a remoralized and revitalized social order.

Both stages of this vision proved problematic, although in the short run it was the political stage more than the social stage that perplexed the movement's founders. Shortly after liberal feminism entered its organizational phase, the Second Empire collapsed during the disastrous Franco-Prussian War of 1870-1871. In its place emerged the Third Republic—in name, at least, the political precondition so crucial to the movement's plans for societal transformation. But rather than embodying the promised land imagined by feminists, the new republic displayed indifference and, occasionally, hostility to demands for women's emancipation. As long as "tyranny" had reigned in the person of Emperor

Napoleon III, this possibility had remained buried beneath a façade of republican unity. Once established, however, the republic responded with great reluctance to feminist demands. Its two major concessions prior to 1889—expansion of educational opportunities for women and legalized divorce—stemmed as much from a desire to mold young people into good republican citizens and to strike a blow at the influence of the Roman Catholic Church as from a willingness to alleviate women's subordination to men. Yet, contrasted to the political alternatives advanced by monarchists, clericals, and Bonapartists, the republic at least enacted some reforms and by its very existence kept alive the hope that women would one day enjoy the full prerogatives of liberal citizenship. Conversely, the liberal feminists feared that, should the republic collapse, then authoritarianism and *masculinisme* would once again combine, ending all prospect for women's emancipation. Where then, feminists had perforce to ask, should they draw the line between criticism and defense of the new republic?

At first, in the wake of the defeat by the Prussians in 1870, the disruption of the Paris Commune of 1871, and the possibility of a successful monarchist resurgence, the republic's precarious position inclined the founders of the feminist movement to favor defense over criticism. But after the political crisis of 16 May 1877 (the *seize mai* crisis), which revealed the strength of republican sentiment, the balance slowly began to shift. Feminists held their first congress the following year and demanded action to end sex discrimination in education, employment, and civil rights. Struck from the agenda, however, was a demand for woman suffrage, which, according to the feminists who opposed it, would have alienated potential republican sympathizers and, if enacted, jeopardized the young republic by delivering countless female votes into the hands of monarchists and clericals.

As the 1880s unfolded, the rift between prosuffrage and antisuffrage feminists split the movement into two antagonistic wings, each of which invoked liberal principles and assessments of the republic's prospects to support its position. The minority of feminists who accorded priority to woman suffrage rallied to Hubertine Auclert and her *politique de l'assaut* (strategy of assault), which held that political rights constituted not only the key to women's emancipation but also the only guarantee that the young republic would ever achieve political viability. An enfranchised womanhood would restore honesty, hard work, and dignity to the nation, the *assautistes* maintained, and put an end to the illiberal rule of the Third Republic's "royalty of sex." The majority of feminists who opposed woman suffrage subscribed to the *politique de la brèche* (strategy of the breach), which accorded priority to obtaining woman's civil emancipation through repeated, piecemeal attacks against the "wall" of masculine prejudice and discrimination, and looked to Maria Deraismes and Léon Richer for leadership. Deraismes and Richer had helped found the French feminist movement at the end of the Second Empire, and in 1878 they cosponsored the first French Congress for Women's Rights. They drifted apart somewhat during the next decade as Deraismes swung around to suffrage while Richer stepped up his attacks against it. But cooperation between them never entirely ceased, and in 1889, amid the festivities accompanying the centennial celebration of the Great Revolution, Deraismes and Richer cohosted the second French Congress for Women's Rights.

The congress of 1889 coincided with a major turning point in the development of liberal feminism. Although skillful managing by Deraismes and Richer guaranteed that the issue of woman suffrage would not mar the proceedings, the momentary reaffirmation of *la brèche* over *l'assaut* bespoke the past more than it addressed the future. Already the splintering that rent the movement in the 1890s had begun, and with Richer's retirement in 1891 and Deraismes's death in 1894 the new leaders of liberal feminism repudiated their predecessors' political priority on the grounds that, as second-generation feminist Jeanne Schmahl put it, "this mixing up of politics and religion with the women's question has been one of the great reasons of the unsuccess of the movement in France."[4] A memory of Deraismes, Richer, and the other feminist pioneers lived on and frequently enough found itself called upon, but this harkening back betrayed as much a desire for symbolic sustenance as a genuine sense of continuity. With the republic no longer so obviously in danger, even the 1889 congress underwent a rapid reinterpretation, becoming less an event toward which the founders struggled for years than an event from which second-generation feminists marked the onset of the struggle.

By then, too, the social aspect of the founders' vision had provoked disquietude within the movement. Suddenly recharged were the paramount issues of constituency and rationale, the issues of with whom and in the name of what to attempt the second-stage task of remoralizing and revitalizing the social order. To the founders, ever mindful of women's collective oppression but ever more wary of threats to the republic, both stages of societal transformation depended less on women as a group than on a constituency of right thinkers—women and men alike imbued with free-thinking, anticlerical, liberal republicanism. Even the founders' contentious exchange over suffrage pivoted on whether the right to vote might spur clerically backward women to right thought. This was a clear guideline, and it helps to explain why Deraismes fought so hard to secure women's admission to Freemasonry, the presumed bastion of right thought, and why, after the traditional lodges balked, she helped just prior to her death to found a "mixed" lodge open equally to both sexes. But this clarity offered scant solace to second-generation feminists who deplored in equal measure the movement's isolation from the mass of "wrong-thinking" women and the movement's heavy dependence on "right-thinking" but otherwise unsympathetic men.

Similarly problematic but much less clear was the founders' rationale, a tension-fused amalgam of equality and equivalence. In the name of equality the founders argued that because women partook of humanity fully as much as men, women too should enjoy the constitutional and legal guarantees embodied in the rights of man, guarantees in the founders' view that had loosed the individual potential of men by freeing them from their hierarchical subordination to the few and that would, if extended to both sexes, loose the individual talents of women as well. In the name of equivalence, the founders contrarily argued that, because women possessed some qualities distinct from and superior to the qualities possessed by men, women too should enjoy the opportunity to impress their unique design onto the social order. At odds with each other, the two rationales also stood at odds with the founders' political and feminist orientations. Politically, for instance, even though women's assumed equivalence could be likened to other forms of self-interest in the pluralist body politic, the sheer magnitude of women as a special interest group radically challenged the liberal assumption that the body social consisted of atomistically separate, individual units. No more than the claims of workers as an economic class, in short, could the claims of women as a sex class find legitimacy within the liberal model of society, a point made abundantly clear by Richer, who in 1889 stressed that he would not demand women's equality "in the name of particular class interests," that instead he would rest his "case, without distinguishing between categories, on the quality of the [individual] human being which encompasses woman as much as man."[5]

Regardless, because the founders, including Richer, nonetheless posed this challenge by asserting that women constituted a group as distinct from men as a group, that the group called woman suffered from an absence of liberty due to its subordination to the group called men, and that women must necessarily secure liberty in order to realize their own potential as well as to regenerate society, the two rationales also interjected considerable ambivalence into the movement's feminist orientation. Occasionally the founders emphasized women's membership in humanity writ large, thus portending an egalitarian social order in which women would assume the status of independent citizens totally unencumbered by any special social-sex role. Much more often, however, the founders stressed women's special role as mother-teachers (*mères éducatrices* or *mères institutrices*), thus designating women as a separate order of beings blessed with "beautiful qualities," such as, according to Deraismes, "sagacity, perseverance, [and] abnegation," and uniquely suited to childrearing.[6] These same "beautiful qualities" would also help to improve the social order outside of the home, the founders maintained, with the result that the rationale of the mother-teacher at times proved effective in winning specific reforms. Yet, however expediently useful in shifting the line that divided the private social world of women from the public political world of men, this rationale implicitly sanctioned the long-standing notion that women and men nevertheless belonged to separate spheres, a notion about which Jenny d'Héricourt's *La Femme affranchie* (*Woman Affranchised* or *The Liberated Woman*) expressed unheeded reservations at the outset of the movement's literary phase in 1860.[7] Hence, in spite of their egalitarian rhetoric and despite their militant challenge of *masculinisme*, the founders of the liberal feminist movement tacitly reinforced the social myth of separate spheres on which women's subordination ideologically rested.

This tacit reinforcement became explicit in the 1890s once the second generation dropped the founders' political priority, thus relaxing the tension that had earlier held the two rationales in an ambivalent balance. Yet, against the long-term disadvantage of reinforcing the notion of separate spheres, the repudiation of the founders' right-thinking politics provided liberal feminists with the important short-term advantage of approaching alternative constituencies. Probes immediately went out, from which developed numerous right-center, center, and left-center feminist groups as well as a short-lived French Federation of Feminist

Societies (Fédération française des sociétés féministes). Concurrently, both the Right and the Left challenged liberal feminism by forming women's groups of their own. Boxed in at the turn of the century by rivals rather than by their predecessors' political rigidity, liberal feminists broke out of their new isolation by joining in 1901 with liberal Protestant moral reformers to found the National Council of French Women (Conseil national des femmes françaises), an affiliate member of the 1888 International Council of Women. In the moral reformers, the liberal feminists found a large, well-organized constituency of women, and by 1914 the National Council had grown from 30-odd groups with 20,000 members to well over 100 groups with 100,000 members. Liberal suffragists meanwhile organized the French Union for Women's Suffrage (Union française pour le suffrage des femmes), which leaped from a few hundred members in 1909 to 14,000 in 1914. By then, too, attuned to the public sentiment that produced 505,972 prosuffrage ballots in an unofficial referendum conducted by *Le Journal* in 1914, no less than fifty departmental, municipal, and *arrondissement* councils had formally endorsed the idea of enfranchising women for local elections.

Although political rights eluded French women until 1944, despite favorable divisions in the Chamber of Deputies in 1919, 1925, 1932, and 1935, and a close defeat in the Senate in 1925, the prewar suffrage support boded well for other reforms as well as for the liberal feminist movement. Aside from the breakthroughs in education and divorce that took place during the movement's formative years and numerous laws to protect working women, which most liberal feminists initially opposed, legislation enhanced women's status in areas ranging from pregnancy-related job security and greater authority within the family to three of the movement's longest-standing objectives: the right of women to witness civil and notarial acts (1897), the right of wives to complete control over their own incomes (1907), and the right of unwed mothers to file paternity suits (1912). The interwar years brought still more reforms as well as a third generation of liberal feminists. A fourth generation then replaced the third, carrying the movement from World War II into the 1970s.

A fifth generation seems unlikely. Not so very long ago, the National Council of French Women, the embodiment of liberal feminism, moved from its long-time headquarters at the Musée Social to the Tour Montparnasse, a steely glass skyscraper whose long, self-satisfied shadows stretch out to Parisians long accustomed to treadling busily, if not complacently, in liberalism. Then in 1980 the National Council vacated the Tour, leaving no forwarding address. Many legal barriers to women's emancipation had fallen during its existence, but many other legal barriers and many more extralegal constraints not only remained but swirled elusively in the separate spheres of a France still gripped tightly by *masculinisme*. In effect, as Zillah Eisenstein has recently suggested, the liberal feminist tradition propounded "a radically important indictment of liberalism and yet an insufficient conception of woman's emancipation."[8] More specifically, according to Suzanne Blaise, a self-described "former poetry teacher, mother and grandmother" and a "militant of the [French] Movement for Women's Liberation (Mouvement de libération des femmes) since 1971," it is only now that French feminism has begun to shift into a "postfeminist" era, building on and at the same time departing from the political "prefeminism" that has endured for nearly two centuries.[9] Yet, whatever the new era may produce, the ongoing struggle for women's emancipation in France must necessarily deal with the liberal feminist tradition and the ambiguous legacy to which its founders contributed.

The account that follows is divided into two interrelated parts. Part I, an interpretive overview, explores in Chapter 1 the conditions and constraints under which French women lived in the nineteenth century and in Chapter 2 the roots and routes from and by which the founders of the movement came to a liberal feminist consciousness. Underlying both of these chapters is the assumption that the constraints against which the founders fought ranged far beyond the moment of their militancy and that at the very least their long generation encountered an even longer century, a century beginning with Rousseau and Napoleon and ending, although in fact it has not yet ended, with Louise Masset twisting into twentieth-century death at Newgate Prison for infanticide. Part II, an analytical narrative, consists of three chapters. The first, Chapter 3, traces the movement's early development from the late years of the Second Empire through the first French Congress for Women's Rights of 1878, focusing in particular on the careers of Maria Deraismes and Léon Richer. Chapter 4 examines the early career of Hubertine Auclert, who jolted the movement by flamboyantly demanding woman suffrage. Chapter 5 details the response of antisuffrage feminists to Auclert, the fragmentation of the movement in the 1880s, and the second French Congress for Women's Rights of 1889. Finally, the Conclusion assesses the founders' contribution to the liberal feminist tradition as well as the ways in which subsequent feminists have dealt with this ambiguous legacy.

TRANSLATIONS AND ABBREVIATIONS

Unless otherwise indicated, all translations from sources cited in French are those of the author. Quotations from works by foreign authors who wrote in English or who had their works translated into English have been taken from and can be identified by the language of the title cited in the notes.

At first mention, the names of French groups appear in English translation with the French in parentheses, for example, the Society for the Amelioration of Woman's Condition and the Demand of Her Rights (La Société pour l'amélioration du sort de la femme et la revendication de ses droits). Thereafter the names appear in a shortened English form, for example, the Amelioration Society.

At first mention, the titles of French publications appear in French with, where appropriate, an English translation in parentheses. Thereafter the title appears only in French.

Three repositories are referred to by their initials in the notes and bibliography: AN for the Archives Nationales, BN for the Bibliothèque Nationale, and BMD for the Bibliothèque Marguerite Durand, all in Paris.

All emphases in quotations are from the original; emphases in the text itself are the author's.

CHRONOLOGY

BEFORE THE FOUNDING: 1789-1858

Great Revolution, 1789-1799

- 1789 Fall of the Bastille (14 July)
  Declaration of the Rights of Man
- 1791 De Gouges's *Declaration of the Rights of Woman*
- 1792 Enactment of divorce by the First Republic (1792-1804)
- 1793 De Gouges's execution during the Reign of Terror (1793-1794)
- 1794 Condorcet's suicide

Napoleonic Era, 1799-1815

- 1804 Napoleonic Code and the establishment of the First Empire (1804-1815)
- 1808 *L'Athénée des dames* outlawed

Restoration, 1815-1830

- 1816 Divorce outlawed (until 1884)

Revolution of 1830 and the July Monarchy, 1830-1848

- 1830s and 1840s   Era of utopian socialist feminism: Niboyet, Tristan, etc.

Revolution of 1848

- 1848 Short-lived outburst of feminism under the Second Republic (1848-1852)
- 1850 Falloux law
- 1851 Deroin's and Roland's imprisonment at Saint-Lazare

Second Empire, 1852-1870

- 1852 Coup by Napoleon III against Second Republic (2 December)

DURING THE FOUNDING: 1858-1889

1858   Proudhon's *La Justice*
      Michelet's *L'Amour*
      Lamber's *Idées anti-proudhoniennes*
1860   D'Héricourt's *La Femme affranchie*
1861   Simon's *L'Ouvrière*
1862   Élisa Lemonnier's professional school for girls
      Daubié received the first *baccalauréat* awarded to a woman
1866   Macé's Education League and the emergence of peace groups
      Daubié's *La Femme pauvre au XIXe siècle*
      Audouard's *Guerre aux hommes*
      André Léo's Society for the Demand of Woman's Rights
      Deraismes's speaking debut
1867   Audouard's petition to French legislature for equal rights
1868   Relaxation of press and assembly restrictions
      Dupanloup's *Alarmes de l'éspiscopate*
      Admission of women to medical schools
1869   Richer's *Le Droit des femmes*
1870   Deraismes's and Richer's Amelioration Society
      Franco-Prussian War (1870-1871)

Third Republic, 1870-1940

1871   Paris Commune
1872   Dumas *fils's Tue-la*
      Deraismes's *Ève contre Monsieur Dumas fils*
1873   Mac-Mahon elected to presidency of Third Republic
      Richer's *Le Divorce*
      Postponement of the first French Women's Rights Congress
1874   Josephine Butler's first trip to Paris on behalf of abolitionism
1875   Deraismes's and Richer's Amelioration Society outlawed
1876   Auclert's Women's Rights Society
1877   *Seize mai* crisis (16 May 1877)
1878   Deraismes's and Richer's first French Congress for Women's Rights
      Auclert's *Le Droit politique des femmes*
1879   Mac-Mahon's resignation
      Beginning of reforms in women's education
      Socialists at Marseilles endorse Auclert's women's rights
      proposal
      First French abolitionist committee
1880   Dumas *fils's Les Femmes qui tuent et les femmes qui votent*
      Auclert's tax strike

1881 Auclert's *La Citoyenne*
     Auclert's census boycott
     Deraismes's vice-presidency of first anticlerical congress
     Deraismes's *Le Républicain de Seine-et-Oise*
1882 Deraismes's brief admission to the Masonic lodge at Pecq
     Auclert's 1,000-signature woman suffrage petition
     Richer's French League for Women's Rights
1883 Richer's *Le Code des femmes*
1884 Divorce reenacted
1885 Suffragist "shadow campaign"
1886 Richer's informal alliance with Pastor Fallot's League for the Improvement of Public Morality
1888 Auclert's marriage and departure for Algeria
     Vincent's Feminist Society "Equality"
1889 Deraismes's and Richer's second French Congress for Women's Rights
     Official Congress of Feminine Works and Institutions

AFTER THE FOUNDING: 1889-1914

1890 First annual Versailles conference
1891 Deraismes's *Ève dans l'humanité*
     Richer's retirement
     Guéroult's *Du rôle de la femme dans notre rénovation sociale*
1892 Third Congress for Women's Rights
     Potonié-Pierre's French Federation of Feminist Societies
1893 Deraismes's "mixed" Masonic lodge *Le Droit humain*
     Schmahl's Advance Messenger
1894 Deraismes's death
     Witness Law
     Musée social
1895 Royer's "Testament"
1896 Maugeret's *Le Féminisme chrétien*
     Fourth French Congress for Women's Rights
1897 Durand's *La Fronde*
1898 The *commerçante* vote
1899 Saumoneau's Feminist Socialist Group
1900 Masset's execution at Newgate Prison (9 January)
     Three women's congresses: Catholic, philanthropic, feminist
     "Seat law"
     Women's admission to French bar
1901 National Council of French Women

1904   Catholic women's first Joan of Arc Congress
1905   Joran's *Le Mensonge du féminisme*
1907   Women's right to vote for *conseils de prud' hommes*
       Wives' right to control own income
1908   Eligibility for *conseils de prud' hommes*
       Auclert's and Pelletier's violent demonstrations on behalf of suffrage
1909   Schmahl's French Union for Women's Suffrage
1911   Richer's death
1912   Paternity law
1914   Auclert's death
       Outbreak of World War I

CONSTRAINTS AND CONSCIOUSNESS: AN OVERVIEW

Part I

CONDITIONS AND CONSTRAINTS: WOMEN AND FEMINISTS UNDER *MASCULINISME*

CHAPTER

1

What we ask of education is not that girls should think, but that they should believe.

Napoleon I

Oh! Monsieur, I haven't any children; I have only daughters.

A Breton farmer

The founders of the liberal feminist movement in France confronted a bleak situation. A pervasive *masculinisme*, underpinned by centuries of monarcho-clerical influence, had arisen to ensnare women in a complex web of legal, socioeconomic, and ideological constraints. In many areas of vital importance to the bourgeoisie, such as politics, higher education, and the professions, women found themselves completely excluded. Where exclusion did not exist, as in the home and in some branches of industry, women found themselves in a subordinate position, subject to the control of men. Exclusion and subordination affected women in a variety of ways, depending in small part on personal differences and in large part on class position. But to the founders of the liberal feminist movement, whose ideological perspective precluded any serious criticism of individualism, the varied effects meant little. In their view, all women not only suffered in common but would continue to suffer until France cast off the prescriptive hierarchy that gave all men dominion over all women and a few men dominion over both. Until that time came, exclaimed Olympe Audouard in the course of declaring a *Guerre aux hommes* (*War on Men*) in 1866, women would remain "neither free nor happy in France."[1]

In their struggle to bring freedom and, by implication, happiness to French women, the founders of the French feminist movement sought to remove from women as a group the constraints that prevented individual women of wealth or talent from taking advantage of the opportunities available to men. Among these constraints, whose strictures became increasingly apparent as the gap widened between the public role assumed by the bourgeoisie as a class and the private role assigned to women as a sex, the most important to France's pioneer feminists were those which had received legal, religious, economic, and educational expression. More subtle but no less influential than these, however, were other expressions of *masculinisme*, the effects of which ranged from "immobilizing" and "deflecting" women in general to "stigmatizing" feminists in particular. Whether overt or subtle, each constraint interacted with the others in support of a single overriding objective: to encourage all women to see domestic life as the only legitimate way to experience their assumed unique and eternal feminine nature. In thus presuming a fundamental link between social role and innate characteristics, *masculinisme* resembled nothing so much as a form of racism in which the presence of female genitalia prefigured a common, unindividualized social destiny for half a population.

THE LAW

The principal statutory constraint on which *masculinisme* rested was the Napoleonic Code. Officially promulgated in 1804, the Code locked women into a "paper Bastille" of legal restrictions.[2] Legend holds that in a museum somewhere is one of Napoleon's chairs, marred by rips and gashes, which the emperor disfigured in a rage when faced by critics who felt the Code treated women too harshly.[3] Whatever the truth of the story, the Code certainly reflected Napoleon's low opinion of women. Female greatness, he asserted in a famous tilt with Madame de Staël, has only one dimension—fecundity. The idea that "genius has no sex" is absurd, he exclaimed; nothing is "more detestable than the woman who thinks." "What we ask of education," Napoleon wrote, "is not that girls should think, but that they should believe."[4] The Code also reflected Napoleon's imperial approach to the organization of society. Every institution required a leader of unquestioned authority. He had provided this leadership for France as a whole; now men, as husbands and fathers, would provide it for the family. Woman belongs to man, Napoleon maintained, as the tree and its fruit belong to the gardener.[5]

In transfiguring the family into a miniature empire, the Code stipulated that, in return for protection, a wife owed obedience to her husband.[6] In the absence of his consent, she could not have a separate residence, obtain a hunting license, or attend a university. He had total control over family property, and without his permission she could neither give, sell, mortgage, nor buy. A wife could not work if her husband forbade it, and whatever she earned in wages or royalties belonged to him. While he lived she had no legal authority over her children, and, regardless of marital status, the Code declared women incompetent to witness certificates of marriage, birth, or death. Children under twenty-one needed parental consent to leave home or marry, but if the parents disagreed the father's consent alone sufficed. Upon a simple request to the courts, a father could imprison his children for various lengths of time without the mother's permission.[7] A father could also assign guardianship to a third party in the event that he predeceased his wife.

A wife's adultery could bring imprisonment of from three months to two years or more; a husband's went unpunished unless he defiled the marriage bed, which, even then, would cost him only a fine of 100 to 2,000 francs. All children born in wedlock belonged to the husband, and he could file a maternity suit if he wished, but no child born out of wedlock or the unwed mother herself could file a paternity suit. Article 324 of the Penal Code sanctioned acquittal for husbands who killed their wives caught in *flagrant délit*. Foreign women who married Frenchmen acquired instant French citizenship; French women who wed aliens lost theirs. In general, announced Article 1124 of the Civil Code, unfit persons included minors, exconvicts, and married women.

In depicting married women as unfit while attributing unquestioned authority to husbands and men in general, the Code also established the legal and "spiritual" premises for a series of judicial and administrative decisions that further lowered the status of women in the course of the nineteenth century. Unless the statutes clearly read in woman's favor, administrators and judges invariably ruled against her. The denial of political rights to women came about in this way, as did the denial of other rights. Married women lost postal privacy, for example, when the courts ruled that in light of "the domestic authority conferred upon him by law" a husband could open his spouse's mail "to seek the proof of an offense against his honor or some grave lapses to the obligations of marriage of which his wife might be guilty."[8] Women lost the right to hunt in 1883 when a Corsican appeals court upheld the conviction of a widow who, in taking up the sport on her doctor's advice, had violated a decree to the contrary by a local mayor. The widow in question drew a fine of sixteen francs and had her gun confiscated.[9]

Single women, divorcees, and widows fared somewhat better under the Code, but in turn they had to confront a hostile society without male "protection." Divorce, available from 1792 to 1816 and again after 1884, therefore amounted to a mixed blessing. Women without husbands could make use of the provisions guaranteeing equal inheritance for offspring, but beyond this the Code did not go. Women enjoyed neither the right to vote nor the right to hold office, which most males lacked as well under the empire of Napoleon I, but men at least had received compensation—the right to domestic dominion.

In only one respect did the Code prove beneficial to women—as a focus of attack for subsequent French feminists. By giving legal articulation to *masculinisme*, it provided liberal reformers with clear-cut objectives and convenient labels. In the name of equality before the law, for example, feminists mounted numerous campaigns in opposition to Article 340, which prohibited paternity suits, and at the end of the century Jeanne Schmahl's Advance Messenger (Avant courrière, 1893–1907) spent over a decade to achieve just two goals: woman's right to serve as legal witness to public and private acts, and a wife's right to dispose of her income without her husband's authorization.[10] But nearly a century had elapsed by then, and Schmahl could work through a movement that had already acquired a generation of experience. The feminists who built that movement were not so fortunate.

THE CHURCH

The Roman Catholic Church constituted another pillar of *masculinisme*. Centuries, as well as opposing views on matters spiritual and temporal, separated Napoleon from Saint Paul. Yet on at least one issue the two men transcended the intervening years and their ideological differences. Both agreed that order required woman's subordination to

man. "The husband is the head of the wife," wrote Paul, "even as Christ
is the head of the Church."[11] In the eyes of France's liberal feminists,
therefore, the Roman Catholic Church not only embodied two millennia
of Pauline *masculinisme*, but it also replicated in spiritual guise the
organizational, ideological, and socioeconomic orientation of Napoleon's
masculinist imperium.

The organization of the Church appalled the founders of the French
feminist movement on two counts. First, as a potential model for political
organization, the Church, in resembling the hierarchical and authoritarian regimes of Napoleon I and Napoleon III, represented the antithesis of
what feminists considered to be the political precondition for women's
emancipation: a liberal republic open to reform from below. Second, in
its policy toward personnel and personal behavior, the Church reserved
its most influential posts to men while forbidding to all of its officials
what feminists and many nonfeminists alike considered to be one of
humanity's unique capabilities—procreation.

In ideology the Church abetted *masculinisme* by emphasizing woman's "natural" domesticity and preaching the importance of confining
women to family life. "Women belong to the family, and not to political
society," wrote Louis de Bonald (1753–1840), a leading spokesman for
traditional, authoritarian Catholicism, "and nature has made them for
domestic cares, and not for public functions." To women fell "almost
exclusively" the task of raising children, he explained, which required
that "all, in their education, ought to be directed toward domestic utility,
as all, in the education of young men, ought to be directed toward public
utility." Nature had admirably distinguished between the sexes, he
continued: "It gives to the one, from the most tender age, the taste for
political and even religious *action*, the taste for horses, for arms, for
religious ceremonies; it gives to the other the taste for sedentary and
domestic works, for household cares, for *dolls*."[12]

Naturally, too, Bonald cautioned, women required a special upbringing. For instance, "The powerful recourse to emulation, so effective in
rearing men, because it awakens in them the most generous passions,
ought to be employed with extreme care in the education of women,
among whom it may arouse vanity, the source of their misfortunes, their
faults, their ridicules." Similarly, because intuition predominated in the
"weaker sex," "we should, in the education of young women, speak to
their heart as much as to their reason. . . because women have received in

sentiment their portion of reason.''[13] Sentiment permitted women to intuit many things without learning them, Bonald added, but men must nonetheless retain unquestioned authority within the family. ''The paternal power is *independent* from other members of the family,'' he emphasized, ''because, if it were dependent, it would not be *power*. It is therefore absolute or *definitive*; because, if it were not, it would be *dependent*, and there would be a power greater than it, that of disobedience.''[14] In short, nature had destined women to play the role of subordinate intermediaries:

> The mother, placed by nature between the father and the children, between the *power* and the *subject*, and by the means or the *ministry* through which is accomplished productive and preservative action, the mother receives from the one in order to transmit to the other, obeys the former in order to have authority over the latter. . . . Thus, if she partakes of man through reason, she partakes of the child, as all physiologists have observed, through the delicateness of her organs, the sensitivity of her nerves, the changeableness of her moods, and we could call her a man-child [*homme-enfant*].[15]

Although numerous individuals throughout the nineteenth century echoed Bonald's view of women as subordinate intermediaries, the latent collective power of Catholic women did not materialize until French feminists succeeded in founding the women's rights movement. Then, reacting against secularization in general and feminism in particular, large-scale, Church-endorsed women's groups fought back by raising the specter of national disintegration. ''In effect,'' wrote Anne Delalande in 1902 in one of the first issues of the right-wing, Catholic ''feminist'' *Le Devoir des femmes françaises* (*The Duty of French Women*), ''if Freemasonry, with its infernal cunning, succeeds in circumventing women, the triumph will be definitive, the French soul and its ideal will quickly die, France will be no more.''[16] Although anxious that paternal abuses within the family should stop, Gabrielle de Villepin similarly warned that legal equality of the sexes was neither possible nor desirable. The Church had granted spiritual equality to spouses, de Villepin argued, but the temporal equality demanded by feminists would violate women's vocation and lead inevitably ''to collisions from which only divorce and free love would result.'' ''The obedience of the wife,'' de Villepin concluded, ''is but an homage rendered to the force that protects her.''[17]

The right-wing Patriotic League of French Women (La Ligue patriotique des françaises), which eleven years after its founding in 1902 had 500,000 members divided into 1,042 committees, also depicted feminism as a threat to France, a "terror polluted by a horde of foreigners, of Freemasons."[18] In itself "liberalism is the reign of the half-measure, of the half-conviction, of the half-virtue," wrote canon Jean Lagardère in 1913, the founder of the 1903 Catholic *La Femme contemporaine* (*The Contemporary Woman*), it "is the triumph of mediocrity," the slippery slope down which people slide little by little toward "the lowest level of morality."[19] Liberal feminism likewise portended nothing worthwhile, reported a French correspondent to the International Service of Catholic Women's Leagues (Service internationale des ligues catholiques féminines), because the ideas of the International Council of Women were anti-Catholic, the president of the National Council of French Women was a Protestant, and one of the latter's most visible personalities was a freethinker. "It would be imprudent to take part in these congresses," the reporter summed up, "where Catholic women will always be in a minority and where they will confront questions that violate our principles."[20] By then, however, Catholic women had already held their first national congress in 1900, and in 1904 they initiated a series of annual Joan of Arc Conferences, thereby symbolically coopting the most famous of France's historic women, whose name, announced the antifeminist National League of Joan of Arc (Ligue nationale de Jeanne d'Arc), stood for "national resurrection and deliverance."[21]

Finally, alongside the persuasive implications of its organization and ideology, the Church also played an overtly antiliberal socioeconomic role in French society. It persistently opposed the separation of church and state and the reintroduction of divorce, for instance, and in education, which all feminists saw as vital to women's emancipation, it held a near monopoly over girls' schools throughout the third quarter of the century as a result of the Falloux law of 1850. Within the economy, moreover, the Church not only supported protective legislation for women workers, against which liberal feminists consistently fought, but also undercut women's wages through convent workshops, provided supervisors for "sweated labor," and on at least one occasion, in 1869, permitted the sisters of Saint Vincent de Paul to send a hundred women to replace strikers at Paris's Magasins du Louvre.[22]

THE ECONOMY

Convent workshops comprised only one small part of a generalized pattern of economic constraints. Most working-class women confronted discrimination on a vast scale in employment opportunities, pay rates, and work conditions, whereas those who did not work found themselves in a state of dependence, unable to ensure by their own efforts the welfare of either themselves or their children. To the liberals who founded the French feminist movement, however, the plight of working-class women assumed only symptomatic importance. Much less jeopardized financially by the collapse of the traditional family economy and imbued in any case with liberal capitalist ideology, the movement's founders accorded primary importance to overcoming the prejudice of domesticism and the discriminatory effects of bourgeois professionalism.[23]

In raw numbers, excluding agricultural occupations, working women totaled over 2.7 million in 1866 and approached 4.5 million on the eve of World War I.[24] The female agricultural work force expanded at approximately the same rate, growing from slightly over 1.8 million in 1866 to more than 3.2 million in 1911. As a percentage of the entire female population, which exceeded the male total throughout the life of the Third Republic, women workers, agricultural and nonagricultural alike, amounted to slightly less than 25 percent in 1866 and nearly 40 percent in 1911.

Among women workers the young and the single predominated. In 1906, for example, over 43 percent of the women aged eighteen and nineteen held nonagricultural jobs, as did more than one-third of the women aged twenty to thirty-nine. Only 20 percent of the nonagricultural female work force was married in that year. Domestic service, clothing, and textiles attracted the majority of women workers, but a significant shift in occupational opportunities occurred during the first two generations of the Third Republic. Better education for women, restrictive labor legislation, and expansion of the tertiary sector brought about a marked increase in the number of women clerks and secretaries and a marked decrease in female domestics. Specifically, between 1866 and 1906, the number of women in domestic service declined from 1,050,735 to 781,200, whereas the number of women employed by banks and commercial establishments rose from 328,000 to 771,000.

Accompanying the shift in women's occupational roles, which reflected the growth of bourgeois economic institutions, came a profound change in attitudes toward woman's place in the work force. Fast disappearing by mid-century were opinions like that of Alexandre Dumas *père*, who years before had warned that woman "would lose all her femininity by stepping foot into an office."[25] With the disappearance of the male secretarial monopoly went as well the context in which sense could be made of a scurrilous anecdote about Madame de Persigny, a purportedly promiscuous representative of the Second Empire's titled elite. While her husband served as ambassador to England, according to a popular tale, Madame de Persigny's taste for embassy clerks led the amused to ask: "Mme. de Persigny is lost; it is impossible to find her." "Well, have you looked carefully under all the furniture? The tables, the buffets, and the secretaries?"[26]

Yet, even as many women gradually gained access to lower-ranking positions formerly reserved to men, most women workers earned far less than their male counterparts. After several decades of relative progress in which wages rose for both sexes, for example, a study by the Office du travail revealed that in the period 1891–1893 women's pay averaged only 3 francs per day in the Department of the Seine and 2.10 in the rest of the country, compared with 6.15 and 3.90, respectively, for men. Only in the cutting and polishing of precious gems did a precious few women earn an excellent and equal wage. At this job both sexes received 9.25 francs per day in the Department of the Seine, whereas outside the Seine women outearned men by 5.15 to 4.63 francs per day.[27] Not included in the study were the depressed wages of female "cottage" workers, who numbered nearly a million at the turn of the century and who earned only 5 to 20 centimes per hour.

The effect of such low wages on working women, 80 percent of whom were not married, received a graphic airing in 1861. In that year, Jules Simon calculated in his study of *L'Ouvrière* (*The Working Woman*) that, barring sickness and unemployment, a woman of the working class could earn about 500 francs per year. Once rent, fuel, clothing, and other essentials had been purchased, though, the average working woman would have only 60 centimes per day for food—"enough not to die of hunger."[28] Female wage rates at the time ranged from 1.30 francs per day in the provinces to 2.10 in Paris; in teaching, the one profession then open to women, more than 4,000 schoolmistresses earned under 400 francs per year. Five years later, Julie Daubié pointed to the link between subsistence wages and prostitution in her critical study of *La Femme pauvre au*

XIXe siècle (*The Poor Woman of the 19th Century*). "The inadequate pay of the urban working woman sometimes drives her, even during a period of industrial prosperity, into meeting her budget by selling her body," Daubié argued; "this is called the fifth quarter of the day [and] during periods of unemployment, this kind of right to work fills the entire day." [29] Understandably, as Elisabeth Weston has recently maintained in the course of estimating the number of Parisian prostitutes at a fairly constant 20,000 during the last half of the nineteenth century, "the rejection of bourgeois ideology about the family, marriage, and sexual morality by prostitutes and other members of the working class was not so much a rejection of ideas as a rejection of a way of life that was sometimes antithetical to survival." [30]

In addition to the low pay, hours were long, twelve to fifteen per day in most cases, and industrial conditions miserable. Seasonal work rivaled the business cycle as a cause of unemployment. Seamstresses labored fourteen hours per day, for example, but only from March to May and September to January. Competition from convent workshops depressed wages for women in general, and the single girls who worked in them, subject to the rule of silence and unable to leave the premises unless accompanied by a nun, seldom made more than 150 francs per year. Factory laws, which liberal feminists opposed in principle, proved inadequate to protect women because they were difficult to enforce and, when enforced, they restricted women's employment opportunities and earnings. [31] Working women also derived little benefit from two of the Third Republic's major reforms in the 1880s: education and unionization. Inadequacy replaced unavailability in women's education in that decade, but, except for a possible correlation between fundamental language skills and secretarial work, the public girls' schools paid scant attention to job or career training. Trade unions won legal recognition in 1884, but for a variety of reasons women workers remained largely outside the movement. In 1900, for instance, women accounted for only 6.3 percent of union membership even though they represented 34.5 percent of the work force.

Although the founders of the French feminist movement reacted to the plight of working women by always demanding equal pay for equal work and by sometimes encouraging unionization, they reacted even more heatedly to the prejudice of domesticism, the notion that women, especially bourgeois women, should not work outside the home. This widespread, deeply held notion rested on three assumptions. The first and most basic assumption, the mytho-biological, depicted women as so naturally and uniquely destined for family life that they should never be permitted to infringe on the male responsibility of making contact with the world outside the home. The second assumption, the legalistic, relied on the premise that, inasmuch as married women were minors in the eyes of the law, they should never be granted the male prerogative of choosing among various occupations. The final assumption, which reflected the capitalist institutionalization of unequal life chances, held that women should not hold jobs because their presence in the work force depressed male wages and contributed to male unemployment.

Individuals representing various schools of thought reiterated one or another of these assumptions with mind-affecting regularity. Liberal republicans like the historian Jules Michelet and the journalist Émile de Girardin, both of whom displayed compassion for working women, sided with positivist Auguste Comte and mutualist Pierre-Joseph Proudhon in asserting that woman's true emancipation depended on freeing her from labor outside the home.[32] Conservatives and Catholics followed the lead of Albert de Mun and Frédéric Le Play who, in demanding factory laws to protect working women, subscribed to the ideal expressed in Pope Leo XIII's *Rerum Novarum* (1891): "Women, again, are not suited for certain occupations; a woman is by nature fitted for home work, and it is that which is best adapted at once to preserve her modesty and to promote the good bringing up of children and the well-being of the family."[33]

At least as provocative to the founders of the French feminist movement as the widespread belief in domesticism was its economic counterpart, the exclusion of women from the bourgeois professions.[34] This exclusion accompanied the increase in size and importance of the middle class, many of whose male professionals closed ranks by instituting formal training, rigorous standards, entry requirements, and state licensing for careers in such fields as medicine, law, and education. Bourgeois women, the married among whom already lacked legal control over their own incomes and property, thus found themselves cut off from the economic roles that signaled success for the male members of their class. In the name of liberal individualism, therefore, France's pioneer feminists demanded the removal of all restrictions that prevented women from competing for the incomes and statuses associated with their class position. These demands in turn gave rise to a strident call for "equal opportunity'' of preparation, a call that embodied the liberal view that competitive success depended on quality education.

EDUCATION

Discriminatory education represented a fourth and, for most liberal feminists, decisive constraint of *masculinisme*. Since the Middle Ages, individuals of various political persuasions had complained about the unavailability and inadequacy of girls' schools, but, as progress through better education became a national myth in the post-1789 era, such complaints assumed a more frantic character. ''Just as today the majority of the members of our society admit that economic growth is the essential objective of the collectivity,'' wrote a French scholar in 1968, ''so in the second half of the nineteenth century they believed in education.''[35]

Statistics reveal something of the significance of the problem in the nineteenth century. Illiteracy affected approximately 40 to 45 percent of the adult population of France in 1851, with women exceeding the men in this group by a ratio of three to two. Two decades later, the overall rate of illiteracy had dropped to 31 percent, but the sex ratio remained constant. In 1872, for instance, only 65 percent of French brides could write their names, compared with 80 percent of French bridegrooms and military recruits. By the time of the second French Congress for Women's Rights in 1889, illiterate brides totaled 15 percent, but male illiteracy had fallen to 9 percent for bridegrooms and 11 percent for recruits. Only in the next decade did the illiteracy ratio begin to vary in women's favor. It stood at six to five for brides to bridegrooms in 1900, and in 1901 illiterate women outnumbered their male counterparts by only 15,914 to 15,269.[36]

This gradual but uneven improvement in literacy during the course of the nineteenth century stemmed in part from public policy. François Guizot, a conservative Protestant who served first as minister of education and then as premier under the July Monarchy (1830–1848), created a nationwide system of primary schools for boys in 1833, and the 1850 Falloux law, although greatly enhancing the role of Catholicism in French education, extended the system to girls. However, neither reform made provision for training women teachers, and, out of deference to the parental prerogative, attendance remained voluntary. Many communities in fact refused to establish girls' schools, and where they did come into existence the Church exercised a predominant influence. In the 1860s

Napoleon III's minister of education, Victor Duruy, attempted to expand as well as reform primary education for both sexes and to create a system of secondary schools for girls. To offset popular fears, Duruy stipulated that only women could teach needlework and that mothers who had doubts about the program could accompany their daughters to class. He also attempted to eliminate religious instruction from state schools, which challenged the clergy's virtual monopoly over girls education and aroused the wrath of the Church. Bishop Dupanloup of Orleans condemned the experiment as immoral, and *L'Osservatore romano*, the official papal journal, threatened Napoleon III with the loss of Catholic electoral support unless he dismissed Duruy. The emperor refused to bow to the threat, and the empress retaliated by enrolling her two nieces in the Sorbonne, but the scale of Duruy's reforms suffered.[37] In 1877, the French Ministry of Education reported that "most lay schools have only one class and employ only one person."[38]

All that began to change two years later, and by the end of the 1880s women had much wider access to education. A law in 1879 required every department to establish a normal school for women primary teachers. Teachers for these schools would receive their education at a special normal school in Fontenay-aux-Roses, founded by decree in 1880. Legislation creating a system of secondary schools for girls passed in the same year, and in 1881 another law located a normal school for women secondary instructors at Sèvres. In the meantime, a bill making primary education free for both sexes passed the Chamber and Senate, and in 1882 elementary instruction became compulsory. Each of these measures reduced the role of the clergy in French education. State scholarships assisted girls to attend secondary schools, which numbered sixteen *lycées* and nineteen *collèges* by 1886–1887. Female teachers also received the vote and eligibility for the Superior Council of Public Education, the chief policy-making committee in the system.[39]

As women acquired greater access to education in the 1880s, the problem of inadequacy came to the fore. In fact, the growth in the number of girls' schools accentuated other deficiencies long associated with women's education in France. Among these deficiencies, failure to grant equal degrees to women ranked as one of the most important. Success through education in general, as well as access to higher education in particular, required a *baccalauréat*. Julie Daubié, who earned a "*bac*" through the University of Lyons in the 1860s, opened the examinations to women, and by 1881 eighty-eight women had earned the degree.[40] Despite Daubié's example, though, the girls' secondary schools that came into existence in the 1880s could award only an inferior "end of secondary studies certificate" (*diplôme de fin d'études secondaires*). Women remained eligible to take the *bac* examinations, but passage demanded a thorough knowledge of Greek and Latin, two subjects absent from the curriculum of the new girls' schools. Not until 1924 did girls' schools offer the same course of study and grant the same degrees as boys' schools.

Another deficiency stemmed from the failure to integrate the new girls' schools into the preexisting system of higher education. Even with the *bac*, women found themselves excluded from most professional training at the university level. Blanket application of an 1802 decree stipulating that "no woman can be lodged or received in the interior of *Lycées* and *Collèges*" had given way to a more liberal attitude in the course of the nineteenth century, but access to specialized programs remained difficult for women.[41] Only in medicine, which Duruy opened to women in 1868, had a breakthrough occurred prior to the founding of the Third Republic. Additional breakthroughs came after 1870, but these brought women face to face with yet another obstacle: the resistance of the various all-male professional associations. A long struggle over internships ensued after Duruy permitted women to attend medical school, for example, and in law, which became available to women at the university level in 1884, the all-male bar refused to admit women until 1900.[42]

The apparent contradiction between the significant expansion of education for French women in the second half of the nineteenth century and its general inadequacy reflected the interplay of social-sexual stereotypes and political exigencies. The stereotypes that infused the educational system emphasized woman's special nature and special destiny. A school inspector at Bordeaux, for instance, linked the two in his 1870 report:

In the girls' schools as well as the boys', the education offers all the guarantees of morality which families could desire. The schools are run by teachers, both nuns and lay-women, who bring to their task, from the standpoint of moral education the most attentive care. Both nuns and laity receive with deference and docility the instructions which are given them by the administration. As I always say, devotion and a sense of duty, generally stronger in persons of this sex, help to compensate for their weakness in other respects.[43]

A report for Paris in the same year reiterated that "the women teachers, both lay and religious render perhaps even greater services [than the men teachers]. Their knowledge and teaching ability leave something to be desired, but they are morally superior, more tactful, and more devoted."[44]

The political exigencies that contributed to the inadequacy of women's education grew out of the new regime's fear that women represented a threat to the republic and that, unless weaned from their superstitious attachment to Church and monarchy, they would undermine French democracy. "Women must belong to Science or to the Church," argued Jules Ferry, one of the chief architects of the expansion, who served as minister of public education in 1879 and as premier twice in the early 1880s. Better education for girls would not only stabilize the family but would also impede the machinations of the Old Regime, that "edifice of regrets, beliefs, and institutions which does not accept modern democracy," Ferry maintained: "In this combat [between liberalism and monarcho-clericalism], woman cannot be neutral; optimists...imagine that she does not take part in the battle, but they do not perceive the secret and persistent support that she brings to that group which is on the run and which we want to drive out forever."[45] Yet, educators must take care lest women lose their femininity, Ferry warned; a woman's knowledge of science need not exceed the requirements of domestic life, nor was it necessary, despite protests from France's liberal feminists, for her to receive professional training.

THE SUBTLETIES OF *MASCULINISME*

In addition to the legal, religious, economic, and educational constraints of *masculinisme*, women found their lives circumscribed by subtle but equally inhibiting attitudes, customs, influences, assumptions, and practices. Operating singly here and in combination there, these socializing agents comprised so intricate a web that at best their overlapping effects can only be apprehended through speculatively combining several such subtleties into themes. Two of the themes examined below attempt to pull together factors that affected women in general: "immobilization" and "deflection." The third theme, "stigmatization," deals with one of the major obstacles confronted by feminists, the widespread belief that feminism constituted an aberrant phenomenon.

French women found themselves immobilized in a number of ways. In respect to spatial movement, the law forbade a married woman to live where she pleased or to leave the country without her husband's consent. No woman, regardless of marital status, could attend political rallies, according to a little enforced but potentially threatening law; nor, according to a custom that constrained women journalists, could women sit in the press gallery of the Chamber of Deputies.[46] Women could appear in public, although their numbers might be regulated in times of crisis, but in doing so they risked humiliation at the hands of the morals police (*police des moeurs*), the enforcement agency charged with supervising the laws regulating prostitution. They also encountered inconvenience in traveling about Paris, where municipal restrooms for men far outnumbered those for women. Women could buy train tickets, but few felt bold enough to travel by rail unaccompanied.[47]

In respect to personal mobility, the law forbade women to wear pants, and popular styles dictated dresses of encumbering length, hats of unwieldy size, and corsets of constrictive and, as a contemporary minority maintained, unhealthy design.[48] Moreover, if the notion of personal mobility can encompass the intimate, the atmosphere of sexual repression in which women lived impeded not only heterosexual and certainly homosexual expression but self-exploration as well. Taboos against the "hideous vice" of masturbation weighed heavily on both sexes, but for women addicted to this form of "hysteria" an 1864 surgical report recommended excising the clitoris and suturing the vaginal orifice.[49] At about the same time, a doctor warned that in girls' schools "onanism must also be the object of vigorous concern; in this case, it is especially necessary to intervene with moral advice, and to exercise the most active surveillance upon students suspected of this vice, not allowing them to put their hands under the table and never leaving them completely alone."[50]

Given these and other restrictions on women's mobility, it is perhaps understandable that exceptional women sometimes adopted male attire, despite the law, or employed male pseudonyms, as in the case of George Sand (Aurore Dupin), Daniel Stern (Marie d'Agoûlt), and André Léo (Léodile Champseix, née Bréa). It is also perhaps understandable that they sometimes tried to create distance between themselves and other women, echoing a version of Madame de Staël's disdainful comment: "I am glad I am not a man, for if I were I would have to marry a woman."[51]

The theme of deflection relates to the influences that guided females into playing feminine social-sex roles and males into masculine social-sex roles, rather than both into more multifaceted androgynous sex-roles. Legal, religious, economic, and educational constraints figured in this deflection, but other equally powerful influences contributed to the feminine–masculine bifurcation of French society. Symbols, or the lack thereof, touch this theme, from "La Belle France," an expression for the French collectivity with "feminine" overtones of moral superiority and honor in need of protection, to statues, street names, and words. To the extent that statues render homage to people deserving of public acclaim, for instance, only a very few of Paris's hundreds commemorate women. At the end of World War II, according to Simone de Beauvoir, there were only ten, three of which honored Joan of Arc. What would have been an eleventh, a late nineteenth-century memorial to feminist Maria Deraismes in the Square des Épinettes, had disappeared by the time of the enumeration.[52] Deraismes, who died in 1894, also had a street named after her, a "first" that elicited a mixed reaction from one of her contemporaries: "The quarter is not beautiful, the street is not pretty; in fact it is a dead end, but at last the principle is secured."[53] The slight recognition accorded to women through statuary and street names showed up as well in French biographical dictionaries, which, as estimated by Jean Larnac in 1929, alloted 92 percent of their entries to men.[54]

Words also contributed to the deflective process. By mid-century, the word *sex* no longer served as a synonym for females, as it had in the seventeenth century when Father Joseph, Cardinal Richelieu's confessor, remarked: "I do not care to see the sex, except shut up and curtained from sight, like so many mysteries not to be regarded save with a kind of horror," or as late as the early nineteenth century when Bonald wrote of "persons of sex" (*personnes du sexe*).[55] Several generations later, Gustave Flaubert recalled the past association in his satiric *Dictionary of Accepted Ideas* by beginning the definition of "woman" with "Member of the sex," but such usage had died out for good during the Restoration (1815–1830), at which time as well the word *femme* supplanted the word *dame* as the general designation for females.[56] However, even without the close association of social role to genitals suggested by the word *sex*, the languages of France supplied hundreds of derogatory expressions for women. Of the approximately 1,500 *Words and Descriptive Terms for 'Woman' and 'Girl' in French and Provençal and Border*

Dialects studied by George C. S. Adams, for example, the vast majority are negative. Only two of the ninety-six words beginning with the letter *t* are neutral, each designating "young girl"; the rest provide a variety of ways to "label" women in their socially assigned sex-roles. Depending on the offense, the "t's" supply ninety-four ways to call women "dirty," "careless," "light," "ragged," "untidy," "babbling," "disheveled," "insipid," "dowdy," "indolent," "wicked," "shrewish," "surly," "slovenly," "licentious," or "hairbrained."[57]

The many words that facilitated the correction of "negative" feminine behavior only complemented numerous "positive" sources of deflection, three of the most important of which were female consumerism, the feminine press, and children's stories. Female consumerism assumed massive proportions during the second half of the nineteenth century as municipal entrepreneurs, particularly Parisians, attempted to tie the provincial market into a new capitalist phenomenon—the department store. The great names in this field acquired their start under the Second Empire—Au Bon Marché in 1852, Le Louvre in 1855, Le Printemps and La Samaritaine in 1865—and their success stemmed in large part from tapping female purchasing power. Middle- and lower-class women could not afford exclusive shops or follow the example of "fashionable women" who changed their clothes six or seven times per day, but they could and would participate to some degree in the arid but everchanging business of style if two requirements were met. Prices had to come down, and the identification of adornment and self, so characteristic of aristocratic circles, had to filter into the ranks of the other classes. The great department stores met the first requirement by stocking less expensive, ready-made goods, and they tackled the identification requirement through advertisements and other promotional gimmicks. Financially the dual assault on women proved spectacularly successful. Aristide Boucicaut, for example, who founded Au Bon Marché in 1852 and who "focused his attention primarily on women, encouraging them to browse and spend money freely," increased his gross tenfold to 5 million francs per year by 1860.[58] Against this background of success with the female walk-in clientele, which made the department store one of the few places where women could move about freely, the prospect of capturing the female provincial market through highly illustrated sales brochures emerged as the next logical step. Indeed, according to historian Maurice Bardèche, the general improvement in women's education in the nineteenth century resulted from two factors: expanded primary instruction and mail-order catalogs sent into the provinces by the large department stores. The new woman addicted to conspicuous consumption that these stores created he aptly called the "client type" (*cliente-type*).[59]

The feminine press, journals about and directed to women, antedated the consumerist phenomenon by over two centuries. The first of this genre in France, *La Muse historique* (*The Historical Muse*), appeared in 1650. By 1800 34 journals had come out, two-thirds during the opening decade of the Revolution. Another 71 appeared by 1845, bringing the total, which included several feminist sheets, to slightly over 100 for the period 1650–1845. Since that time and as a correlate of improved female literacy, an additional 200 to 300 titles have seen the light of day. Many of these publications proved to be short lived. Of the 71 that appeared during the first half of the nineteenth century, for example, 49 folded within two years, and only 16 survived five years or more. But the few that did survive, especially those that lasted into or originated under the Third Republic, tended to acquire enormous readerships. *Le Moniteur de la mode* (The Fashion Monitor) of 1843–1919 had 200,000 subscribers in 1890, for instance, and *Le Petit Écho de la mode* (*The Small Echo of Fashion*), which still exists, leaped from a run of 5,000 copies in 1879, the year of its founding, to 175,000 in 1884 and to 210,000 in 1893. Newspapers and magazines of a feminist persuasion, in contrast, had runs of only a few thousand until 9 December 1897, when, during the movement's second generation, *La Fronde* printed 200,000 copies of its first edition.[60]

In content, the feminine press abetted deflection by promoting frivolity and emphasizing woman's domestic role. The identification of adornment and self that characterized the business boom in women's goods found an ally in many of the journals of this genre. Dozens of publications, some of which depended in whole or in part on industry subsidies, promoted the latest in "*mode*," "*vogue*," "*fashion*," "*toilette*," "*nouveauté*," and "*bon ton*."[61] Like the short-lived *Musée des modes parisiennes* (*Museum of Parisian Fashions*) of 1843, they inundated their readers with "designs of elegant fashions, sketches of ridiculous fashions, discussions of the latest feminine products, the clamor of the salons."[62] The emphasis on woman's domestic role appeared in titles such as *La Mère de famille* (*The Family Mother*), *La Femme chez elle* (*Woman at Home*), and *Le Bon Ange du foyer* (*The Good Angel of the*

Hearth). The first of the Roman Catholic journals of this type, *La Mère de famille* (1833–1836), contributed to a trend that grew in strength throughout the nineteenth century. This trend effected a juncture between moral imperatives, the "duties" of woman as wife and mother, and the social entity that dominated bourgeois society, the conjugal family. The juncture in turn amounted to a veritable cult, regardless of religious overtones, as sociologist Évelyne Sullerot observed.

The woman is very forcefully integrated into [the family] by tradition and her role is narrowly dictated to her; while at the same time her moral sense is molded in such a way that she tends to think that she is the one who deliberately chooses, desires, freely accepts that place, that role, that destiny.[63]

The third deflective influence, children's stories, arose out of a combination of factors whose precise formula is as difficult to determine as the impact of the stories themselves. Heated exchanges over breast-feeding and swaddling at the end of the eighteenth century engendered a voluminous, wide-ranging inquiry into childrearing in the nineteenth century. Women found themselves doubly burdened as a result, saddled simultaneously with heavier child-related responsibilities and fewer outlets for their own creativity. For some, especially those who wrote for the feminine press, children's stories represented the best and, to a certain extent, the only available way to reconcile the contradictions of the double burden. Consequently, dozens of literary-minded, child-oriented, middle-aged, Christian women sought relief from the double burden by devoting their talents to the service of youth. The women who wrote for *Le Journal des femmes* (*The Women's Journal*) of 1832–1838, for example, authored enough stories to fill fifteen pages of bibliography. With reprintings, which numbered thirty in forty years for Alida de Savignac's *Les Petits Garçons d'après nature*, the quantity of paper consumed by such works alone proved enormous. One might ask along with Évelyne Sullerot:

But what influence have they had, *really*, these women story tellers who soothed the infancy of so many children and inculcated into them this moral current, these clichés of vocabulary, these religious impulses, this subdued Manicheanism and this view of society, their place and their duties that mark a mentality, a sensibility, even when the adult does not retain a very clear memory of them![64]

The final theme, feminism as an aberrant phenomenon, concerns the emergence of the idea that women's emancipation represented an illegitimate social objective, and that feminists, as proponents of this objective, deserved a full measure of contempt and ridicule.[65] Rather than a product of determined, organized opposition, the "stigma of illegitimacy" that opponents of women's emancipation attached to feminism represented the cumulative effect of a wide variety of general impressions and selectively interpreted incidents. Rare were those like Théodore Joran, who devoted a considerable portion of his journalistic career to combatting the "lie of feminism," and even then Joran found it unnecessary to go beyond literary assault. Institutionalized *masculinisme* could usually supply whatever additional support the antifeminist cause might need. Joran's 1905 work on *Le Mensonge du féminisme* (*The Lie of Feminism*) won the acclaim of the French Academy, for example, and his 1913 attack on *Le Suffrage des femmes* (*Women's Suffrage*) earned him the budget prize of the Academy of Moral and Political Sciences.[66] Through works like Joran's, *masculinisme* acquired new, more up-to-date reinforcement, and, as a corollary, feminists found themselves singled out for specific, derogatory treatment. On a collective scale antifeminism assumed a significance inversely related to either the constancy of its purveyors or the strength of the feminist movement.

The stigma of illegitimacy drew its operative force in part from a plethora of "guilts by association." At the deductive level, feminists could hardly avoid the popular assumptions that denigrated women in general. These ran a metaphysical gamut of special natures and special roles, each of which tended to undermine feminist credibility. Women were only large children in the eyes of Jean-Jacques Rousseau, for example; to others they were even less.[67] "Oh! Monsieur," responded a Breton farmer to an inquiry by Ernest Legouvé, "I haven't any children; I have only daughters."[68] For those who admitted women's potential for postinfantile development, there existed other negative assumptions. Many believed along with priest Félicité de Lamennais that women lacked the ability to think: "I have never met a woman capable of following an argument for half a quarter-hour."[69] Or, if women's minds proved sound, they lacked moral integrity: "Madame, remember this," adjured police prefect Lacour to an English opponent of the official regulation of prostitution, "that women continually injure *honest* men, but no man ever injures an honest woman."[70]

On an inductive level, feminists found themselves associated with a multitude of individual women who had transgressed the standards of *masculinisme*. These too ran a gamut, the whole of French history. Sometimes, as with Marie Antoinette, the individual might be referred to by name. At other times, the reference was less precise. Was the *philosophe* Antoine-Léonard Thomas thinking of Catherine de Medici and her role in the Saint Bartholomew Day's Massacre of 1572, for instance, when he wrote that women "lack that calm strength that knows how to stop: all that is moderate torments them"?[71] Occasionally the individuals had only a collective identity. The Goncourt brothers, for example, who considered Rousseau to be a great liberator of women, employed the phrase "pillow government" to characterize what they saw as the debilitating influence of a few women on the Second Empire's ruling elite; and a great many French citizens under the Third Republic attributed the destruction during the Paris Commune of 1871 to another small group of women, the *pétroleuses* (women arsonists).[72] Myth mingled with reality in these attributions, but the effect remained: feminists suffered from having to contend simultaneously with particular assumptions about women in general and with the generalized "sins" of their various "sisters" in particular.

The stigma drew additional force from attacks on specific actions and practices of women. Some of these attacks bore directly on feminist endeavors. In his *Alarmes de l'épiscopat justifiées par les faits* (*The Episcopate's Alarms Vindicated by the Facts*) of 1868, for example, Bishop Dupanloup warned against the proliferation of professional schools for women, for which Élisa Lemonnier had founded the prototype in 1862. After a lengthy tirade against positivism, pantheism, materialism, atheism, and Darwinism, Dupanloup announced the "truth" that "we are confronted by a profound and vast enterprise of impiety directed against the faith of young French women. . . . And it is clear that if such a system of education spreads and prevails for the girls of our country, it would not take two generations, it would take only one to make of France a nation of the ungodly and a people such as have never been seen under the sun."[73]

Other attacks focused on activities pursued by feminists and nonfeminists alike. Jules Barbey d'Aurevilly, for instance, seized on women's literary works to assert that men alone had the capacity to engage in abstract thought. "Speak to [woman] neither of deduction nor reason," Barbey d'Aurevilly urged, "she will obey nothing other than blind unreflective impulses."[74] The slightest acquaintance with female publications would reveal their sex-determined inferiority: "Study their works. . . . At the tenth line, and without knowing whose they are, you are forewarned, you smell woman! *Odor di femina.*" The blue-stockings (*les bas bleus*), as Barbey d'Aurevilly called them, resurrecting a derisive label of English origin, had forsaken their principal function: reproduction of the species. They had attempted to become men, but "male faculties are as radically lacking in them as the organ of Hercules to Venus de Milo."[75]

A fourth and final way in which the stigma garnered force stemmed from the belief that "uppity" women had attempted to disrupt the natural, albeit revolutionary, evolution of French society. The National Assembly in 1850 subscribed to this belief and nearly succeeded in depriving women of their one and only political right, the right to petition the legislature.[76] Women's participation in the utopian socialist movements of the 1830s also aroused hostility because, as a turn-of-the-century feminist put it, those movements amounted to nothing more than "an enormous orgy where giants endowed with the appetite of ogres gorged themselves on monstrous feasts and innumerable loves."[77] But, above all, the Great Revolution of 1789 served as the principal source for this belief.

Within *philosophe* circles preceding the events of 1789, Jean-Jacques Rousseau, who emerged as the foremost antifeminist spokesman, perceived women as depraved beings whose primary duty in life consisted of constant service to the sex they had "originally" wronged. "All education of women should be relative to men," he ruled: "To please them, to be useful to them, to be loved and honored by them, to counsel them, to console them, to render their lives agreeable and sweet; these are the duties of women at all times."[78]

In contrast, the Marquis de Condorcet articulated a more advanced position, urging equal education and the right to vote for women, and during the Revolution's initial phase his stand seemed to prevail.[79] Women contributed significantly to the course of events, at first through spontaneous actions like the march on Versailles in October 1789, then through organized endeavors, such as clubs, vigilance committees, pamphlets, and manifestos. But, as euphoria gave way to fear, the Revolution moved leftward and a reaction set in against women. Condorcet's suicide in 1794 symbolized the shift in attitude, and the same Reign of Terror that hounded him to death quickly proceeded to close the women's clubs and to arrest their more prominent members. A few women received death sentences, including Olympe de Gouges who had written a *Déclaration des droits de la femme et de la citoyenne* (*Declaration of the Rights of Woman and the Woman Citizen*) in 1791 and had petitioned the National Convention for the right to act as defense counsel to Louis XVI.[80]

As important as the individual fate of these women, however, was the attitude displayed by their persecutors. To the Jacobin Chaumette, an expriest, militant women were "degraded beings who wish to avoid and violate the laws of nature." "Since when," he asked, "is it permitted to women to abjure their sex and to make themselves men?"[81] Despite women's virtues, pronounced Amar, "it is nonetheless true that they cannot apply themselves to work, to fill the jobs or the occupations to which men are destined."[82] Like Chaumette, Amar belonged to the Jacobin faction, and his views reflected those of his more illustrious colleagues, Marat and Robespierre. But the Jacobins were not the only ones to espouse this Rousseauvian interpretation of women. Hébert, although executed by the Jacobins, subscribed to it, and the Thermidorians who overthrew Robespierre ordered women to remain in their domiciles under pain of arrest should more than five assemble together in public.[83] The regime created by the Thermidorians withstood, in turn, a challenge by a man of like mind. "French citizens," proclaimed Babeuf, leader of the Society of Equals, "you are under the regime of c. . . The Pompadours, the Dubarrys, the Marie-Antoinettes live again, they are the ones who govern you, to whom you owe a great part of the calamities that assail you and the deplorable retrogression that kills your revolution."[84] Three years after Babeuf's execution, Napoleon assumed control of France. In nurturing what the Revolution begot, Napoleon confirmed the idea of woman "as an inferior race that an undefined and quasi-divine curse rendered irretrievable."[85] Thus, in addition to the innumerable institutional and social constraints that impeded their efforts, feminists found themselves excluded from the principles and at odds with the work of their nation's revolutionary heritage. "The fourteenth of July is not a national celebration," suffragist Auclert typically exclaimed, "it is the apotheosis of masculinity."[86]

THE FAMILY

The various constraints of *masculinisme* had a specific and immediate objective, namely, to direct women into family life. There, held the proponents of *masculinisme*, women would find what familialists in the next century called "fulfillment"—the satisfaction of accomplishing tasks uniquely suited to the female disposition. There, too, women would find a haven from the corrupting influences of society as well as "protection" from their own mental and physical flaws. "Women belong to the family," Bonald had written in 1802; at the end of the century, during an 1891 debate on labor legislation for women, Count Lemercier drew cheers from Left and Right alike for the same thought:

Ah? do not forget that it is woman who makes the family, and the more you leave her to her domestic hearth, the more you leave her in her own milieu, the more you assure the peace and the prosperity of the family.

Now, the peace of the family is the peace of society.[87]

However, the type of family toward which *masculinisme* and capitalism compelled women in the nineteenth century exhibited a number of new and startling characteristics. How and why these developed is a matter of some controversy, but the end product has received apt description in the imaginative work of Philippe Ariès.[88] By the nineteenth century, according to Ariès, a new concept of family had begun to carry the day:

This powerful concept was formed around the conjugal family, that of parents and children. This concept is closely linked to that of childhood. It has less and less to do with problems such as the honor of a line, the integrity of an inheritance, or the age and permanence of a name: it springs from the unique relationship between the parents and their children. . . . What counted most of all was the emotion aroused by the child, the living image of his parents.[89]

In several respects, particularly in its historical evolution and in its grip on nineteenth-century French society, the new concept reflected the aspirations of the middle class. In that sense at least the new concept can be described as "bourgeois," and, although material need prevented many of the French from putting the new concept into practice and the widespread utilization of child and female labor in the early stages of industrialization contradicted the ideal, this concept of the family increasingly pervaded the whole of French society. "Starting in the eighteenth century," Ariès observed, "it spread to all classes and imposed itself tyrannically on people's consciousness."[90]

The emergence and institutionalization of the new family concept had an enormous impact on nineteenth-century French women. As family life more and more became the only legitimate sphere for women's lives, women found themselves harnessed to an institution whose general contours bore little resemblance to earlier family types. Gone were the days of the "big house" where friends, clients, relatives, and protégés streamed in and out at all hours of the day. Gone too were the "general purpose" rooms where people slept, danced, worked, and ate without aid of timetables, especially for meals. In their place emerged the café, the office, and the "modern" home with its dining room, drawing room, bedrooms, and so forth. Within and without, the home had become specialized, no longer serving as the locus for the larger social dynamic. Everywhere as the new pattern of home and family spread, wrote Ariès, "it reinforced private life at the expense of neighborly relationships, friendships, and traditional contacts."[91] "One is tempted," Ariès reflected, "to conclude that sociability and the concept of the family were incompatible, could develop only at each other's expense."[92] Women, especially women of the middle class, as "homemakers" par excellence, thus found themselves "privatized," prohibited not only from meaningful involvement in public affairs but physically removed from proximity to them as well.[93]

In addition to its insulating effect on women, the new-style household fostered other changes of consequence. Where finances permitted, for example, women found themselves simultaneously confined to the home and cut off from the kind of productive labor that generated exchange value. This condition not only left women in a state of dependency vis-à-vis the men in their lives but laid the base for relegating women's market influence to consumption. Furthermore, through its practice of spatial segregation, the bourgeois family accentuated class divisions. Physical distance began to take the place of moral distance, from which Ariès adduced:

It was all as if a rigid, polymorphous social body had broken up and had been replaced by a host of little societies, the families, and by a few massive groups, the classes. . . . The old society concentrated the maximum number of ways of life into the minimum of space. . . . The new society, on the contrary, provided each way of life with a confined space. . . . Each person had to resemble a conventional model, an ideal type, and never depart from it under pain of excommunication.

The concept of family, the concept of class, and perhaps elsewhere the concept of race, appear as manifestations of the same intolerance toward variety, the same insistence on uniformity.[94]

Although the general contours of the new family pattern raised obstacles of critical importance to feminists, particularly with respect to issues of class and the "creeping isolation" that left women divided and scattered, these broad effects represented only half the problem. The other half stemmed from transformations within the internal structure of the family. Each of the family's primary components underwent a process of redefinition similar to that of the family unit itself. New subconceptions of fatherhood, childhood, and motherhood emerged as the new-style family developed. As a result, women found their "legitimate" sphere of life doubly narrowed, first by being confined to the home when possible and second, by playing there a limited, although not necessarily unpleasant, role.

Of the three subconcepts, fatherhood proved the most ambivalent as well as the most vulnerable to feminist criticism in the nineteenth century. But this vulnerability derived less from the new subconcept than from the traditional legal and institutional prerogatives that fathers exercised over wives and children, prerogatives whose origin lay in the world of Old Regime patriarchy and the masculinist ideology of men like Napoleon I, Louis de Bonald, Joseph de Maistre, and Frédéric Le Play. Untrammeled paternalism in the form of an absolute right to possess and to dispose of family matters constituted the essence of this view. "Our most fatal error," wrote Le Play, "is to disorganize by State encroachments the father's authority in the family, the most natural and the most fruitful of autonomies, that which conserves the social bond, in repressing original corruption, in raising young generations in respect and in obedience."[95] Under the new family concept, in contrast, the significance attached to possession declined in favor of a new prime ideal, affection, "the most important trait of the modern family."[96] But at mid-point in the nineteenth century, this trait, already a century in the forming, exerted only a leavening influence on the older ideal. Although a few of the worst patriarchal abuses gave way, notably primogeniture, the emergent ideal of fatherhood preserved its reactionary character by simply adding a dose of familial sentiment to the considerable prerogatives that remained.

Compared with the new subconcept of fatherhood, which amounted to little more than sentimental patriarchy, the subconcepts of childhood and motherhood represented drastic departures from the past. The modern idea of childhood, unknown in the Middle Ages, developed in the course of the sixteenth and seventeenth centuries, Ariès observed, and "as attitudes towards the child changed, so did the family itself." Indeed, by the end of the seventeenth century, the child had become "an indispensable element of everyday life, and his parents worried about his education, his career, his future." During the eighteenth and nineteenth centuries, "this return of children to the home" gathered additional momentum. Formal education eclipsed apprenticeship as "it was recognized that the child was not ready for life, and that he had to be subjected to a special treatment, a sort of quarantine, before he was allowed to join adults." Within the family, which increasingly cut itself off from the world, all the energy of the group focused on "helping the children to rise in the world, individually and without collective ambition." Children, as a result, found themselves subjected to special dress codes, special vocabularies, special hygienic regimens, and so forth, with the effect that "family and school together removed the child from adult society."[97] Once removed, children became dependent as never before on their immediate families, which, given the privatization of family life and the outside "responsibilities" of fathers, meant dependency on their mothers.

The link between the new subconcept of childhood and the new subconcept of motherhood can hardly be overemphasized. Without the counterweight of large-scale social reforms, mothers, or mother surrogates, could not avoid the consequences of increasingly dependent children in increasingly isolated and nuclearized households. Nor could the young girls in such households avoid the counterdependency that compelled them toward a similar destiny, that made them as "little mothers" to little brothers the unwitting agents of *masculinisme*.[98] As long as men occupied themselves with activities outside the home and "sociability" remained on the decline, women had of necessity to assume individual responsibility for the daily care of their children. Sometimes, even, this necessity contained a high level of voluntarism, as with the many noblewomen who in reaction to the Revolution of 1789 "consciously adopted domesticity for moral reasons, for the good of their souls, but also for political reasons—for the good of France and in particular, for the good of their class.[99] Regardless of its causal significance, though, necessity had little to do with the force of the new notion of motherhood. Its strength lay, instead, in a series of assumptions about women and their motherly instincts, assumptions so laudatory and eventually so popular that necessity seemed to reflect virtue. The woman who failed to live up to these assumptions might be called a ''dragon woman'' (*femme-dragon*). But the virtuous, child-centered woman would be called a ''child woman'' (*femme-enfant*), or, as in the late eighteenth and nineteenth centuries, a mother-teacher (*mère-éducatrice*).[100]

The ideal of the mother-teacher called on women to instill a sense of duty and religiosity in their offspring, to instruct them in elementary subjects, and to supervise until marriage the upbringing of daughters. Popular handbooks depicted the mother-teacher as the ''universal agent of humanity's regeneration'' and urged women to be ''serious and dutiful, modest and prudent, disciplined, sensitive and loving.''[101] Moreover, the mother-teacher's responsibility involved not only coping with her offspring's extended childhood but asserting as well a new attitude toward birth itself. No longer would she experience, as in the seventeenth century, ''a sense of alienation from the whole reproductive process that reduced [her] to a mere instrument of destiny.''[102] Instead, she would experience that ''modern invention,'' maternal love. Through the new attitude toward birth and the proper exercise of her educative responsibilities, the mother-teacher would, as the new subconcept held, share a kind of purity with her children. Loss of purity could result from too much contact with affairs outside the home; however, if women remained true to their ''destiny'' by fulfilling their duties as wives and mothers, they (and the schools) would carry out society's most precious charge, the forming of the next generation.

CONCLUSION

In reviewing the policies of the Great Revolution's National Convention (1792–1795), Évelyne Sullerot asked what the Convention's reputation would be today had it treated Jews as it treated women. However, the scope of the question might easily be broadened to include the whole of the French experience since 1792. ''Racism begins when the definition of the excluded individual conjures up an allusion to his *nature*,'' Sullerot explained:

Consequently, all the individuals who partake of that *nature* which carries within it the inferiority will be assimilated to a group, even though certain of the individuals may be intelligent and others stupid, certain honest and others cheats, certain strong and others weak. Therein is the essence of racism.[103]

Therein as well was the essence of *masculinisme*. Beneath the fanfare of revolution and counterrevolution, which lent an aura of profound change to developments in nineteenth-century France, the status of women inexorably declined. Repeatedly the centuries-old mechanism of "male racism" and the politics of the moment went hand in hand. Even in the home, the one sphere where woman's supposed "nature" entailed serious responsibilities, men exercised the final say-so on all matters of importance. Legalists defended this situation on the grounds that woman's subordination had nothing to do with sex but stemmed instead from the need to preserve "public order" and to "maintain the unity and integrity of the family." But, as the National Council of French Women reported in 1912, there existed "a certain number of laws which affect woman and which one can hardly explain without resort to that idea, no doubt primitive, of the inferiority of the feminine sex to the masculine sex."[104] Rather than in pragmatism, such laws had their roots in what Françoise d'Eaubonne called *phallocratisme*.[105]

As a statement of *masculinisme*, therefore, the significance of the Napoleonic Code was as much symbol as substance. The other constraints, particularly the ideological ones that twisted themselves around the minds and hearts of women, carried at least as much weight. They were the ones that provided the sociopsychological base from which the law and the other institutional fetters seemed rightly and naturally to flow. Thus, in their confrontation with *masculinisme*, the founders of the liberal feminist movement in France found themselves locked in battle with a way of life so ordinary as to defy awareness and so complete as to inhibit protest. In the form that it assumed at mid-point in the nineteenth century, *masculinisme* amounted to nothing less than a totalitarianism of the commonplace.

CONSCIOUSNESS AND CONTRADICTIONS: ROOTS AND ROUTES OF FEMINIST AWARENESS

CHAPTER

2

Victim of the prejudiced who still oppose the intellectual improvement of woman, I have labored all my life without reward to enlighten a blind humanity that has only raised obstacles to the development of my philosophical work, closing schools, [university] chairs, and laboratories to me. All that I know I have seized through determined struggle and I have had to forget all that had been taught to me in order to learn anew for myself.

I shall carry with me into the tomb useful truths that others will have to discover again. Because I have had the misfortune to be born a woman, I have lacked all means of expressing, expanding, and defending my thoughts, and I have done only the smallest part of what I could have done. I shall die cursing human stupidity and deploring having been born into an epoch of intellectual decadence, into an aging world gripped by a senile dementia, that under the pretext of art, turning its back on reason, is ready once again to return to backwardness and to abandon itself to a new era of morbid mysticism that will entail its retrogression and social dissolution.

Clémence Royer, "Testament," 1895 (BMD)

Pressed from the one side by the institutional constraints of *masculinisme* and from the other side by the overriding myth of women's general inferiority but domestic superiority, most nineteenth-century French women found themselves subtly wedged into a narrow niche of bondage and illusion. Over them men collectively exercised a classic suzerainty, a form of rule in which, as Sheila Rowbotham put it, ''a dominant group is secure when it can convince the oppressed that they enjoy their actual powerlessness and give them instead a fantasy of power.''[1] In reaction to this form of dominion, the founders of the liberal feminist movement in France sought first to dispel the illusion of woman's ''natural'' subordination and then to replace the ''fantasy of power'' with substantive power. To effect either objective, however, the founders had themselves to acquire an awareness of woman's subjection under *masculinisme*. While statements like Clémence Royer's above reflect such an awareness, they in turn provoke the question of how the founders themselves came to a consciousness that was liberal and feminist at one and the same time.

Although the answer to this question remains fundamentally obscured by the profoundly subjective nature of the process, the founders of the liberal feminist movement nonetheless gave frequent expression to the kind of conceptual and normative sensibility commonly called consciousness. They, like their contemporary and twentieth-century counterparts generally, underwent an experience of ''reality transformation'' that led them to identify women conceptually as a group distinct from men and normatively to judge the disparity between the two groups as injurious to women. In effect, as Joan Cassell has suggested, they ''switched worlds'' through a revolutionary ''process of resocialization, where the previous structure of reality is dismantled and meanings are radically reassigned.'' What had been thought of as ''natural'' became historical. What had been felt as personal became political. Slowly or rapidly, partially or wholly, they redefined self and society, assuming new identities, biographies, beliefs, and behaviors. But above all they assumed in consciousness a new commitment, the struggle for women's emancipation.[2]

In manifesting this commitment, the founders of the liberal feminist movement displayed an outlook that fused two experientially inseparable but analytically distinguishable elements. One element can be called the ''roots'' of consciousness; the other, the ''routes'' to consciousness. By ''roots'' is meant the direct and vicarious experiences that jolted the founders into a reality resonant with the literal and metaphorical screams of women; by ''routes,'' the interpretive paths that enabled the founders to explain to themselves the anguish and the injustice of their new reality. Neither element can be known except as it found tangible expression in the writings and actions of the people who had already committed themselves to women's emancipation. Nor can the dynamic between the elements be precisely delineated, because "root" experiences seemingly fostered further interpretation, and, conversely, "route" explanations seemingly evoked additional reality.

Yet, however elusive the interaction between the two elements, the founders of the liberal feminist movement displayed a fusion of the two sufficient to set themselves off as unique within French society. In general, aside from the gulf that immediately separated the founders from the indifferent, this fusion marked the movement as a singular phenomenon in contrast to three configurations of more or less determined opposition. One configuration opposed both feminism and liberalism, another rejected liberalism but accepted feminism, and a third objected to feminism but endorsed liberalism. Against the configuration that opposed both, the founders struggled without confusion. In relation to the other two configurations, the founders confronted the problem not only of how to move nonliberal feminists to liberalism and nonfeminist liberals to feminism but also how to spur those who partook somewhat of each to become more active in both.

Because such problems emerged only after the founders had come to a consciousness, however, the question remains of what indeed caused the "reality transformation" that led some nineteenth-century women and men to create the liberal feminist movement in France. What in effect jolted them into a new reality, and along what interpretive paths did they travel in search of explanations? The "roots" of this consciousness can be found in various manifestations of the rights and righteousness of man, one flagrant example of which sparked the revival of literary feminism in the late 1850s. The "routes" to this consciousness can likewise be found in variety, particularly in the influence of utopian socialism, liberal republicanism, reformism, and womanism and feminism. Overarching both, moreover, loomed an historic convergence of woman's new image as mother-teacher with the everyday conditions in which women lived, a convergence that, especially among bourgeois women, narrowed the gap in which women in times past had generally found space and time for themselves.

THE RIGHTS AND RIGHTEOUSNESS OF MAN

The contemporary world of men presented a disturbing picture to the founders of the liberal feminist movement in France. Everywhere in the

West men seemed alive to the possibility of freeing themselves from ancient forms of oppression. But, although women usually helped to translate such possibilities into reality, the men once freed invariably refused to relinquish the age-old oppression of *masculinisme*. Rather, consistent with Évelyne Sullerot's observation that "as civilization asserts and refines itself, the gap between the relative status of men and women widens," the extension of the rights of man to ever greater numbers of men not only seemed to benefit men much more than women but also seemed to evoke from men a disdain toward women akin to righteousness.[3]

Varied were the developments that marked the widening gap. Whereas the "romantic woman cult" kept "women so perfectly colonized they policed one another,"[4] for example, nationalist movements in the eighteenth and nineteenth centuries wrested independence from foreign political domination for Americans, Brazilians, Germans, Italians, and a host of other peoples in Europe and the Western hemisphere. In the sixteen years from 1848 to 1864, serfs gained legal freedom in Austria and Russia, and slaves won manumission in the United States. Jews had obtained equality in France during the Revolution of 1789, and, although their progress remained spotty, other Jewish nationals, notably in England, also secured liberty in the course of the nineteenth century.

Varied, too, were the reactions of the founders of the liberal feminist movement in France to these developments. Liberal antipathy toward Russian autocracy impeded forceful comparisons of serfs with women, and, after the Franco–Prussian War (1870–1871), patriotism provoked feminist complaints about naturalized Prussian males enjoying the rights of French citizens rather than a comparison of Germany's recently attained independence with women's continuing dependence.[5] Where emancipation occurred within a liberal context removed from French national interests, however, a sharp "root" contrast emerged. The pioneer suffragist Auclert, for instance, cited Jewish women as "veritable modern Judiths" who alone among the victims of *masculinisme* saw that sex equality entailed human equality without distinctions of race or cult. She also drew on Abraham Lincoln's Emancipation Proclamation to contrast the advance of American blacks to the unrelieved bondage of French women and to call for nonviolent "John Browns" to arise in the name of women's emancipation.[6] Indeed, another French feminist later wrote in reference to the long struggle of American women to end slavery, "Our personal opinion is that they would have done better (we speak not at all in the name of egoism, but only in the name of justice and morality!) to claim the emancipation of women before demanding the liberty of African and American slaves."[7]

Within France itself, men retained their reactionary gains over women despite the Second Empire's authoritarian debasement of earlier revolutionary advances. Universal manhood suffrage became a façade for one-man rule under Napoleon III, but women had not even the illusion of the vote. Press and assembly laws crippled freedom of expression, but on women alone between 1852 and 1881 fell prohibitions against newspaper directorships and political commentary.[8] Twice, for example, Olympe Audouard fell afoul of the gap in rights. In the mid-1860s imperial officials forbade her to publish a political review, *La Revue cosmopolite* (*The Cosmopolitan Review*), on the grounds that women lacked full citizenship, and in 1870 they broke up a speech by her on divorce, even though her text rested in part on the emperor's *Idées napoléoniennes* (*Napoleonic Ideas*).[9] No feminist could claim that men stood equal to each other under the Second Empire, but even their truncated liberties cast them well above women, "the French pariahs."[10]

Yet, if one "root" of consciousness lay in the widening gap between women as a group and men as a group, the other "root" lay in the absence of scarcely any gap at all between women and abusive male righteousness. No matter the number, at least a few women suffered the harsher penalties for adultery or the absence of any legal recourse in a system of justice that condoned "crimes of passion." Some, too, had husbands who fully exploited their financial rights, a legal prerogative that, for instance, cost Juliette Lamber the initial proceeds from her pioneer feminist work of 1858 on the *Idées anti-proudhoniennes sur l'amour, la femme, et le mariage* (*Anti-Proudhonian Ideas on Love, Woman, and Marriage*).[11] More no doubt suffered from the prohibition against paternity suits, and the morals police roved the thoroughfares, hassling at random any woman who conformed even slightly to its profile of the unregistered prostitute.[12] More yet probably bore witness to the folk adage that "women and omelets are never beaten enough,"[13] and what but terror could have stalked the woman who knew that popular myth prescribed sexual intercourse with a virgin as the cure for syphilitic men?[14] It must have been with less surprise than disgust that Arria Ly, a second-generation feminist who had taken up residence in a tiny Southern village, encountered a municipal councilor who responded to her complaints of harassments by exposing himself.[15]

However typical Ly's experience, the founders of the movement hardly needed to undergo male abuse personally. They had only to read the daily press. There, amid advertisements for perfumes and parasols, they could vicariously experience an endless account of abortions, infanticides, abductions, suicides, maimings, and murders.[16] The blood of victimized women ran thick across the pages, and when life itself was not at stake, jealousy-provoked acid disfigurements burned their way into headlines and column fillers. Although the founders of liberal feminism disagreed with the politics of anarchist-feminist Louise Michel, who scoffed at them for expecting legislators, even women legislators, to prevent the prisons and the sidewalks from continuing to vomit legions of unfortunates one onto another,[17] they nonetheless partook of her anguish. On the French Senate rested the blame for every spouse who had violently died due to the absence of divorce and, abetted by the Chamber of Deputies, for every child who had perished due to the absence of women's right to file a paternity suit, Auclert charged: "How much longer will the sewers choke with tiny cadavers; how much longer will betrayed women kill themselves or mutilate their seducers; how much longer will spouses who loathe one another execute each other, before the legislators take action?"[18]

As the 1800s spun out, French feminists collected three thousand signatures on a petition begging Queen Victoria to spare the life of Louise Masset, a teacher condemned to death for infanticide. Rather than attempting to sift through the specifics of Masset's case, they argued instead that the crime itself bore brutal witness to the reality of women's subordination, to the extenuating circumstance of pervasive *masculinisme*. On 9 January 1900, the appeal for mercy having failed, Masset's execution at Newgate Prison ushered in another century.[19]

More so than from occasional confrontations with unwarranted death, however, the feminist redefinition of reality sprung from struggles for a decent life against obstacles as endless as they seemed senseless. Among these obstacles, the ones connected with education proved especially—and illustratively—provocative. When Julie Daubié broke the *baccalauréat* sex barrier at the University of Lyons in the 1860s, for example, only the timely intervention of the elderly François Barthélemy Arlès-Dufour (1797–1872), who personally traveled to Paris, enabled her to gain physical possession of the degree from the recalcitrant minister of public education. Daubié also became one of the first women to earn a *license ès lettres*, and three years before her premature death in 1874 she founded the Association for the Emancipation of Woman (Association pour l'émancipation de la femme), with Arlès-Dufour as president. But despite the precedents she set, by 1890 women had received only 202 nontraditional degrees: 35 medical doctorates, 69 *bacs* in science, 67 *bacs* in letters, 16 *licenses*, and 2 degrees in pharmacy. Dependent from the beginning on tutorial assistance to surmount the inferior curricula of their own segregated secondary schools, the women in the class of 1897 additionally encountered a new regulation by the national university administration forbidding them to wear pants or to ride bicycles. In the following year male students jeered the first women to attend the École des Beaux-Arts.[20]

In the next year, a decade after the second French Congress for Women's Rights of 1889, the question of what jobs women might qualify for with just their own secondary degree prompted a delegation from the French League for Women's Rights (Ligue française pour le droit des femmes) to visit Alexandre Millerand, minister of commerce and industry. Of Millerand, a socialist in violation of his party's policy of nonparticipation in bourgeois cabinets but a past advocate of women's rights, the delegation inquired whether he would live up to his earlier statements by hiring ministry personnel without regard to sex. Millerand agreed but with the proviso that women possess equal credentials, meaning the *bac*. Reminded that girls' schools could only grant the standard "end of studies certificate," Millerand advised the delegation to take its complaint to the Ministry of Public Education.[21]

That recourse hardly portended redress. The Ministry of Public Education not only oriented the newly expanded system of girls' schools toward domestic training, but it also awarded its woman's prize of 1891 to Georges Guéroult's *Du rôle de la femme dans notre rénovation sociale* (*The Role of Woman in Our Social Renovation*). Guéroult, whose *Rôle* also won a first prize from the National Society for Encouragement of the Common Good (Société nationale d'encouragement au bien), maintained that too much education would draw women away from agriculture and lead to a break-up of the family. Along lines spelled out by Bishop Fénelon in the seventeenth century, he argued that household skills and religious indoctrination would suffice to enable women to accomplish their honorable role as guardians of the home and upbringers of children. "Instead of *bachières*, *licensiées*, *doctoresses*, make good Christians, good house-wives, educated women without doubt," Guéroult urged:

I am in favor of education as much as can be, having the honor to belong myself as member and laureate to a Society for Popular Education and Childrearing (Société d'instruction et éducation populaire), but an education limited to conform to their sex, their condition, the mission that Divine Providence has confided to them; make girls modest, pious, reserved, charitable, thrifty.[22]

And useless, Auclert charged when the secondary system, with its worthless diploma, went into operation in 1881.[23]

THE REVIVAL OF LITERARY FEMINISM: LAMBER AND D'HÉRICOURT

By the time Guéroult's award-winning essay appeared, the liberal feminist movement, after a long generation of propagandizing and organ-izing, had developed a general, if imperfect, critique of *masculinisme*. In the beginning, however, liberal protests against *masculinisme* assumed the form of highly individualistic responses to specific provocations. Although these responses isolated issues around which organized protest soon formed and provided insights from which a systematic interpreta-tion of liberal feminist reality eventually emerged, they were essentially reactive in character. At "root" they sprang from angry reactions to male righteousness, and only a few went beyond the parameters of the initial provocation. These few, notably the works by Juliette Lamber and Jenny d'Héricourt, lived on and contributed to the consciousness of later feminists. The others barely survived the moment of their publication.

Two of the shorter-lived protests came from the pen of Olympe Audouard in the mid-1860s, and both sprang from a reaction to Procura-tor General Dupin's attack in the Senate on women's "frantic" addiction to luxury. In the first of two pamphlets, Audouard stressed the impor-tance of the fashion industry to the French economy and castigated the hypocrisy of males who blamed "good" women for dressing well and then lavished finery on courtesans.[24] In the second pamphlet, originally delivered as a speech, Audouard broke no new ground but won over her audience by flipping the attack back on Dupin:

A horrifying pest, *an evil that spreads terror*, is ravaging French society!...This scourge, this pestilential evil, this enemy of all good social economy is LUXURY...[But] much more disastrous than the luxury of women is that of men (Yes, very good! very good!). You see: these men have invented clothes for the morning, the afternoon, the woods, the track, the evening, the hunt: useless fantasies, prolific in ruinous expenses.[25]

Similarly, Audouard's lengthier 1866 declaration of *Guerre aux hommes* (*War on Men*) represented a reaction to the Second Empire's ban on her political review. Against the many men who made sport of woman by trading on her faults while forgetting the sex of their own mothers, sisters, and daughters, Audouard struck back in *Guerre* by dividing men into fifteen "villainous types" ranging from the "toad" and the "chameleon" to the "sphinx" and the "skilled compromiser of women." Among the types could no doubt be found the man from whom she separated in 1860 and the imperial magistrates who squelched her business career by ruling that she could not spend her own dowry, even to bring up her children, without first paying her husband's debts.[26] She also returned in *Guerre* to the luxury charge, countering that misery, not finery, ruined women. Solely attributable to men, this misery not only accounted for why "woman is neither free nor happy in France"[27] but also provoked Audouard the following year into petitioning the legislature for equal civil and political rights.[28] The legislature paid no heed, but her use of the petition foreshadowed a tactic repeatedly employed by feminists under the Third Republic.

More enduring in their impact on subsequent feminist consciousness than the works of Audouard, who eventually drifted off into spiritualism, were two of several responses that sprang somewhat earlier from reactions to the single most provocative embodiment of mid-nineteenth-century *masculinisme*, Pierre-Joseph Proudhon. The first among equals in an antifeminist troika that included Jules Michelet and Auguste Comte, Proudhon wielded so enormous an influence over the French working class that in 1866, a year after his death, the French section of the International Workingman's Association, founded by Karl Marx and Friedrich Engels in 1864, paid tribute to his memory by formally resolving that women should be barred from work outside the home. That memory might never abandon such advice, Proudhon singled out women for special treatment in 1858 in the third volume of *La Justice dans la révolution et dans l'église* (*Justice in the Revolution and in the Church*) and again in *La Pornocratie ou les femmes dans les temps modernes* (*The Rule of the Harlots or Women in Modern Times*), a half-finished work published posthumously.[29]

The scope of Proudhon's assault on women went far beyond matters of dress; in his eyes they wallowed in inferiority. Men exceeded them in physical strength by a ratio of three to two, and, according to Proudhon, because muscle power correlated to brain power and brain power to moral sense, men had the same edge in intelligence and righteousness. Qualitatively, woman possessed not only "a false mind, irremediably false" but also constituted "the desolation of the just." Quantitatively, Proudhon exponentially calculated, because society depended on a combination of strength in the form of work, intelligence in the form of science, and moral sense in the form of justice, "the total value of man and of woman, their relationship to each other and consequently their share of influence, will be as $3 \times 3 \times 3$ is to $2 \times 2 \times 2$, that is as 27 is to 8."[30]

Woman had only a limited capacity for improvement, Proudhon maintained, and only through marriage and within the context of the family, the basic element of society, could she play any worthwhile role. At most education should enable her to cultivate her "beauty," her "charm," and her "juvenile grace," qualities that would permit her to assume a proper relationship to man. "As the face of woman is the mirror in which man acquires respect for his own body," Proudhon reflected, "so the intelligence of woman is also the mirror in which he contemplates his genius."[31] Further, because "equality of civil and political rights would mean that the privileges and grace that nature has bestowed on woman would become bound up with man's utilitarian faculties," society committed no injustice in discriminating against her. On the contrary, without such discrimination, "woman, instead of being elevated, would become denatured and debased," entailing apocalyptically "the end of the institution of marriage, the death of love, and the ruin of the human race."[32] Separated from men by a natural barrier "like that placed between animals, by a difference of race," woman had no claim to emancipation. Indeed, Proudhon exclaimed, "I should incline, rather if there were no alternative, to exclude her from society."[33] Short of that, husbands should enjoy complete dominion over their wives, including the right to kill if faced with adultery, immodesty, treason, drunkenness, debauchery, wastefulness, obstinate insubordination, or theft.[34] In the category of theft fell jobs, which working women by definition stole from men. "Property is theft," too, Proudhon argued in 1840 with great revolutionary effect among workingmen, but, at the height of the revolution that broke out eight years later, he divined for women only two options in life: housewife or harlot (*ménagère ou courtisane*).[35]

It was from reaction to the third volume of *La Justice* that sprang the strongest responses to Proudhon's views. No less than four book-length rejoinders flew off the presses between 1858 and 1860, each partly provoked as well by the fact that imperial censors initially banned all of *La Justice* except for the sections on women.[36] In *Les Femmes dans cent ans* (*Women in a Hundred Years*) of 1859, Hermance Lesguillon responded with a proposal for marriage reform, specifically urging that spouses submit to a mandatory reconsideration of their vows at the end of seven years. The next year, Adéle Esquiros argued in *L'Amour* (*Love*) that only by liquidating the "inequality that kills love" could marriage work: "We do not love a slave, we do not love a master."[37] More sweeping and ultimately more influential, however, were the other two works: Juliette Lamber's *Idées anti-proudhoniennes* and Jenny d'Héricourt's *La Femme affranchie*.

Rushed to print in just two months,[38] *Idées anti-proudhoniennes* reflected the decision of its twenty-two-year-old author to speak out rather than "to oppose to his reasons mixed with injuries the disdainful silence that ordinarily rewards those who speak a certain language." Lamber asserted that Proudhon, as a man, represented force, whereas she, as a woman, represented weakness, "but there is one thing above force, the truth." "The cause that I defend will succeed, but not without combat and effort," she maintained: "It needs to be defended against some, against many. Yesterday, it was against the adversaries of progress; today, against M. Proudhon; tomorrow perhaps, against the friends of progress and misunderstood liberty."[39] At the moment, though, it was Proudhon's "power of proselytism" that particularly alarmed Lamber:

His doctrines on woman are extremely dangerous; they express the general feelings of men who, regardless of the party to which they belong, progressives or reactionaries, monarchists or republicans, Christians or pagans, atheists or deists, would be delighted to discover the means of reconciling at the same time their egotism and their conscience in a system that would permit them to preserve the benefits of exploitation based on force, without having to fear protests founded on right.[40]

In turning to Proudhon's specific charges, Lamber granted that he probably meant well; she too objected to women's passion for frills. She also acknowledged the backwardness of contemporary women, and some years later she warned that, because in France ambition seemed to come to women before the search for merit, "we must first require of those we emancipate the proof that demands for their rights rest on knowledge of their capacity, that is to say, their duties."[41] Nonetheless, as an advocate of liberal individualism as well as a proponent of the notion that civilized progress depended on the supplanting of "might" by "right," she could abide neither Proudhon's opposition to equal opportunity nor his verbal smokescreen for force.

Instead, Lamber proposed "functional equality," an equivalence theory that accepted special natures and separate spheres in principle but demanded a redefinition of both in practice. "Women must be educated thoroughly, and, wherever possible, professionally," she argued. "They must be made productive. Work alone has emancipated man. Work alone can emancipate woman." Still, she hedged, let me not "be accused of undervaluing woman's role in the family; I, like Proudhon, believe that a woman's first duty is to be wife and mother." It was just that "family life need not absorb all woman's activities, physical, moral and intellectual," she added: "The part of a broody hen is honourable without doubt, but it is not suited to everyone, neither is it so absorbing as it is represented."[42] Especially in light of Proudhon's opinions, a danger antithetical to individual freedom lay in trying "to determine in advance the respective roles of men and women and to imprison either in occupations imposed by their respective sex."[43] Moreover, even if their respective natures were different, progress required the cooperation of men and of women as equals. "A mere glance at the history of mankind will suffice to show," Lamber asserted, "that among nations civilization is in proportion to the part played by woman, to her influence, to her moral worth; and as civilization increases, the greater will be the value set upon the position accorded to woman."[44]

Two years later, in 1860, Jenny d'Héricourt published the other major response to Proudhon. An older, experienced writer with an established reputation, d'Héricourt had already written an article on "Proudhon and the Woman Question" for the *Revue philosophique* (*Philosophical Review*) of December 1856.[45] She seized on the publication of *La Justice* to answer Proudhon and others of similar persuasion in *La Femme affranchie:*

réponse à MM. Michelet, Proudhon, É. de Girardin, A. Comte et aux autres novateurs modernes (1864 English translation: *A Woman's Philosophy of Woman: or Woman Affranchised. An Answer to Michelet, Proudhon, Girardin, Legouvé, Comte, and other Modern Innovators*). In a manner similar to Audouard's subsequent *Guerre*, d'Héricourt explained her position and declared her objective:

In marriage, woman is a serf.
In public instruction, she is sacrificed.
In labor, she is made inferior.
Civilly, she is a minor.
Politically, she has no existence.
She is the equal of man only when punishment and the payment of taxes are in question.
I claim the rights of woman, because it is time to make the nineteenth century ashamed of its culpable denial of justice to half the human species.[46]

Why, she asked, should women criticize Michelet's ostensibly sympathetic *La Femme* (*Woman*) and *L'Amour* (*Love*)? "Because to him woman is a perpetual invalid who should be shut up in a gynaeceum," she answered. He differed from Proudhon only in style: "The first is as sweet as honey, and the second as bitter as wormwood.... We will therefore castigate him [Michelet] only over the shoulders of M. Proudhon, who may be cannonaded with red-hot shot."[47]

D'Héricourt's other targets received more gentle treatment. She made a distinction between Comte's "priestly" assertion of woman's inferiority and his positivism, a mode of analysis she hoped others would employ to a better end. Legouvé, Girardin, and the "other modern innovators," mostly utopian socialists, received praise for compassion but blame for enveloping the woman question in mysticism:

Excuse me, brothers, from joining in your theological discussion; my wings are not strong enough to follow you into the bosom of God, in order to assure myself whether he is spirit or matter, androgynous or not, binary, trinary, quarternary, or nothing of all these. It is enough that you all grant that woman should be free, and the equal of man.[48]

Granting woman free and equal status in theory did not, however, absolve them from the implications of their view that men and women are but two parts of the same whole or of their neglect to recognize the role of masculine force in society:

I permit myself only a single observation; that your notion of the couple. . .tends fatally to the subjection of my sex. . . .*In social practice*, this unity is manifested by a single will, . . . and the individuality that prevails in our society is that which is endowed with strength of arm; the other is annihilated, and the right given to the couple is in reality only the right of the stronger. The use that M. Proudhon has made of androgyny ought to cure you of this fancy.[49]

In effect, although she shared with Lamber an attachment to liberal individualism and an aversion to identifying "right" with "might," d'Héricourt moved away by degree, if not absolutely, from accepting special natures and separate spheres in principle. She even questioned the likelihood that most women possessed the aptitude to rear a child, as over against giving birth to it. The two sexes should of course be "perfectly equal in rights," she concluded, but "woman must not claim her rights as a woman, but only as a human person and a member of the social body."[50]

Yet, although d'Héricourt's book was hailed in the United States as the best reply to Proudhon and other masculinists, Lamber's *Idées anti-proudhoniennes* exerted a much greater influence in France.[51] Later feminists expressed appreciation of d'Héricourt's motives but felt that the "violence of her words unfortunately negated the force of her argument."[52] In the opinion of Jane Misme, who founded *La Française* (*The French Woman*) in 1906 and helped found the French Union for Women's Suffrage in 1909, Lamber rather than d'Héricourt "personified at one and the same time feminine influence, such as it was formerly accepted, and feminine action as it is permitted today [1931]." The contrast remained, Misme wrote, despite Lamber's long withdrawal from the movement:

The *Idées anti-proudhoniennes* were, for a long time, the only contribution that their author made to feminism. . . .[Lamber's book] was without contradiction the most explosive and the most effective. *La Femme affranchie*, by Jenny d'Héricourt, which appeared two years later and which also responded to Proudhon but without defending Daniel Stern and George Sand, and in an arid form, was much less important.[53]

This difference of reception also stemmed in part from a combination of personal pique and length of personal contact. Both Lamber and d'Héricourt frequented the salon of Charles Fauvety, editor of the *Revue philosophique*, where, according to Lamber, d'Héricourt appeared as a conceited, bigoted, dogmatic "bluestocking of the most objectionable type." D'Héricourt reciprocated the disdain. "Would you believe it," she exclaimed to Fauvety, "that young lady actually dares to take upon herself to underline Proudhon." When Lamber expressed concern about the preparation of *Idées*, acknowledging that she lacked the experience of veterans, d'Héricourt responded: "Veterans! Veterans! You mean me, doubtless. Well, if you defend some of us [women], you are very impertinent to others."[54] How much these exchanges, recorded in a biography of Lamber published during World War I, affected feminist opinion is difficult to say. But to the extent that the living interpret the dead, Lamber had a decided advantage. Not only did she become, as Madame Adam, one of France's foremost political figures, who, among other things, trumpeted revenge against Germany for twenty years through her *La Nouvelle revue* (*The New Review*, 1879–1899), but she also, after remaining aloof from the feminist movement in its early years, returned to the cause of women's rights by joining Jeanne Schmahl's very conservative Advance Messenger in 1893. Moreover, she died in 1936, a century after her birth, outliving d'Héricourt, who in 1890 died at sixty, by decades.[55]

Considerably more important to the fate of *La Femme affranchie* than either its tone or d'Héricourt's feud with Lamber was another factor: d'Héricourt's failure to adopt the correct "line." Lamber acknowledged that feminists might confront opposition from the "friends of progress and misunderstood liberty" but only as a "perhaps" and not until "tomorrow." Consequently, she limited her protest to the immediate adversary, Proudhon. In contrast, d'Héricourt sensed that Lamber's "tomorrow" had come. Revolutionaries, she noted, had abandoned women twice before, in 1789 and in 1848, and a third betrayal seemed imminent. She therefore went beyond Proudhon, whose *La Justice* so flagrantly violated woman's aspirations, in order to expose others whose honey-sweet sentiments also perpetuated *masculinisme*. Although Lamber no doubt believed that nations advanced "in proportion to the part played by women," d'Héricourt accorded it priority. To the advanced thinkers, to the democrats, to the friends of freedom, to the Michelets, Legouvés, and Girardins, she issued a stern warning:

Woman is ripe for civic liberty, and we declare to you that, from this time on, we shall regard as an enemy of progress and the Revolution anyone who comes out against our legitimate claim, just as we shall rank among the friends of progress and the Revolution those who speak out for our civic emancipation—even if they be your enemies.[56]

The warning proved prescient but impolitic. By criticizing others than Proudhon, d'Héricourt challenged the prevalent belief that political, economic, and social progress for France as a whole would automatically benefit women. Writing at mid-point in the Second Empire, when republicanism dominated the thoughts of many advanced thinkers, she asserted in effect that a proper attitude on the woman question alone should distinguish friend from foe. Lamber disagreed, but other more devoted feminists also disagreed; they viewed liberal republicanism as the essential precondition for reforms of all types, including those affecting women. Thus, in attacking so many "friends of freedom" and in suggesting that common cause with republicans might disserve women, d'Héricourt placed herself outside the political parameters that marked the woman question's "legitimate" field of debate. Toward the end of the generation that built the movement, feminist Léon Richer remarked that his greatest error had been to be right at the wrong time.[57] D'Héricourt might easily have said the same, but whereas Richer had been wrong by only a few decades, d'Héricourt missed her moment by a century or more.

The lopsided reaction of subsequent feminists to d'Héricourt's and Lamber's books reflected attitudes of critical importance to the emergent movement. Later feminists could easily identify with the anger that prompted the two works because they too confronted articulate spokesmen for *masculinisme*. They could also identify with the constraining ambience in which Lamber and d'Héricourt wrote because the discriminatory trend in favor of the rights of man and daily contact with the righteousness of man also constituted the roots of their own consciousness. Nevertheless, most subsequent feminists could not accept d'Héricourt's conclusions. From their vantage point, she had permitted her uneasiness to flow not only into a questioning of the liberal vision of society but also into a querying of the assumption that woman's primary duty lay in wifehood and motherhood. Hence, they repudiated her views. In the long run, that reaction damaged the cause of women's emancipation in France. Yet, that reaction also illustrates one of the central difficulties of feminist consciousness in the nineteenth century. For, if direct and vicarious experiences of *masculinisme* lay at the root of feminist consciousness, there were no clear markers indicating which interpretive route the struggle to emancipate women should take.

ROUTES TO LIBERAL FEMINIST CONSCIOUSNESS

As evidenced by the many alarms, crises, revolutions, and reactions that swept France between 1789 and 1914, expressions of discontent proved nearly as varied as the conditions from which discontent flowed. To every configuration assumed by French society during these years there emerged in theory at least an alternative and an alternative to the alternative. Once jolted into the reality of woman's systematic subordination, the founders of the liberal feminist movement thus faced a bewildering situation. Having no desire or capacity to separate themselves from French society, they wrestled with the question of how much to change and in what direction. Had *masculinisme* become so pervasive that only a complete and radical transformation could eliminate it, or could it be ameliorated through reforms that left existing institutions intact? And what of other injustices: war, poverty, pornography, censorship, child abuse, animal abuse? Should the struggle to emancipate women focus exclusively on women as if nothing else mattered? Or should feminism concern itself with other forms of oppression, and, if so, which ones? In principle was justice indivisible? In practice could the woman question be answered without reference to other questions? Only the questions seemed clear. In order to effect a transformation of their new reality, French feminists had first to find doctrines by which to define themselves, channels through which to express themselves, and allies with whom to align themselves. Switched into the world of *masculinisme*, they had, in short, to find routes by which to interpret and alleviate the conditions and constraints that women confronted.

UTOPIAN SOCIALISM

Utopian socialism offered one interpretive route. The titular founder of this school of thought, Henri de Saint-Simon (1760–1825), wrote scarcely a word about women.[58] But his intellectual heirs accorded an extraordinary importance to the woman question. Books touching on the subject included the mystical but insightful *Théorie des quartre mouvements* (*Theory of Four Movements*) by Charles Fourier (1772–1837), *De l'Égalité* (*On Equality*) by Pierre Leroux (1797–1871), and the novel *Voyage en Icarie* (*Journey to Icarie*) by Étienne Cabet (1788–1856). Newspapers displaying a similar interest included the Saint-Simonian *Le Producteur* (*The Producer*) and *Le Globe* (*The Globe*), Victor Considérant's Fourierist *La Phalange* (*The Phalanx*) and *La Démocratie pacifique* (*The Peaceful Democracy*), and *La Tribune des femmes* (*The Women's Tribune*) of 1832–1834, the first feminist journal to appear in France after Napoleon I suppressed *L'Athénée des dames* (*The Athenaeum of Ladies*) in 1808.[59]

Emphases varied among individual thinkers, but in general the utopian socialists espoused a critique of *masculinisme* that involved new definitions of society, the couple, man, and woman. Woman's subordination found apt description in Cabet's *La Réalisation d'Icarie* (*The Realization of Icarie*) of 1846:

Woman is actually a slave, not individually like the negress, or the ancient slave, or the woman of bygone times over whom her husband had the right of life and death and especially repudiation, but women *en masse* are the slaves of men *en masse* who leave them no rights and impose on them all the laws dictated by their [male] caprice and their [male] egotism.[60]

Utopian socialists attributed this subordination to the past when "antagonism," the exploitation of "man by man," reigned supreme. But, as Saint-Simon himself observed, a new era of affection and cooperation had begun to dawn, an era in which "national hatreds are diminishing every day and the people of the earth who are ready for a total and definitive alliance present us with the beautiful spectacle of humanity gravitating toward *universal association*."[61]

One impediment to universal association stemmed from the Christian identification of woman with the flesh and the flesh with sin. Prosper Enfantin (1796–1864) believed that Christianity, supported by the institution of private property, had created prostitution, perverting legitimate physical desire and the sacred rights of beauty. To this "disorder of the flesh," Enfantin opposed the "rehabilitation of the flesh":

We wish to rehabilitate the flesh, and to sanctify physical beauty by bestowing upon it a social importance which . . . it must today obtain through fraud. . . . Yes, truly, the flesh repressed and martyred by the Church for so long is today free from this heavy burden; but it is in a state of disorder. Today the flesh causes destruction as it did at the time of the appearance of Christ, and it is still the shame of the world. . . .

Look at the people. They sell their bodies to labor; they sell their blood to war; they sell their daughters' flesh to pleasure and to shame. For a piece of bread the world contorts them, commits them to toil and to the appeasement of passion; it prostitutes the people both in their strength and in their beauty.[62]

In order to overcome "antagonism" and its associated "disorder," men and women had to throw off the burden of the past and adopt a new social ethic: love. Love would permit the passage from social egotism to social altruism, from "antagonism" to "associationism." It would also render violence unnecessary.[63]

The vision of a society transformed without violence into associations based on love left a critical issue unresolved—the future status of women. All utopian socialists called for sex equality. As Enfantin wrote, "The equality of man and woman, without which there is exploitation of one-half the human genre by the other, is the law of the future, the sole moral law that it is possible to conceive."[64] Some, like Fourier, attributed superior qualities to women: "I am justified in saying that woman in a state of liberty will surpass men in all mental and bodily functions that are not ascribed to physical strength."[65] But how would this "moral law" and these superior "functions" be expressed?

In their quest for an answer, one faction of utopians stressed the primacy of the couple and marriage. Single women should have the same rights as single men, wrote Pierre Leroux, but only love and marriage could emancipate women. "She loves, she is loved, *la voilà femme*," he rhapsodized: "It is through marriage that the condition of woman has been ameliorated, it is through marriage, the equality of love, that the emancipation of woman will truly take place."[66] Couples should freely choose each other in the reconstructed society of the future, but to anticipate marital disunion ran "contrary to the ideal." To Leroux and others like Olinde Rodrigues, "the cessation of love, separation and divorce are tantamount to death before death."[67]

Another faction attacked marriage for failing to take human differences into account. Fourier held the institution directly responsible for woman's subordination. "Marriage is the tomb of woman's liberty, the principle of all feminine servitude," he declared. "Daughters are compelled to become housewives and wives to confine themselves to the home and to be faithful, even though three-quarters of them have no taste for family work, are capricious in love, predisposed to adornment, to gallantry, and to dissipation."[68] "Marriage is prostitution by law," scoffed Claire Demar, one of the editors of *La Tribune des femmes*, whose experience of the contradiction between conventional morality and a desire for freedom ended in her suicide.[69]

Some individuals might desire permanent unions, admitted Enfantin, but couples should endure only as long as they meet each others' needs:

We have profound feelings or lively, enduring, or transitory feelings; we are reserved, modest, moderate, patient, or very enthusiastic, loving glory, brilliance, passion, etc. Either of these forms is good, the one wants to conserve, the other wants to innovate.... The one is immutable, the other is changing.[70]

For the many who preferred a change of "place, things, habits, society, and finally husbands and wives," argued Enfantin, divorce represented a right, not a misfortune. It cannot be, wrote one of Enfantin's followers, "that the *exclusive love* of one man for one woman lasting their whole lives is a law or even a universal tendency of mankind":

I deny that this precept conforms and is applicable to the nature of *all* men and *all* women without *exception*.... I say, then, that to fight and to overthrow the principle of Christian love we would need merely to declare that a religion which saw in celibacy the state most favorable to salvation and the one closest to perfection was too ignorant of human nature to have been capable of giving marriage a solid and stable base.[71]

Enfantin's ideas undoubtedly influenced the turn-of-the-century feminist who described utopian socialism as a "monstrous orgy where giants endowed with the appetite of ogres gorged themselves on monstrous feasts and innumerable loves."[72] However, on the individuals who built the feminist movement, utopian socialism had a profound and salutary effect. Through it, Rowbotham observed, "a number of women emerged with a new conception of their own dignity and worth"; "it gave them the confidence to express themselves and provided them with the courage to formulate conceptions about their own possibilities, which would have been inconceivable to women a generation before.''[73] Even in the late 1870s and 1880s, when French socialism became less utopian and more militant, Saint-Simonianism and Fourierism continued to exert a strong influence on the founders of the French feminist movement.

This influence stemmed in large part from utopian socialism's vague, sentimental egalitarianism, which enabled feminists to avoid too narrow a commitment to any particular reform, and from its advocacy of peaceful change, which meshed well with liberal feminism's identification of *masculinisme* with violence.[74] The first feminist newspaper outside Paris, Eugénie Niboyet's 1833 *Le Conseiller des femmes* (*The Women's Adviser*) of Lyon, bore its imprint, and the first feminist daily, Niboyet's 1848 *La Voix des femmes* (*The Voice of Women*), managed a brief life with the help of subsidies from Saint-Simonian banker Olinde Rodrigues.[75] Many of the reforms proposed during the Revolution of 1848, which coincided with the young adulthood of most of the founders of the liberal feminist movement, reflected the influence of utopian socialists or other profeminist socialists like Louis Blanc and Constantin Pecqueur. Between 1848 and 1849, feminist Jeanne Deroin, a disciple of Saint-Simon and Cabet, created a women's club, a feminist newspaper, and a worker's association. She also ran for a seat in the National Assembly in a precedent-setting act of protest against woman's exclusion from the recent enactment of universal manhood suffrage.[76] In the late 1860s, utopian socialism inspired several cooperatives, including Nathalie Lemel's Stew-Pot (La Marmite) and Marguerite Tinayre's Society of the Just of Paris (La Société des équitables de Paris).[77]

In 1871 the Paris Commune engaged in additional experimentation along utopian socialist lines. None of these efforts effected lasting institutional changes of benefit to women, but the tie between feminism and utopian socialism remained strong. In contrast to the vast French majority who manifested hostility or apathy toward women's emancipation, utopian socialists not only repeatedly attempted to improve woman's lot but paid in suffering for their failure. A veritable Who's Who of socialist feminists figured among the deported and exiled after the Revolution of 1848 and the Paris Commune of 1871: Pierre Leroux, Louis Blanc, Victor Considérant, Jeanne Deroin, Pauline Roland, Nathalie Lemel, Marguerite Tinayre, André Léo, and Paule Mink. Undoubtedly, too, had she not succumbed to an untimely death at the age of thirty-one in 1844, Flora Tristan, a self-described "pariah" and author of *L'Union ouvrière* (*The Workers'*

Union) who also sought to link feminism and socialism, would have figured on this list.[78]

It was no mere coincidence then that, even though utopian socialists accepted the notion of special natures and rejected the concept of separate spheres more in theory than in practice, the emerging feminist movement drew heavily on their ideas and personnel. Arlès-Dufour, the elderly fellow who personally picked up Daubié's *bac* and who served as president of her short-lived association, was a loyal follower of Enfantin's cult.[79] Virginie Griess-Traut, a convinced Fourierist who donated 50,000 francs to Considérant's utopian socialist "school" called the École sociétaire phalanstérienne, actively participated in the founding of the first ongoing group in 1870, the Society for the Amelioration of Woman's Condition (Société pour l'amélioration du sort de la femme).[80] And the French League for Women's Rights, established in 1882, included several practicing utopians from the Familistère de Guise, created by Jean-Baptiste-André Godin in 1859.[81] The doctrines of Saint-Simon and Fourier provide a "just and incisive critique of our current [social] organization," wrote feminist Maria Deraismes. Liberals had no cause to fear them because "of all the socialist ideas, the bourgeoisie has, by design, only held back from communism, inasmuch as neither Saint-Simon, nor Fourier had ever professed the division of riches." On the contrary, she argued, they wanted salaries to "become proportional to capacities and they accorded a very large role to genius, to talent."[82]

The slogans employed by the French feminist movement during its formative years also reflected utopian socialist influence. Two came directly from the pen of Charles Fourier. In one he linked man's emancipation to that of woman: "Everywhere where man has degraded woman he has degraded himself, everywhere where he has ignored the rights of woman he has himself lost his own rights."[83] In the other he linked women's emancipation to progress in general, an interpretation of history to which Lamber, d'Héricourt, and their liberal feminist successors resoundingly gave voice. "The change in a historical epoch can always be determined by the progress of women toward freedom," Fourier pronounced, "because in the relation of woman to man, of the weak to the strong, the victory of human nature over brutality is most evident." Hence, "the degree of emancipation of women is the natural measure of general emancipation,"[84] or alternatively, "*the extension of privileges to women is the general principle of all social progress.*"[85]

Another statement frequently quoted by French feminists came from Victor Hugo, the Second Empire's most illustrious republican exile. In acknowledging his debt to Enfantin and upon hearing of the death of utopian socialist and feminist Pauline Roland in 1854, Hugo declared, "The eighteenth century was the century of man, the nineteenth century will be the century of woman."[86] Yet, although utopian socialism provided the founders of the liberal feminist movement with slogans for women's emancipation and with insightful critiques of *masculinisme*, it imparted neither a vision of large-scale societal transformation nor, despite Deraismes's disclaimer, an acceptable political-economic theory. For this the movement's founders turned elsewhere.

LIBERAL REPUBLICANISM

Liberal republicanism, and particularly its left-wing variant known as radical republicanism, provided this "elsewhere." Indeed, the founders of the liberal feminist movement developed such close ties to republicanism that the interplay between the woman question and the political question emerged during the movement's early years as the dominant consideration in the struggle to emancipate women. Or, to put it more pointedly, the republican "connection" became the tie that bound the founders to a problematic "politics first" orientation. With the possible exception of d'Héricourt, however, none of the feminists who helped forge the tie anticipated the extent to which the Third Republic itself would one day obstruct their efforts. Nor, in retrospect, is it easy to see how the founders of the liberal feminist movement could have avoided the republican attachment.

Republicanism offered an attractive interpretive route to those who chafed at the constraints of *masculinisme*. In the middle decades of the nineteenth century, according to Roger Soltau's characterization, it comprised a blend of logic and sentiment, effecting a fervor of quasi-religious enthusiasm:

The Democrat [or republican] is usually an emotionalist, a sentimentalist in both the good and the bad sense of that much ill-used term; he [or she] is a mystic, and his [or her] politics are to him [or her] a faith that often replaces religion; his [or her] belief in the Republico-Democratic organization of society is largely a matter of intuition, of the heart having its reasons that Reason knoweth not—a faith that made him [or her] risk prison, exile and deportation, and that kept alive during the four years of bitter disillusionment that were the Second Republic [1848–1852] and the eighteen years [1852–1870] of the half *opéra bouffe* [comic opera], half tragedy that we call the Second Empire.[87]

The democrat believed in the potential goodness of ordinary people, a belief that meshed well with aspects of socialist thought. In a sense, the republican was an "underdeveloped socialist":

[And] what differentiates him [or her] from the Socialists is often a matter of tactics rather than of principle; he [or she] believes first in the conquest of political weapons: the vote, the abolition of the hereditary principle, and relegates to a distant future the economic reorganization of society which is the Socialist's primary aim.[88]

In time republicanism would also relegate feminism's primary aim to a distant future. But in the context of the 1860s the republican ideal portended a society freed of the old injustices and open to reform from below. This ideal had a special interpretative appeal to the Second Empire's feminists who could reflect on how, after 1789 and 1848, political reaction had gone hand in hand with resurgent *masculinisme*. At worst, republicanism promised an open society in which feminists could conduct their campaign exempt from hassles like the brief ban imposed on d'Héricourt's *La Femme affranchie* or the disruption of Audouard's divorce speech. At best, republicanism might produce a society cleansed of the Church, the Napoleonic Code, and other illiberal fetters and place France on the path of rational, scientific progress. Republicanism seemed to complement much of what the utopian socialists espoused, with the added advantage of encompassing the whole of society and sidestepping the issue of private ownership of productive property. Interpretively construing their new reality in terms of the republican promise thus made sense to the movement's founders who, holding clericalism and the authoritarian Second Empire responsible for woman's plight, imagined that a liberal republican France not only would permit them to express their grievances but would also respond quickly and efficaciously.

This hope had a pragmatic as well as an ideological dimension. Republican sentiment prevailed among the Second Empire's several thousand exiles and deportees, maintaining a link of opposition to the empire between emergent feminists in revolt against *masculinisme* and others who sought an end to political authoritarianism.[89] Within France, the radical (and not so radical) republican opposition to imperial rule included a number of prominent historians, journalists, and politicians who expressed concern for women. Consistent with Michelet's view that woman "must have a household, she must be married,"[90] their opinions tended to the traditional, but they nonetheless focused attention on the woman question. They also demanded reform of some of the worst abuses. In 1866, for example, a committee of legal experts recommended marital equality through abolishing Article 213 of the Napoleonic Code, which required wives to swear obedience to husbands. On the committee sat the host Jules Favre, Jules Simon, Joseph Garnier, Émile Acollas, Charles Vacherot, Frédéric Morin, Charles Lemonnier, André Cochut, Jean-Jules Clamageran, Paul Jozon, Jules Ferry, Courcelle-Seneuil, Paul Boiteau, Henri Brisson, Charles Floquet, Hérold, and Doctor Clavel— together a pretty fair sampling of soon-to-be prominent liberal Protestant republicans.[91]

The founders of liberal feminism themselves had multiple contacts with republicanism. Aside from belonging with d'Héricourt to the republican salon of Charles Fauvety, for instance, Lamber, after publishing *Idées anti-proudhoniennes* and remarrying, established her own salon, through which as Madame Adam she introduced the radical republican Léon Gambetta to Parisian political life. Feminist Deraismes also ran a republican salon and in the 1880s assumed control of a newspaper entitled *Le Républicain de Seine-et-Oise* (*The Republican of Seine-et-Oise*). Richer, Deraismes's closest collaborator, began his career as a journalist for Adolphe Guéroult's moderate republican *L'Opinion nationale* (*The National Opinion*) and later became editor-in-chief of *La République radicale* (*The Radical Republic*). Deraismes and Richer led the moderate, antisuffrage wing of French feminism during the 1870s, but in the 1860s all liberal feminists expressed a transportive faith in republicanism as the necessary first step to women's emancipation.[92] Even after the founding of the Third Republic in 1870, when a suffragist minority within the feminist movement began to attack the new "democracy" for perpetuating the old *masculinisme*, faith in republicanism remained strong. However imperfect the new political order, the founders of the liberal feminist movement held fast to the republican promise that had engendered in them such high hopes during the last years of the Second Empire.

REFORMISM

An explosion of reformism rocked France during the second half of the nineteenth century, offering liberal feminists yet another route for interpreting, and possibly redressing, the reality of *masculinisme*. From reformism, generally, feminists obtained a fuller awareness of the world into which they had switched. Through it, specifically, they acquired a sense of what in detail to focus on while awaiting the final republican reckoning as well as a set of allies with whom to cooperate in bringing about change. At the same time, however, because reformism and feminism projected complementary rather than identical realities, the founders of the liberal feminist movement eventually confronted in reformism the twofold dilemma of how theoretically to decide between essential and marginal causes as well as how practically to pursue essential causes with marginal allies or marginal causes with essential allies.

Almost any reform issue could attract at least some support from liberal feminists.[93] Most endorsed dress reforms, for instance, especially efforts to abolish the corset, and all supported the reestablishment of divorce, for which feminist Richer drafted the law that Alfred Naquet guided to passage in 1884.[94] Most objected to the way men referred to women, but not much energy went into Auclert's proposal for wives to keep their family name or for all adult women to use ''Madame.''[95] Efforts to outlaw vivisection also loomed small to most, but Deraismes passionately sought it, and out of a similar concern second-generation feminist Marguerite Durand founded a still-functioning pet cemetery just north of Paris at Asnières. The association therein expressed of *masculinisme* with brute force and barbarism also turned a few to vegetarianism and many more to temperance. In thought, despite Comte's antifeminism, positivism with its linear, rationalist interpretation of history, proved congenial to most liberal feminists, and Auclert's *La Citoyenne* (*The Woman Citizen*) took for its first masthead motto positivist Émile Littré's description of the future citizenness as ''the woman who enjoys full rights within the state.''[96] In belief, spiritualism too proved popular, with Audouard achieving a prominence in it second only to Allan Kardec (1804–1869), France's foremost spiritualist. Yet, excepting the campaign for divorce and the philosophical underpinning of positivism, none of these causes profoundly affected the collective disposition of liberal feminism.

Rather, it was from four other causes and two associated cadres that the founders of the liberal feminist movement derived interpretive inspiration. The four causes were anticlericalism, educationism, pacifism, and European abolitionism—the campaign to abolish governmental regulation of prostitution. The two cadres were the Freemasons and the Protestants. Together these causes and cadres formed a network in which the boundary between issues and individuals blurred but through which liberal feminists found essential objectives and essential allies.

Anticlericalism and its correlate, free thinking, went hand in hand with radical republicanism, which perceived the Roman Catholic Church as a bastion of superstition and an enemy of progress. Liberal feminists had their own bone to pick with the Church, literally in the sense that the myth of Adam's rib continued to serve as a justification for women's subordination, and figuratively in that they saw Catholicism as the linchpin of authoritarianism and *masculinisme*.[97] Mutual hatred of clericalism thus formed one of the strongest ties binding feminism to republicanism as well as one of the issues on which an extensive exchange of ideas and personnel took place between feminists and reformers. Under the Second Empire, for instance, Richer wrote a weekly column entitled "Letters d'un libre-penseur à un curé de village" ("Letters from a Free thinker to a Village Priest") for Guéroult's anticlerical *L'Opinion nationale*, and during the early years of the Third Republic Deraismes helped to organize the first anticlerical congresses.[98] Indeed, in their critique of *masculinisme*, liberal feminists forged so strong an interpretive link between clericalism as the foe of republicanism and the republic as the friend of women's emancipation that throughout the movement's first three decades they aligned themselves with republican intellectuals and radical polemicists who, as Paul Gagnon observed, "were not merely anticlerical as a matter of politics but anti-Catholic as a matter of faith."[99]

Inextricably connected to anti-clericalism was the issue of education, the principal battleground on which the "forces of order" and the "forces of change" confronted each other in nineteenth-century France. Liberal feminists viewed improved education not only as a prerequisite for women's equal participation in French society but also as a necessity for full realization of the mother-teacher ideal. In their view, *masculinisme* had reduced woman to ignorance and then had attributed the ignorance to her "nature." Feminists thus encouraged self-help efforts like Élisa Lemonnier's professional school for girls, founded in 1862,[100] and organized groups like the 1866 Society for the Demand of Women's Rights (Société de la revendication du droit des femmes) to promote equal, free, compulsory, and lay education. Their concern for education also brought them into contact with individuals like Ferdinand Buisson, a Protestant who helped to reform the Third Republic's school system and who eventually became the foremost male advocate of woman suffrage in France, and groups like Jean Macé's Education League (Ligue de l'enseignement), founded in 1866. The success of Macé's League, which grew to 17,856 members grouped into fifty circles by 1870, in turn provided an organizational model for Richer's French League for Women's Rights, founded in 1882. From his side, Macé supported women's emancipation by, among other things, financially backing Jeanne Deroin's short-lived *L'Opinion des femmes* (*Women's Opinion*) and personally joining Richer's League.[101]

Macé also participated in the upsurge of pacifist activity that swept France in the 1860s and that attracted liberal feminists generally. He joined a League for Peace (Ligue pour la paix) in 1862 and in 1867 collected forty-eight signatures, half German and half French, against war from residents in the vicinity of his hometown, Beblenheim, Alsace.[102] Also in 1867, Frédéric Passy founded in Paris the League of Peace (Ligue de la paix), which later operated as the Friends of Peace Society (Société des amis de la paix) and finally as the Arbitration Society (Société de l'arbitrage), while at the same time divorce advocate Naquet and Napoleonic Code critics Lemonnier and Acollas helped to form the League of Peace and Liberty (Ligue de la paix et de la liberté). Earlier, between 1858 and 1863, a third major peace organization had come into existence, the League of Public Good (Ligue du bien public).[103] None of these groups espoused conscientious pacifism like the Quakers', but all demanded abolition of permanent armies and international arbitration of disputes. Liberal feminists rallied to this type of pacifism out of a general concern for human welfare and because it conformed to their belief that *masculinisme* embodied the rule of ''might'' over ''right.'' In turn, as with education reform, peace advocates reciprocated by endorsing women's emancipation, the purpose, for example, of a resolution passed at the second congress of the League of Peace and Liberty in 1868.[104] ''War against war'' summed up the pacifist objective, and Émile de Girardin wrote a series of articles under that title.[105] But the slogan itself came from the pen of Edmond Potonié-Pierre, whose wife Eugénie helped to found the liberal feminist movement.[106] Indeed, pacifism eventually became a criterion for determining membership in the movement, and in 1909 the National Council of French Women expelled Jeanne Deflou's French Feminist Studies Group (Groupe française d'études féministes) and the Ariège Committee of Feminine Progress (Comité ariègeois de progrès féminin) for their opposition to it. It also alarmed the French government, but after an intense investigation the Interior Ministry reported with relief in 1915 that with the onset of World War I the earlier espousal of pacifism by liberal feminists had largely ceased.[107]

Abolitionism swept into France from across the channel in the 1870s.[108] Led by the English woman Josephine Butler, who first recruited in Paris in 1874, it attracted support from radical republicans, who saw governmental regulation of prostitution as a threat to civil liberties, and from feminists, who viewed prostitution as a typical byproduct of *masculinisme*. Although more concerned with moral reform than women's emancipation, the abolitionists nonetheless developed a "nascently feminist" critique of male despotism, the penultimate French symbol of which was the women's prison of Saint-Lazare. Many feminists thus rallied to Butler, and at the end of the decade Deraismes assumed the vice-presidency of the French Association for the Abolition of Regulated Prostitution (Association française pour l'abolition de la prostitution réglementée). Conversely, from the ranks of abolitionists emerged liberal feminist leaders like Sarah Monod, the first president of the 1901 National Council of French Women, and Francis de Pressensé, one of the founders of the 1911 League of Male Voters for Women's Suffrage (Ligue d'électeurs pour le suffrage des femmes). But, as the latter two dates indicate, the convergence of abolitionism, moral reformism, and liberal feminism occurred after the turn of the century. During the years of its founding, the liberal feminist movement remained cooperatively but distinctively independent.

Behind these reform issues stood two cadres, the Freemasons and the Protestants, both of which helped to coordinate the struggle for change. Episodes typical of how French Freemasonry provided coordination occurred at Le Havre and Metz in the late 1860s. In 1868, Ferdinand Santallier, the director of the *Journal du Havre*, created a Peace Union (Union de la paix). The union had its own journal with 1,500 subscribers, and Saint-Simonian Arlès-Dufour figured among its honorary members, but the bulk of its support came from several Masonic lodges in the vicinity.[109] The year before a professor at the *lycée* of Metz founded the first branch circle of Macé's Education League. The prefect at Moselle immediately authorized the circle, but the local bishop excommunicated the professor, who also headed Metz's Masonic lodge. All over France other lodges similarly supported peace and education projects, accompanied usually, as at Metz, by conflicts with local Catholics. Of the connection between Freemasonry and the Education League, Macé, a Freemason himself, wrote: "The two institutions are certainly independent of each other, but they are sisters as well, very certainly, their principle being the same: war on ignorance and on intolerance."[110]

Inasmuch as liberal feminists also saw their struggle as a "war on ignorance and on intolerance," they too turned to Freemasonry for support. The Masons in turn expressed an interest in women because, as the republican politician, Mason, and feminist José-Maria de Hérédia put it in 1878, woman "is the last fortress that the spirit of obscurantism opposes to human progress."[111] Consequently, although the lodges continued to bar women from full membership, Freemasonry nonetheless provided liberal feminists with public forums from which to expand their call for women's emancipation and with personal contacts through which to approach the French political world. The latter proved especially important when in the 1880s, as Mildred Headings reported, by their own estimate "the Freemasons claimed that the large majority of the deputies, ministers, councilors of all kinds, and officials were Freemasons."[112] At the highest level of government, at least twenty-one Freemasons served as prime minister under the Third Republic, and no less than nineteen Freemasons held the critically sensitive post of minister of public education. Many of the Masons were also Protestants, furthermore, and, whether they belonged to lodges or not, Protestants also frequently held cabinet offices in numbers inversely related to their proportion in the population at large.[113] Hence, through reformism the founders of liberal feminism encountered personalities and projects that left a deep interpretive imprint not only on what the movement should seek but also on how the movement should seek it.

WOMANISM AND FEMINISM

In addition to utopian socialism, liberal republicanism, and reformism, the founders of the feminist movement derived interpretive insights into *masculinisme* from two other sources, womanism and feminism itself. By womanism is meant the general trend that developed in nineteenth-century France to single out women for special scrutiny and study. Indeed, according to a report by lawyer Jules Tixerant to the French League for Women's Rights in 1911, more books appeared on women under the Second Empire than at any other time in French history.[114] In part this interest originated with aristocratic and bourgeois women who, having personally experienced the Great Revolution, wished to define a role for women in postrevolutionary France. "Like almost all of the educators, doctors and moralists, they thought they were only refurbishing and enlarging the traditional (and for them natural) role—that of the perfect wife-companion and the inspiring mother-teacher."[115] Womanists objected both to the frivolous "feminized society" of eighteenth-century France and to the "meddling women" who played active revolutionary roles. Stressing instead, according to Barbara Pope, "woman's indirect, spiritual influence, as wives and mothers of citizens," womanism complemented feminism in pinpointing specific abuses and in exposing gynophobic sores in the French social body. It also found an echo in "patriarchal feminists" like Ernest Legouvé and Richer, who sought in women's emancipation to regenerate society through improving woman's status within the family.[116]

Womanism manifested itself in a variety of ways: in novels like André Léo's *Un Mariage scandaleux* (1862), *Une Vieille Fille* (1864), and *Un Divorce* (1866); in documentaries like the third edition of Alexandre Jean-Baptiste Parent-Duchâtelet's two-volume study *De la Prostitution dans la ville de Paris* (1857) and Louis Reybaud's *Études sur le régime des manufactures, Condition des ouvriers en soie* (1859); in histories like Clarisse Bader's *La Femme dans l'Inde antique* (1864) and *La Femme biblique* (1866); in drama like Alexandre Dumas's *La Dame aux camélias* (1852) and *L'Ami des femmes* (1864); in mother-teacher tracts like Pauline Guizot's *Lettres de famille sur l'éducation* (1824) and Clarisse Beaudoux's *La Science maternelle* (1844); and in a host of newspaper and magazine articles, pamphlets, brochures, and university studies. Between 1864 and 1869 at least three works addressed the subject of "women in the nineteenth century," and toward the end of the century the number of law dissertations on women increased from 14 in 1884-1885, to 30 in 1894-1895, and 51 in 1904-1905.[117] Fifty-four percent of these dealt with issues arising out of marriage, but, regardless of the focus, they reflected the growing trend of popular, professional, and academic concern for the position of women in society.

The other source of insight into *masculinisme* was feminism itself. Once founded, the feminist movement provided an obvious interpretive route. Soon after leaving the convent in which she grew up, for example, Hubertine Auclert heard about feminism and immediately left for Paris to join the movement. Marguerite Durand, actress turned journalist, drew an assignment to cover the 1896 Women's Rights Congress and stayed. The next year she founded *La Fronde* (1897-1905, 1914), the first French newspaper run entirely by women.[118] Isabelle Bogelot attached herself to the movement almost as a matter of course; she had been raised in the home of feminist Maria Deraismes.[119] But these and other recruits enlisted in an effort that had already achieved a degree of consolidation. Such was not the case for the movement's founders, who had had to fashion an organization out of whole cloth.

The whole cloth, however, presented at least three workable qualities. The first consisted of convoluted snags and rips, connoting the subordination and abuse to which *masculinisme* subjected women. The "root" meaning of these rents in the social garment was clear to feminists: women had been drop-stitched out of the otherwise progressive fabric of French society. The second and third qualities might be likened to threads: one running backward into time; the other stretching across national boundaries. One enabled feminists to draw on the past for support; the other brought sustenance and direction from foreign contemporaries.

When French feminists looked at the past, they saw not only a pattern of increasing male oppression but repeated attempts by individuals and groups to throw off that oppression. Since the fourteenth century, when Christine de Pisan published the first of her protests against *masculinisme*, the 1399 *Épître au dieu d'amour* (*Epistle to the God of Love*), "forerunners" of feminism had advanced arguments in favor of women's emancipation.[120] In the sixteenth century, these forerunners included Louise Labé, François de Billon, Henri Estienne, Pierre de Bourdeille (Brantôme), and the woman who in Simone de Beauvoir's opinion "did the most for the cause," Marguerite de Navarre.[121] In the seventeenth and eighteenth centuries, salons provided forums for collective protest, while Marie de Gournay, Poulain de la Barre, and the *philosophes* wrestled individually with what had become known as the "woman question."[122]

The revolutions of 1789, 1830, and 1848 engendered new pleas for women's emancipation and new forms of protest, particularly women's clubs.

Thus, by the second half of the nineteenth century, liberal feminists could look back on a tradition of protest hundreds of years in the making. Nothing like a consistent "line" had arisen, but the legacy of protest enabled feminists to avoid an historical vacuum and to experience a sense of continuity. The legacy also supplied "useful" heroes such as Joan of Arc, whose image inspired feminists until right-wing Catholics coopted her during the first decade of the twentieth century; the Marquis de Condorcet, whose death date became women's annual day of celebration on the eve of World War I; and Olympe de Gouges, who drew up a *Declaration of the Rights of Woman* to supplement the Great Revolution's *Declaration of the Rights of Man*. De Gouges's execution during the Reign of Terror lent a haunting air to Article 10 of her *Declaration*: "Woman has the right to mount the scaffold; she ought also to have the right to mount the tribune."[123]

Foreign developments influenced French feminism in several ways. Among the most widely read works on women in nineteenth-century France, two came from England—Mary Wollstonecraft's *A Vindication of the Rights of Woman* (1792) and John Stuart Mill's *The Subjection of Women* (1869)—and another came from Germany, August Bebel's *Woman Under Socialism* (1883).[124] The Anglo-Saxon and Scandinavian countries appeared as beacons with respect to both organized feminist efforts and practical legislative gains. American women held the first Women's Rights Congress at Seneca Falls, New York, in 1848, and the Wyoming Territory led the Western world in granting full political rights to women. In 1851 Jeanne Deroin and Pauline Roland avowed from their cells in Saint-Lazare: "Sisters of America! Your socialist sisters of France are united with you in the vindication of the rights of woman to civil and political equality."[125] In response, the second National Woman's Rights Convention, meeting at Worcester, Massachusetts, delegated Lucretia Mott to correspond with French feminists. Those with firsthand knowledge of the United States included Olympe Audouard, who traveled there in the late 1860s, and Communard Élie Reclus, who paid a brief visit to two American utopian communities during his post-1871 exile.[126] From the other direction came the American feminist Susan B. Anthony, who spent part of 1883 in Paris and, although struck "deaf and dumb" by the language barrier, left impressed by three experiences in particular, according to Elizabeth Cady Stanton's son Theodore: "the interment of Laboulaye (the friend of the United States and of the woman movement); the touching anniversary demonstration of the Communists, at the Cemetery of Père La Chaise, on the very spot where the last defenders of the [Paris] Commune of 1871 were ruthlessly shot and buried in a common grave; and a woman's rights meeting, held in a little hall in the rue de Rivoli, at which the brave, farseeing Mlle. Hubertine Auchet [Auclert] was the leading spirit.[127] Four years later, Elizabeth Cady Stanton herself spent six months in Paris, during which time, she subsequently recalled, several of the most prominent liberal feminists paid her a visit:

To one of our "at homes" came Mlle. Maria Deraismes, the only female Free Mason in France, and the best woman orator in the country; her sister, Mme. Féresse-Deraismes, who takes part in all woman movements; M. Léon Richer, then actively advocating the civil and political rights [*sic*] of women through the columns of his vigorous journal; Mme. Griess Traut, who makes a specialty of peace work; Mme. Isabelle Bogelot, who afterward attended the Washington Council of 1888, and who is a leader in charity work; the late Mme. Emilie de Morsier, who afterward was the soul of the International Congress of 1889, at Paris; Mme. Pauline Kergomard, the first woman to be made a member of the Superior Council of Public Instruction in France, and Mme. Henri Gréville, the novelist.[128]

Hence, by the time Bogelot sailed for the United States in 1888 as the first official representative of the liberal feminist movement in France, extensive contacts had already developed between French proponents of women's emancipation and their counterparts on both sides of the Atlantic.

VIRGINIE GRIESS-TRAUT: A REPRESENTATIVE FEMINIST

In coming to consciousness the founders of the liberal feminist movement in France experienced a multifaceted "reality transformation." The "switch" from acceptance to rejection of *masculinisme* projected them into a struggle to dismantle the obstacles to women's liberty and, simultaneously, to assert women's influence over a wide range of national and international problems. Indeed, the reform interests of individual feminists occasionally proved so strong that the line separating changes projected in the name of women and changes predicated on the "use" of women became blurred. Still, although combinations and emphases varied from one individual to another, the typical founder of the liberal feminist movement exhibited a range of interests similar to that of one of the women whom Elizabeth Cady Stanton met on her 1887 visit to Paris, Virginie Griess-Traut.

Griess-Traut, whose gift of fifty thousand francs to the École sociétaire phalanstérienne revealed both her Fourierist utopian socialism and her wealth, belonged to three feminist groups.[129] She served for decades as vice-president of the Amelioration Society, which she helped found with Deraismes and Richer in 1870, and later joined Richer's French League for Women's Rights and Maria Martin's Women's Solidarity (Solidarité des femmes), established, respectively, in 1882 and 1891. Among feminist goals, she fought in particular for the right of business women to vote for the judges of commerce tribunals (the *commerçante* vote) and for coeducation. "Everybody is in agreement on the urgent necessity to assure to the country enlightened women, exempt from errors of superstition and sincerely republican," Griess-Traut wrote of the latter: "The means for attaining this goal are simple. Just do for girls what has been done for their brothers. Coeducation leads directly. . . [to] peace and concord without and within, in the state and in the family."[130] She also fought to abolish governmental regulation of prostitution, arguing that either the morals police should be suppressed or prostitutes should be made eligible for state pensions.

A free thinker, Griess-Traut attended the 1881 Anticlerical Congress as part of the Amelioration Society delegation, but her principal reform interest was peace. After the Franco-Prussian War, for instance, she demanded the neutralization of her native Lorraine rather than revenge against Germany, and, like her husband who prior to his death in 1882 had been one of France's foremost pacifists (as well as a cofounder of the Amelioration Society), she belonged to numerous antiwar groups: the French Society for Arbitration Between Nations (La Société française d'arbitrage entre nations), the International Union of Women for Peace (L'Union internationale des femmes pour la paix), the International League of Workers for Peace (La Ligue internationale des travailleurs pour la paix), the Worker Friends of Peace (Les Travailleurs amis de la paix), the Universal League of Women for Peace and the Union of Peoples (La Ligue universelle des femmes pour la paix et l'union des peuples), and Charles Lemonnier's International League of Peace and

Liberty (La Ligue internationale de la paix et de la liberté). With her old friend Lemonnier, Griess-Traut exulted that "to abolish royalty, this would be virtually, to abolish war; to establish the Republic, this would be, virtually, to establish peace and liberty."[131] Griess-Traut died on 9 December 1898, at the age of eighty-five, from injuries caused by a fall. A life of serious devotion to just causes had preserved her youth, feminist colleague Maria Pognon observed, making her an excellent example for others.[132]

CONCLUSION

By the late 1860s the stage was set for a revival of organized feminism in France. In itself that was not unusual. Somewhat in advance of Eastern Europe and somewhat behind the Anglo-Scandinavian world, the liberal feminist movement in France fell neatly into line with the struggle for women's emancipation that swept the West in the nineteenth century. What distinguished the struggle in France from the struggles elsewhere, however, was the way in which the consciousness of French liberal feminists emerged from the fusion of the historic position of women in the West generally with that of women in France specifically.

The founders of the liberal feminist movement in France stood close to the moment when two long-standing trends converged. One trend involved the images of woman; the other involved the actual conditions of women's lives. In imagery *woman* had for centuries "existed" along a sharply polarized good-evil spectrum. At the saintly end of the spectrum, the extraordinary "good" woman received reverential respect, as in medieval Mariolatry and in the Saint-Simonian quest for a "female messiah," whereas at the devilish end the extraordinary "bad" woman garnered scorn, as in Tertullian's belief in *her* as the "devil's gateway" and Prefect Lacour's conviction, expressed to Josephine Butler, that a "bad" woman could always ruin a "good" man. Yet, although some women attempted to approximate the reverential ideal and others fell victim to the counter-ideal, neither of the extreme images directly affected the actual conditions in which women lived their daily lives. Rather, even where convents provided an institutional path to reverence, most women day in and day out faced circumstances that permitted only a modest measure of saintliness or sinfulness. Placed between what myth prescribed but conditions proscribed, they in effect lived out their lives in a gap delimited by any number of mundane circumstances but relatively free from mythic *woman* constraints.

Within this gap, women at all levels of society held a status roughly comparable to that of men during the early modern era. "Neither feudalism nor the Church freed women," Simone de Beauvoir observed of the masses, but with the abolition of serfdom "husband and wife lived on a footing of equality in small rural communities and among workers; in free labor woman found real autonomy because she played an economic and social part of real importance."[133] At the opposite end of the social hierarchy, according to Margaret H. Darrow, noblewomen had only the power to influence—to beg favors from royalty and to dispense favors to lesser ranks—but in this "they did not differ very much from their husbands. Although men had a wider sphere of influence—the army and the Church, for example—they were most often in the same relationship to power as the women."[134] Among the bourgeoisie in between, Hilda Smith argued, women may have gained new educational opportunities during the Renaissance, but "women were actually better off during the medieval period when the general ignorance of both men and women was greater, and the lack of a good education was not considered such a serious flaw."[135]

This rough equality hardly made the early modern era a golden age for women, but over the next few centuries the gap itself gradually closed, thereby eliminating the space in which women had formerly found at least some options. In imagery the older polarization gave way to the eminently realizable mother-teacher ideal, a comparatively pedestrian destiny that stripped women of their assumed power to save or destroy society directly but strapped them tightly to the present through their assumed talent to mold the future indirectly. Simultaneously, with the growth of commercial and industrial abundance, the conditions of women's lives changed, making it possible as never before for more and more women day in and day out to live out their lives as just wives and mothers. Although only among the bourgeoisie at first, the gap disappeared, slowly in fact but suddenly in impact, leaving women by the mid-nineteenth century with increasingly optionless lives.

In the meantime, as everywhere in the West the gap closed shut between what women should be and what women could be, everywhere, too, the status gap between women as a group and men as a group yawned ever wider. Indeed, according to William O'Neill, "The gap between women's narrowed sphere and men's expanding one appears to have reached its greatest extent at a time when liberal and libertarian ideas were in ascendance.''[136] Women, especially bourgeois women, and even more especially the bourgeois women from whom the liberal feminist movements in France and elsewhere drew their support, thus confronted a transformed reality before they themselves underwent the reality transformation called consciousness.

Yet, although the founders of the liberal feminist movement in France came to consciousness in part by reacting to developments that transcended national boundaries, they also ''switched worlds'' in reaction to developments specific to French society itself. Especially in attempting to interpret women's subordination, they turned their anguish against all that in their view embodied illiberal authoritarianism as well as *masculinisme*, notably imperial ''despotism'' and the Church, and aligned themselves with a divergent array of critics and reformers. Some of these critics espoused feminism for positive ends, hoping first to emancipate women and then to employ women's energy and talent to remake society; others saw it as a negative necessity, fearing the potential destructiveness of an unenlightened womanhood. Still others cared hardly at all about women's emancipation but cooperated with feminists in opposition to common enemies. Thus, although at ''root'' its main outlines reflected conditions common to the nineteenth-century West, liberal feminist consciousness in France also displayed ''route'' characteristics uniquely determined by the historic peculiarities of the society in which it developed.

THE MOVEMENT: A NARRATIVE

Part II

CRISIS AND COOPERATION: MARIA DERAISMES, LÉON RICHER, THE STRATEGY OF *LA BRÈCHE*, AND THE CONGRESS OF 1878

CHAPTER

3

Woman being one of the two great factors of humanity and civilization, all good as well as evil resulting only from the mixed action of the two sexes, let us recognize that any law, any institution that does not bear the imprint of the human duality will be neither viable, nor durable.

Maria Deraismes, 1882

The question of women is no longer a narrow question, the utopia of some EMPTY MINDS; IT IS A UNIVERSAL QUESTION.

Léon Richer, 1878

In the twenty years that elapsed between the publication of Juliette Lamber's *Idées anti-proudhoniennes* in 1858, and the first French Congress for Women's Rights of 1878, the founders of the liberal feminist movement moved from literary to organized protest. No sooner had this transition begun in the late 1860s, however, than they confronted a series of disruptive events, notably the Franco–Prussian War of 1870–1871, the

A version of the material presented in this chapter appeared earlier as "Maria Deraismes, Léon Richer, and the Founding of the French Feminist Movement, 1866–1878," in "Women during the Third Republic," ed. Karen Offen, a special double issue of *Third Republic/Troisième République*, nos. 3–4 (1977), 20–73. Reprinted by permission of *Third Republic/Troisième République*.

Paris Commune of 1871, and the convolutions of the early Third Republic. Each of these events had multiple immediate and long-range effects
on the movement. The international conflict brought an instant suspension of feminist activity, as concern for women's emancipation gave way
to a general concern for national emancipation. The conflict also led
Juliette Lamber, as Madame Adam, to separate herself from the movement's founders in order to trumpet "revenge" againt Germany. France
ended the war by signing a disastrous armistice in January 1871, whereupon the Paris Commune erupted. The ensuing civil disorder cost the
movement dozens of feminist Communards, whose fates ranged from
death to imprisonment or exile, and spawned a wave of "petrophobia"
which strengthened the prevailing belief in two types of women: the
"bad" who, like the *pétroleuses* (women arsonists), go berserk under
stress, and the "good" who either remain at home or perform social
nurturing like nursing. However, the issue that had the greatest effect on
the movement involved the long drawn-out dispute over the Third Republic.

The founders of the French feminist movement could not imagine
women's emancipation in a nondemocratic society. A liberal political
order in which change could come from below constituted in their
perception the essential precondition for any improvement in woman's
situation. For women to be free, France had to be freed from authoritarian
institutions, which meant in effect that liberal republicanism took prece-
dence over feminism whenever political crises arose. Such crises abounded
throughout the Third Republic, but in the 1870s the dangers seemed
particularly acute. Five years passed before a constitution emerged in
1875, and it was not until 1878 that the republic seemed stable enough for
feminists to organize the first French Congress for Women's Rights.
Republican victories in the wake of the crisis of 16 May 1877 played a
critical role in the timing of this event, and, equally important, the
sponsors of the 1878 Congress had by then developed an approach that
they hoped would permit renewed efforts on behalf of women's emancipation without jeopardizing the fragile democracy.

This approach was called *la politique de la brèche* (the strategy of
the breach). Designed to reconcile the movement's primary goal of
women's emancipation with the essential republican precondition, the
"breach" accorded an exclusive priority to women's civil rights and
called for an attack on the "wall" of male privilege at its weakest points.
Women's political rights figured in this approach as a desirable ideal, but

only at a future date. In the view of the *brèchistes,* pressing for the immediate enactment of woman suffrage would provoke additional and unnecessary opposition to the more realizable civil reforms and, if enacted, fuel a resurgence of authoritarianism by delivering millions of female votes into the hands of clerical and political reactionaries. Hence, if the *politique de la brèche* foreshadowed a lengthy struggle to obtain only piecemeal benefits, as French suffragists charged, it nonetheless offered the possibility of at least a few gains without risk to the republic. It also held out the prospect of obtaining political rights without struggle because, according to the *brèchistes,* once women secured full civil equality their enfranchisement would follow as a matter of course. In outline form, the *politique de la brèche* closely resembled the reformist approach of the governing political faction in the 1880s, the Opportunists, who, confronted by a plethora of problems, decided to take up issues one at a time—*sérier les questions.* Above all, however, it reflected the judgment of the movement's two principal figures, Maria Deraismes and Léon Richer.

MARIA DERAISMES

Deraismes was well into her thirties by the time she became a militant feminist.[1] Born in Paris in 1828, she lived out her youth at Pontoise (Seine-et-Oise) in a Voltairean milieu fostered by her liberal republican father. One of five offspring, of whom only she and an older sister survived childhood, she received the type of education usually reserved for sons. She mastered Latin and Greek; studied law, political economy, music, painting, and philosophy; and eventually acquired, according to one of her admirers, the ability to analyze "all the antisocial egotisms."[2] This learnedness enabled her to grapple with bold avant-garde thinkers such as Auguste Comte and John Stuart Mill and to respond with telling effect to the masculinist diatribes of writers like Jules Barbey d'Aurevilly and Alexandre Dumas *fils.* It also provided her with a means of escape from the intellectual prison in which most nineteenth-century French women languished.

Substantial wealth made escape all the easier. Her father amassed a fortune as a wholesale merchant trading with America out of an office on the rue Saint Denis in Paris. His death in 1852, followed by that of her mother nine years later, left Deraismes a rich *rentière* (bondholder) with an income of 50,000 to 70,000 francs per year. Intelligence and wealth combined to reinforce her independent disposition. Unlike her sister Anna and despite a close relationship to Alexandre Weill, author and journalist, Deraismes never married. "Why am I not married?" she once asked laughingly. "There could be several reasons, but the truth is that I have not met a man who pleased me, or if I have met him, I did not see him." As much as oversight, however, it was insight into the servile position of married women that prompted Deraismes to remain single.[3]

Deraismes's literary career began inauspiciously in the early 1860s with a series of theatrical comedies, only one of which played outside the confines of her home.[4] She turned to feminist themes in 1865 with the publication of two pamphlets on women: *Aux Femmes riches* and *Thérésa et son époque*.[5] Then came a spate of articles for various journals, including *Le National, Le Grand Journal, L'Époque,* and *Nain jaune.* When in 1869 Léon Richer founded *Le Droit des femmes*, Deraismes contributed to its introductory issue and to many subsequent numbers. By then she was well on her way to developing the writing talent that later brought her admission to the Société des gens de lettres. She had also by then established herself as an "orator of great talent," a quality of critical importance to any militant in nineteenth-century France.[6]

Deraismes's debut as a speaker brought her into contact with personalities and causes that marked her entire career. Freemasons sponsored the Sunday "philosophical conferences" at which she first spoke, and throughout her lifetime she fought to open Masonic ranks to women. The principal organizers of these conferences, Jules Labbé and Léon Richer, served as editors of Adolphe Guéroult's *L'Opinion nationale (National Opinion)*, a stridently anticlerical sheet that meshed well with Deraismes's devotion to freethinking. The timing of the event, 1866, coincided with a concerted effort on the part of republicans to liberalize, if not topple, the Second Empire and prepared the way for the explosion of conferences that greeted Napoleon III's relaxation of assembly restrictions in 1868. Contacts made at the Grand Orient on the rue Cadet, where the conferences took place, also helped Deraismes's salon become one of the foremost centers of liberal republican opposition to Napoleon III. Finally, by accepting Richer's invitation to become the first woman to address these assemblies of Freemasons, freethinkers, and republicans, Deraismes not only made valuable contacts and discovered her talent for speaking, but she also entered into a cooperative relationship with her host that foreshadowed the founding of the feminist movement in France.

Richer's invitation to speak at the Grand Orient met with reluctance from Deraismes until unexpected help came from Barbey d'Aurevilly, who aroused her ire by singling out women writers as denatured "blue-stockings."[7] In one of his many derisive critiques, Barbey d'Aurevilly venomously focused on the "faults" of sixty-seven-year-old Eugénie Niboyet, a feminist militant who had demanded women's rights during the Revolution of 1848. The critique of Niboyet ran in the *Nain jaune* of February 1866, and within the month Deraismes, offended by Barbey d'Aurevilly's abusive tone, committed herself to speak out. Even then, however, she became frightened at the last moment and begged Richer to speak for her, but he, "wholly encouraging her, pushed her onto the stage and, as her beautiful and sympathetic qualities elicited much applause, she quickly recovered herself."[8]

Her presentation proved electric, according to an eyewitness: "From the outset, she conquered her listeners. Her voice was very resonant, her elocution fluent, her language pure, witty, subtle without being unkind, well projected. With this [came] much good sense and vast erudition. The success was total."[9] Nervousness kept Deraismes away from the issue of women's emancipation on this occasion, but over the next four years she repeatedly analyzed such feminist themes as "woman in society," "woman before the law," "woman in the novel," and "woman such as she is." After the 1868 assembly law went into effect, Richer booked programs into other sites around Paris and recruited additional women speakers, including André Léo and Paule Mink, who along with Deraismes had a great effect on popular opinion. But, although "the journalists in their reports were astonished at the aplomb of women speaking in public" and despite her own conviction that "the influence of the spoken word is superior to that of the written word" and that "the oratorical method has always been the most powerful ally of social transformation," Deraismes developed a preference at odds to her acclaim.[10] "Unfortunately," wrote one of her colleagues, although "very independent, rich, positioned to dispose of her time as she pleased, [Deraismes] gave speeches only rarely, the success left her indifferent. She preferred the circle of her friends to the rostrum, the intimate chat to the speech. And then, undermined by a terrible disease [exacerbated by an accidental childhood poisoning] that brought her acute suffering, she avoided fatigue."[11]

In addition to her speaking debut, the year 1866 marked Deraismes's entry into one of the Second Empire's earliest feminist organizations, the Society for the Demand of Woman's Rights. Founded in the home of André Léo, the Society included such disparate members as Paule Mink, Louise Michel, Néomie and Élie Reclus, Maria Verdure, Eliska Vincent (Girard) and her sister Florestine Mauriceau, Louise David, Ranvier, Madame Jules Simon, and Caroline de Barrau. Republican sentiment and an interest in woman's lot held the group together under the Second Empire, but individual differences prevented large-scale cooperation. Anticlericals like Deraismes objected to the moderate religiosity espoused by Madame Simon and her husband Jules; Caroline de Barrau's interest in inmates of the Saint-Lazare women's prison reflected the group's concern for prostitutes but represented a philanthropic tendency out of step with the activist orientation of Mink, André Léo, and Michel; and in general the group split along class lines, as evidenced by the Communard careers of the Reclus, Mink, Michel, André Léo, and Verdure. Consequently, the Society settled on a goal that, given the innumerable constraints on women, represented a consensual minimum: better education for girls. The Society survived into the Third Republic, but once girls' education began to improve in the late 1870s and 1880s it merged with the Society for the Amelioration of Woman's Condition, founded by Deraismes and Richer in April 1870.[12]

Initially called the Association for Women's Rights (Association pour le droit des femmes), the Society for the Amelioration of Woman's Condition provided the collective base from which Deraismes and Richer imposed their personal leadership on feminism's first generation. Their propaganda arm had appeared the year before in April 1869, when, with financial backing from the utopian socialist Arlès-Dufour and in the face of a "formidable burst of laughter," Richer took advantage of a new press law to found *Le Droit des femmes (The Right of Women)*. Richer served as both president of the Amelioration Society and editor-in-chief of *Le Droit des femmes*, but it was Deraismes who conducted the group's day-to-day activities and helped to keep the fledgling newspaper alive with monetary and literary contributions. On 11 July 1870, Deraismes, assisted by Richer, presided over the first feminist banquet in France.[13] Eight days later France declared war on Prussia.

The seriousness of Deraismes's physical disability manifested itself in the course of the Franco–Prussian War. A bout of emphysema led her to quit Paris and her infirmary in the Faubourg Saint-Denis for a period of convalescence at Saint Malo. There she joined the local republican committee and accepted an invitation to speak at a neighboring theater. She chose the subject "Republic and Monarchy," and, although she had considerable success, "she paid for this success by vomiting blood and her shaky health forced her to remain silent for four years." [14] While recovering she turned her full attention to writing and in short order published a major feminist work in 1872, *Ève contre Monsieur Dumas fils* (*Eve against Mister Dumas the Son*) and a tract extolling the virtues of republican patriotism in 1873, *France et progrès* (*France and Progress*). [15]

Ève contre Dumas fils sprang from a reaction to the second of two postwar incidents that infuriated Deraismes. The first involved the sentencing of three Communard women to death for arson in September 1871. Deraismes disclaimed any sympathy for their conduct but excoriated the verdict as unjust and discriminatory, a perfect example of masculinist justice. The Fourth Council of War had failed to take into account either the extenuating circumstances or the collective nature of the crime. The condemned women had followed orders issued by men who, Deraismes maintained, were both older and better educated. In short, "there were women arsonists (*pétroleuses*) because there were men arsonists (*pétroleurs*)." Yet, she pointed out, of the seventeen male leaders of the Commune who had recently undergone prosecution only two had received death sentences. More galling still was the council's implication that the convicted women had shamed their sex. The two sexes are equally human, she asserted, and the one should not be judged more harshly than the other. [16]

The second incident stemmed from a *cause célèbre*, the Dubourg affair. In 1872 a man by that name summarily executed his adulterous wife, an occurrence so common that no particular importance attached itself to the slaying until Henri d'Ideville intrepidly suggested in *Le Soir* that women like the late Madame Dubourg ought to be pardoned, not killed. The result was a veritable explosion of print, very little of which supported d'Ideville. Alexandre Dumas *fils* proved violently critical. He had earlier referred to Communard women as female animals who resembled decent women only when dead. Now he published a book-length defense of Dubourg's act, aptly entitled *Tue-la (Kill Her)*, and then issued a brochure, *L'Homme-femme (Man-Woman)*, in which he reiterated the Biblical stricture that woman is to man as man is to God.

The Creator conceived man as movement, Dumas explained, whereas woman was but form. It followed therefore that, if a wife sullied her husband's good name, he had every right to kill her; indeed, honor required it.[17]

In *Ève contre Dumas fils*, Deraismes rose to the defense of d'Ideville in particular and women in general, anticipating by almost twenty years her other major feminist work, the 1891 *Ève dans l'humanité* (*Eve in Humanity*).[18] She dismissed Dumas *fils* as poorly educated and uncreative, the fortunate legatee of a well-known father. Only in the eyes of people who knew nothing could he pass as a *savant*. Many thoughtlessly shared his attitude, however, which helped to explain woman's enslavement to man. But, she asked, "what had been the result obtained by the servitude of women?" The answer was obvious. Humanity found itself weakened, deprived of half its force. Two hostile camps had emerged within society, the one vying with the other in general discord, while morality, the foundation of all order, had vanished due to the duplicity of man's double standard. Fortunately, Deraismes observed, the principle of democracy logically and necessarily entailed the emancipation of women. The revolutions of 1789 and 1848 had begun a process that the new republic would continue: "The Republic seems this time to want to strengthen itself, and the rights of the women who march at its side are beginning to be a question that must be reckoned with. Let us persevere in our efforts. Every truth has its hour."[19]

The strident, aggressive, and hopeful tone of Deraismes's response to Dumas *fils* characterized her entire career. At the first women's rights banquet a listener challenged her for neglecting to speak of women's duties. Women's duties have received too much attention, she snapped: "What we claim is what we do not have."[20] The roots of woman's oppression branched deep into the soil of intolerance, Deraismes said on many occasions. In past ages women had often dominated their menfolk, just as in more recent times individual women of exceptional merit had led armies and governed nations.[21] The lot of most women, however, had worsened over the years. Revolutions had offered brief glimmers of hope, as had the doctrines of Saint-Simon and Charles Fourier. But men had abandoned women in both 1789 and 1848, and the new schools of thought had attracted too few followers.[22] It was therefore necessary to begin anew. Since the mid-nineteenth century the struggle for women's rights had all but collapsed, Deraismes remarked in 1883: "I have resuscitated it; I have once again put it into the limelight; I have examined it, studied it under all its points of view, under all its aspects."[23]

According to Deraismes's examination, the Church had to bear a major responsibility for woman's subordination. Its theology deprecated woman, its obscurantism reason, and no society could advance without the total participation of the one and the full utilization of the other. Women had to throw off the influence of priests, which could be done only by establishing a system of universal, rational, scientific, and patriotic education. Women had also to guard against false science. Many still believed that the father alone determined the character of offspring, despite proofs to the contrary by Linné and Buffon, whereas others sought evidence of female inferiority in the dubious findings of phrenologists. Woman was in a state of transition, Deraismes observed: man-made institutions, not natural laws, had retarded her, and only through a wider range of experiences could she overcome her defects.[24]

Furthermore, Deraismes argued, without the aid of women the Third Republic could not hope to survive. The new democracy was rent through and through with contradictions: "Founded on rights, it had at its base the violation of rights."[25] Its governmental structure permitted a fraction to represent the nation, and one sex all humanity. Its leaders denied woman a voice, claiming her sentimentality would disrupt the political process, whereas in truth feelings were inseparable from reason, and men as well as women were guided by both.[26] Republicans rightfully feared the Church's influence over women, but why then did the men in power allow priests to preach and to teach? Could they not see that to escape from her contemporary bondage woman had only two options, the fanaticism of religion or the license of prostitution?[27] Far from being an exact science, politics was among the most general of disciplines. Its school was life, and its goal the synthesis of all factors, especially the fusion of the male and the female elements. "When woman has taken the place assigned to her by nature," Deraismes informed the Freemasons of Pecq in 1882, "you will have strong chances of assuring to the republican edifice durability and indestructibility."[28]

An emancipated womanhood would bring more than just political stability to France. For, "by her constitution and the nature of her mandate," Deraismes proclaimed, woman is "the moral and pacific agent par excellence."[29] Woman possessed innate talents in four critical areas, Deraismes believed. Educationally, she presented a superior example to children, being more reserved and more in possession of herself than man. Morally, "the senses have less of a grip on her; she has come to regulate passion, to subordinate it to duty."[30] Economically, woman knew through her household tasks both the price and the sanctity of life. Finally, woman was a peacemaker. "It is banal to repeat that war and armed peace are the obstacles to all real progress," Deraismes reflected, "but the elimination of woman from universal suffrage necessarily means the prolongation of the bellicose spirit." Reason had already begun to displace martial glory as a source of grandeur, she claimed, and we "can strongly affirm that this weakening of military prestige is the sign of the advent of woman." The potential benefit of woman's domestic virtue to the whole of society was incalculable: "She will bring to public life her beautiful qualities: sagacity, perseverence, abnegation." Without full utilization of these qualities, society must inevitably suffer: "Woman being one of the two great factors of humanity and civilization, all good as well as evil resulting only from the mixed action of the two sexes, let us recognize that any law, any institution that does not bear the imprint of the human duality will be neither viable, nor durable."[31]

Considerable confusion lay at the heart of this analysis, especially as regards the apparent contradiction between the belief in woman's innate qualities, which presumably would bring instant improvement to society once women secured greater freedom, and woman's backwardness, which could only be overcome through education and experience. Despite this confusion, though, which appeared over and over again in the writings of nineteenth-century French feminists, Deraismes espoused a dual orientation that opened to her a vast field of action on a variety of fronts. One side of this orientation emphasized the "political ideal" that only a liberal republic could enable women to live freely. The other side stressed what might be called the "woman ideal," that no republic could survive unless women played within it the fullest possible role. In theory Deraismes invested each side of the orientation with equal value. In practice, however, the political side assumed operative priority, with the result that the feminist cause frequently received less than a full measure of Deraismes's energy and money.

Upon her return to Paris from Saint Malo, Deraismes immediately plunged into the struggle against reactionary Bonapartists, Legitimists, and Orleanists. When Victorien Sardou's *Rabagas* cast aspersions on the young republic's virtue, she broke silence and at her favorite Capucines's

Hall gave voice to "her republican indignation, her ardor as a citizen wounded in her convictions, and all the vehemence of an apostle who fights to defend her faith."[32] Such vehemence also left her a marked person, and in the aftermath of the antirepublican crusade that toppled Adolphe Thiers in 1873, Interior Minister Buffet outlawed her feminist group. Richer pleaded the Amelioration Society's cause in *Le Droit des femmes*, but the ban continued until after the crisis of 16 May 1877 restored a republican majority and the 1878 Women's Rights Congress demonstrated the feminist movement's moderation.

Deraismes reacted to the ban by expanding her political role. During the course of the 1877 crisis she rallied her home district and succeeded in securing the election of Monsieur Sénard, the first republican deputy from the Department of Seine-et-Oise. Faced with monarchist Premier de Broglie's prohibition of public assembly, Deraismes had turned her beautiful Pontoise property of Mathurins into a campaign headquarters. There, recorded one of her colleagues, she engineered Sénard's victory by improvising "household conferences whose success drew people... from the entire department; often several hundred came; during those days, the salon was too small and they trampled on the prohibition of M. de Broglie and on the flowers in the garden."[33] In 1881 Deraismes increased her political influence by taking over a newspaper, *Le Républicain de Seine-et-Oise*. She abandoned it five years later when her hand-picked republican slate swept to victory in the 1885 election. Thereafter the intimacy of her salon on the rue Cardinet kept her in touch with leading radical republicans. Through it she led her friends in opposition to General Boulanger in the late 1880s, offsetting in part the influence of his foremost backer, the wealthy Duchess d'Uzès.

In the meantime, Deraismes assumed a prominent role in organizing opposition to clericalism in France. Consistent with her participation in Richer's philosophical conferences and her oft-repeated view of the Church as an obstacle to progress and as an arm of *masculinisme*, she stepped up her campaign against "the empire of the Church and the authority of the priest" in the wake of the republican victories at the end of the 1870s. In 1879 she attacked the notion of Catholicism as a civilizing force in a *Lettre au clergé français* (*Letter to the French Clergy*).[34] Two years later at the Grand Orient she served as vice-president of the first Anticlerical Congress in France, which called for separation of church and state, civil interment, divorce, and equal rights for men and women.[35] Her role in this event turned out to be larger than expected: the president of the congress, Deputy Victor Schoelcher, "attended little, presided rarely, and in sum it was Maria Deraismes who directed the event with as much tact as authority." Deraismes also authored the resolution that called for "men, and especially free-thinking men, to treat their wives as their companions in their meetings, circles, groups, and to work to achieve legal recognition for them as their equals." "It is understood," the resolution concluded, "that political rights are included in the word: Equality."[36] In 1885 local anticlericals paid tribute to her by electing her president of the Seine-et-Oise Federation of Free-Thinking Groups (La Fédération des groupes de la libre pensée de Seine-et-Oise).

Devotion to republicanism and anticlericalism brought Deraismes into contact with French Freemasonry, which provided much of the ideological and organizational support for these two causes. It saddened and angered her that Freemasons excluded women from full membership because she believed the effect of that policy was to drive women into the arms of the Church. But as long as clericals opposed rational scientific progress, she maintained, it was necessary to support their opponents. And despite a constitutional prohibition against admitting "slaves, women, fools, stupid atheists, immoral and dishonored people," a minority of Masons like Richer and Victor Hugo sought to open the ranks to women. An apparent breakthrough for Deraismes came in January 1882, when a lodge at Pecq (Seine-et-Oise) admitted her. "The door you have opened will not be closed again on me or on all the legion that will follow me," she exlaimed to her Masonic brethren. Six months later the door closed. Pecq's parent organization slapped the lodge with a suspension, forcing it to recant by once again barring Deraismes. A decade passed, and then in 1893 Deraismes retaliated by founding a special lodge with cooperation from Clémence Royer and Senator Georges Martin, *vénérable* of the lodge "Freethinkers of Pecq" ("Libres penseurs du Pecq"). Taking the name "Human Rights" (*Le Droit Humain*), the new lodge admitted men and women on an equal basis. Traditional lodges refused to recognize the hybrid, but it flourished nonetheless, spreading to America, Africa, and several European countries. It survives today under the name Mixed and International Human Rights (Droit humain mixte et international).[37]

Within the contours of her grand design for a lay and liberal republican France, Deraismes focused considerable attention on details of particular parts. Some of the details, such as her advocacy of governmental decentralization, had little to do with the woman question. Other details bore on it rather directly, like her support of the French wing of Josephine Butler's crusade to abolish state regulation of prostitution. Several details bridged the gap between the political ideal and the woman ideal, reflecting Deraismes's interest in moral regeneration. In defense of the family, for example, she campaigned against novels "with their contemptible heroes, their exploitation of scandal and their destruction of 'principles and sentiments.'" Duty must temper pleasure lest the family collapse: "The phalanx of bastards and foundlings are the innocent victims of this pleasure."[38] In opposition to the realism of Émile Zola, Deraismes maintained that "the ideal is the true goal of literature and it alone can guide humanity toward great things and open to it large horizons":

He who would deny the ideal must deny progress....M. Zola robs man of his moral liberty. Under the pretext of science, he arbitrarily exaggerates a general law [of heredity]. He offers us every chance to descend and none to rise; this is the fatal law. According to his system, what ought we to become? Who knows? Perhaps poisonous mushrooms?[39]

A similar moral perspective led her to oppose vivisection and to join both the French Society against Vivisection (Société française contre la vivisection) and the Popular League against the Abuse of Vivesection (Ligue populaire contre l'abus de la vivisection). "I see you full of blood, of blood up to your necks, but it is not yours," Deraismes wrote of those who experimented on animals:

Ah! What a happy generation you prepare for us there [in your laboratories]. Cast a glance at all those adolescents who, on the pretext of studying and learning, petrify their heart, blind their sentiment, killing, finally, in them the principle of all emotion; praising themselves for seeing suffering and remaining unaffected.

Coupled with Darwinism, vivisection portended euthanasia or worse. Indeed, a young man imbued with just such ideas had not so long ago killed a woman who had befriended him because, Deraismes related, he considered her a "vulgar being who lived more vegetably than intellectually." "I am convinced," she concluded, that France "will disabuse itself of this new invasion of barbarians, and will justify, one more time, its imperishable motto: Right, Justice, Humanity."[40]

The imperishable motto excluded communism.[41] Eliminating class antagonism was imperative, Deraismes maintained, "because that opposition of interests forcibly creates a multiple, heterogeneous politics, inevitably engendering disorder and perturbation." In place of such antagonism, there should emerge a "persistent crusade against misery" in order to establish "the most favorable conditions for [individual] physical, intellectual, and moral development." Such conditions, however, could never materialize under communism:

Thank God, we can rest assured, because that faction [the communists] is composed of only the most ignorant and least honorable individuals....Communism is repugnant to nature....It is absurd. Certainly it is not impossible to seize riches violently, but what remains inalienable, indivisible, immovable are the sources that produce them: talent, genius, knowledge, character, beauty, health, etc. These are riches that cannot be expropriated and cannot be held in common.

Extensive reforms had to be undertaken, but only with moderation. No justice could come from "turning society upside down, of displacing injustices, of raising on high what had been on low and vice versa." Rather, a just society required "successively introducing, after hard examination, profound study, and partial experimentation, the modifications, the reforms, where they are indispensible and the most legitimately claimed." To this end and in contrast to the communism she loathed, Deraismes praised the doctrines of the early utopian socialists, who not only sought women's emancipation but who also elaborated a "just and incisive critique of our current [social] organization." Liberals had no cause to fear them, she asserted, because neither Saint-Simon nor Fourier "had ever professed the division of riches. They wanted, on the contrary, salaries to become proportional to capacities, and they accorded a very large role to genius, to talent."

Toward the end of her life, Deraismes acknowledged the existence of two schools of feminism, liberal and protectionist. Protectionists stressed woman's unique character and advocated selective reforms such as the abolition of woman's right to work at night. Liberals eschewed special legislation and demanded integral reform, desiring all laws to apply equally to the two sexes. Deraismes, as her frequent pronouncements suggest, sided with the liberals. Indeed, in 1889 she helped organize an independent women's rights congress because the directors of that year's centennial exposition intended to impose as president of the offical women's congress Alphonse Daudet, a leading exponent of special laws for women. Liberty represented the first need of all human beings, Deraismes intoned at the opening session, and it alone could foster initiative, development, and progress. The rights of liberty are indivisible, she explained, and the enactment of special laws for women could only demean the sex that legislators pretended to serve.[42]

The reforms on which Deraismes concentrated fell far short of her liberal, integral rhetoric. Convinced that the feminists of 1789 and 1848 had erred in demanding too much too soon, she selectively employed *la politique de la brèche* to shelve a variety of proposals. She initially downplayed women's political rights, leaving only civil disabilities, and even within this category she limited her activism to a handful of issues. Her most sweeping objective was better education for women, followed closely by claims for the reestablishment of divorce, woman's right to file a paternity suit, and the abolition of state-supervised prostitution. Less important to French women as a group but vital to the interests of the property-owning class to which she belonged were three of Deraismes's most ardently sought reforms: the right of wives to dispose freely of their own income, the right of women in general to witness public and private acts on the same footing as men, and the right of business women to vote for and serve on commerce tribunals.[43]

With the exception of education for women, which improved in the 1880s as republicans sought to wean women from the Church, and divorce, whose reestablishment in 1884 also reflected the politics of anticlericalism, only the business women's vote made headway during Deraismes's lifetime. She launched her campaign for it by sending out 17,000 circulars to women merchants and shopkeepers but received only two responses, one of which was slightly abusive. In 1883 she turned directly to the Chamber of Deputies with a petition in the name of her feminist group. Six years later the Chamber capitulated, but the Senate balked when a survey revealed that seventy-nine of ninety-six chambers of commerce objected to the measure. Finally in 1894, as Deraismes lay dying of cancer, the Senate passed an amended version of the bill, permitting business women to vote but prohibiting them from holding the judgeships themselves.[44]

Deraismes's career elicited a variety of reactions. Many of her contemporaries, unconvinced of the need for women's emancipation, identified her with the revolutionary and philosophical excesses so long associated with feminism. They saw her as simply a more refined version of the *pétroleuses*, dangerous to moral and social order and a threat to the family.[45] Even a majority of Freemasons viewed her as "a kind of monster," possessed of an essence distinct from that of other women.[46] More recently, a French critic has faulted her for giving "to feminism a cerebral character that removed from it all possibility of action on the majority of women of her epoch."[47] In general, throughout the movement's first two generations, Deraismes's call for an extension of liberalism to women alarmed the bourgeoisie, whereas working-class people distrusted her because of her upper-class background.

The contemporaries whom Deraismes called her *consoeurs* (co-sisters) also tended to be critical. Feminist Jane Misme, founder of *La Française*, gave her credit for being the first militant "who has brought to the cause the prestige of a personality of high value and the influence of a socially privileged situation." Deraismes also deserved recognition for organizing "the nucleus of an army" and for introducing "to the combatants a plan of attack." Especially in urging her followers to concentrate on piecemeal reforms, Misme emphasized, Deraismes advanced a strategy that others could employ with great success. Where Deraismes erred was in permitting feminism to become identified in the public mind with causes "more or less revolutionary":

Maria Deraismes, prudent enough to strike from her action, if not from her doctrine and from her discourses, the demand for woman's political rights, was a political woman, directrice of a journal, party militant, and, above all, apostle of free thinking and Freemasonry. But feminism would only have a chance to be more generally understood and accepted when its propaganda, detached from all political, philosophical or religious taint would reveal it clearly for what it is: a cause of general interest.[48]

It thus seemed clear, Misme charged, "that Deraismes's political passions impeded her feminist activity" to such an extent that what she gave to women with one hand she took back with the other.[49]

Of like opinion was Jeanne Schmahl, whose Advance Messenger waged a successful campaign over fourteen years (1893–1907) for the witness and income reforms. In Misme's view, Schmahl and her moderate allies, notably Madame Adam and the Duchesse d'Uzès, had far outdistanced Deraismes in "the art of taking up issues one at a time and in plucking ripe fruits." Schmahl in turn agreed with Misme that Deraismes had erred badly in linking feminism to political and religious issues. "Until women have got the franchise they can neither be Republicans nor Monarchists," Schmahl maintained, "it is therefore foolish to stamp them beforehand as belonging to this or that political camp." French women had rallied slowly to feminism "not only because they are profoundly ignorant of its signification, but because they disapprove of the socialistic and irreligious attitude of most of the leaders." Deraismes also deserved blame for the movement's fragmentation, a development that coincided with Schmahl's entry into feminism. She "was despotic," Schmahl wrote in 1896, "and lacked that primordial quality of great leaders—a quality that has ever been one of the distinctive characteristics of all great generals—the ability to recognize and utilize talent and merit in the rising soldiers of her army."[50]

More critical still was Marie Dronsart, who asserted that, although "Maria Deraismes was assuredly *someone*; one should acknowledge and deplore it all the more that she put her beautiful intelligence to the service of many erroneous and subversive ideas." Fortunately the situation had begun to change, Dronsart wrote two years after Deraismes's death: "Moderation and patience were entering into feminine councils, and the omnipotence of Maria Deraismes was weakening; other women were coming to the fore and making themselves heard; that was very painful to her [in her last days], because for twenty years, she could say: 'Le feminisme, c'est moi' [I am feminism]." As an advocate of Catholic bourgeois "family feminism," Dronsart had no difficulty in agreeing with Misme and Schmahl that Deraismes erred in tying feminism to anticlericalism:

Christian morality is treated more than contemptuously; its divine founder has discovered nothing; the priests, without exception, are condemned as malefactors, born enemies of societies, of light and of justice....This is what the admirers of Maria Deraismes style as the "dialectic without passion."...State socialism was dear to her and the so-called free society of which she dreamt would have been so protected, guarded, regulated, that individual initiative would be annihilated in a stroke and roped like no theocracy or autocracy would have known how to invent.[51]

Deraismes's domination of Seine-et-Oise's political fortunes left her susceptible to charges of hypocrisy as well. Suffrage-oriented feminists led by Hubertine Auclert repeatedly castigated her in the 1880s for devoting and donating too much to republicanism in her home department and too little to the struggle for women's political rights. Her wealth evoked a further reproach at the time of her death. An obituary notice of March 1894 pointed out that Deraismes left her entire income to her sister, making no provision for the movement:

So rich, would she leave nothing to continue her work of feminine emancipation?. . .She permitted the hope that after her death she would not forget the emancipators. There are some grave deceptions here. Poor groups which went into debt to buy the wreath [for Deraismes's funeral] are spreading recriminations in hindsight against what they call forgetfulness, not to say treason.[52]

Shortly thereafter a motion to add Deraismes's name to the offical title of the group she founded ended in failure. A majority of its members, while acknowledging her leadership, felt such an honor would be a slur on the reputations of other feminist pioneers.[53]

Many of the barbs flung at Deraismes reflected the passage of time. As Misme conceded, Deraismes anticipated by twenty years the large-scale entry into feminism of bourgeois women, especially Protestant enthusiasts of moral regeneration.[54] This influx began at the end of Deraismes's life and eventually resulted in the founding of the National Council of French Women in 1901. By then, however, the Third Republic had achieved relative stability, and, despite the Dreyfus affair, the political fears of Deraismes's generation, which reached its majority during the abortive Revolution of 1848, no longer seemed so germane. Much of the groundwork for the movement had emerged by then as well, which for the first time in France enabled a second generation of feminists to build directly on the consciousness and dynamic of its immediate predecessor. Deraismes nonetheless remained dissatisfied with her accomplishments. "Justice!" she pronounced on her death bed, "in it I believe with all my soul, but I have searched for it in this world and I have not found it; perhaps it will be elsewhere."[55] For this earthly quest, however, she bequeathed a sense of direction to her successors, whether or not they fully appreciated it. Indeed, wrote the liberal feminist Léon Abensour in 1921, "many contemporary feminists have, without moreover always rendering unto Caesar that which belongs to him, borrowed ideas, facts, and arguments from the works of Maria Deraismes."[56]

LÉON RICHER

Deraismes's mentor and closest associate in the movement was Léon Pierre Richer, whose devotion to women's emancipation earned him the accolade "the women's man" (*l'homme des femmes*) from his sympathizers. Compared with Deraismes, the "talented polemicist" and "golden-voiced" orator, he was a "tranquil and serious man" and, according to Simone de Beauvoir, "the true founder of feminism in France." He shared Deraismes's liberal political outlook, and at the time of their first meeting he held the post of *vénérable maître* in the Masonic lodge Mars et les arts. His origins were relatively humble, at least in contrast to Deraismes's. Born in 1824 in the Department of Orne west of Paris, he worked for eleven years as a notary's clerk for the Orleans Railroad. He was married, and both his wife and a son Paul assisted him in founding the French feminist movement.[57]

Journalism constituted Richer's major avocation, and toward the end of the Second Empire he quit his job in order to pursue a newspaper career. He contributed to *L'Alliance réligieuse* and the *Libre conscience* of Henri Carle at first and later became editor-in-chief of the daily *République radicale*. He also collaborated for years on the *Petit Parisien*, writing under the name of Jean Frollo. When he applied for permission to found *Le Droit des femmes* in 1869, the prefect of police reported his financial situation as sound and his political views as liberal. By then he had acquired a reputation for controversy, due in large part to a weekly series entitled "Lettres d'un libre-penseur à un curé de village" ("Letters from a Free Thinker to a Village Priest") for Adolphe Guéroult's *L'Opinion nationale*. In reaction to this column, Richer recalled, atheists and materialists reproached him for not going far enough, whereas priests from all corners of France sent him their maledictions. For the first of many times he found himself branded as a destroyer of faith, a troubler of consciences, and an arch enemy of the family.

Richer shared Deraismes's faith in *la politique de la brèche*, and a eulogy at the time of his death in 1911 praised him for avoiding utopian schemes and for seeking social "amelioration without disruption."[58] While he lived, however, suffrage-oriented feminists considered him "a reactionary and an opportunist.'' Woman's political rights struck him as a desirable ideal, but he ardently opposed every effort to enact them immediately. ''The feminine mind,'' he remarked, ''was still too crushed by the yoke of the Church.''[59] If women voted the republic would not last six months: ''It is enough for us to have to struggle against reactionaries of the masculine sex without giving to these partisans of defeated regimes the support of millions of female ballots subject to the occult domination of the priest, the confessor.''[60]

Richer therefore concentrated on removing women's civil disabilities. Every issue of the journal he edited between 1869 and 1891 carried a critique of French law. On the inside cover in two columns he listed relevant points of the Napoleonic Code and how he proposed to amend them. In the mid-1870s his proposals centered on male abuses outside marriage and woman's subordination within it. Specifically he railed against loopholes in the law that punished men only when they *habitually* corrupted minors or used *force* in seducing girls over fifteen. Women ought to have the right to file paternity suits, he maintained, just as men could initiate maternity inquests, and fathers should be held responsible for the care of illegitimate children. Betrothals should be treated as contracts, enabling the jilted party to sue for breach of promise, and women's right to bear witness in criminal proceedings should be extended to cover all public and private acts. To improve marriage, Richer called for conjugal equality in rearing children, handling personal wealth, disposing of household property, and belonging to family councils. Husbands should also suffer the same severe penalty as wives for adultery, thus eliminating the double standard that condoned male immorality outside the family domicile. In order to guarantee the sanctity of marital unions, he demanded divorce in place of the hypocrisy of legal separation, ''which breaks marriage without dissolving it, separates spouses without disuniting them, and opens the door to shameful compromises.''[61]

Between 1872 and 1883 Richer published four books on the woman question.[62] The first was a book of quotations, *Le Livre des femmes* (*The Women's Book*). The last two, *La Femme libre* (*The Free Woman*) of 1877 and *Le code des femmes* (*The Code of Women*) of 1883, covered a wide range of issues. The second, which caused a sensation when it appeared in 1873, was entitled *Le Divorce*. Louis Blanc wrote the introduction, and the text elaborated Richer's ideas for a model act. Alfred Naquet, the ''father'' of divorce, took up the proposal and managed it through the legislature eleven years later. The resultant law, which Richer termed "a magnificent victory," restored a right suppressed since 1816. Richer viewed it as immensely beneficial to women, pointing out that of the 3,286 legal separations in 1882 wives had secured 86 percent. But the grounds for divorce fell short of expectations. The law of 1884 required demonstration of cause in the form of adultery, grievous injury, or criminal conviction, the Senate having struck mutual consent from the bill. Nevertheless, Deraismes expressed pleasure that the grounds of adultery applied equally to either spouse, and suffragist Hubertine Auclert saw in Naquet's decade-long campaign a source of inspiration for future feminist efforts.[63]

The reestablishment of divorce appeared to confirm Richer's belief that his was an epoch ripe for reform.[64] But the euphoria rapidly vanished. Richer ranked woman's right to file a paternity suit next in importance to divorce. He demanded it for years (as Deraismes did for the *commerçante* vote) but failed repeatedly. Not until 1912 did the Senate approve the bill, and by then Richer had been dead for several months. In the meantime, other aspects of his program fared better, especially, as a result of Schmahl's efforts, the rights of women to bear witness and of wives to control their own income. But perhaps Richer's greatest achievement in a career that spanned a half-century was his first. Shortly before the Second Empire struck down the Faculty of Medicine's sex barrier, a fight in which he also played a prominent role, Richer threw his influence behind Julie Daubié's successful struggle to open *baccalauréat* examinations to women. The victory they won, so crucial to the liberal notion of "equal opportunity," helped to pave the way for many subsequent breaches of the male-dominated education system.

Although Richer's sex afforded him more opportunities to influence legislation directly, his importance to French feminism had little to do with actual legal reform. Like Deraismes, Richer's main contribution to the cause of women's emancipation lay in his role as one of the movement's foremost organizers and propagandists. Also like Deraismes, though, Richer imparted to liberal feminism a contradictory rationale for women's emancipation. Both he and Deraismes accorded centrality to the family, on the reconstruction of which they thought the fate of the Third Republic depended. "It is an inevitable fact," Richer wrote, "that tyranny in the family gives birth to tyranny in the state."[65]

Yet, even more than Deraismes, Richer linked woman's assumed nature to a familial destiny. Nothing distinguished woman's intellectual potential from that of man, he argued, but, because equivalence marked the sexes, the family constituted woman's primary sphere for action, "her preferred environment, her natural atmosphere." Through work woman had to free herself from her dependence on man, and through education she had to free herself from her ignorant attachment to monarchism and clericalism, but "nobody intended by that," he disclaimed, "to give her the absurd advice that she should abandon her sex."[66] Neither her schools nor her jobs had to be the same as those of man. "No," he exclaimed in 1872, "woman should remain woman.[67] In 1877, he approvingly cited the motto of Susan B. Anthony's and Elizabeth Cady Stanton's 1868 newspaper, *Revolution*: "Principle, Not Policy—Justice, Not Favors—Men their Rights and Nothing More—Women Their Rights and Nothing Less."[68] But the ambivalence remained. Although Richer staked the future well-being of France and the family on woman, for her emancipation he could only urge, hoping in his words "perhaps to avoid any misunderstanding," conformity to the ambiguous principle of "*equality* in difference," of "variety within the oneness of the species."[69]

THE AMELIORATION SOCIETY AND *L'AVENIR DES FEMMES*

In April 1870, in one of their last acts before the deluge of foreign and civil war, Deraismes and Richer established the Association for Women's Rights. Imperial officials, as well as conservatives during the early Third Republic, objected to the use of the word *right* in the title, holding that only the government could stipulate what was a "right." The group therefore changed its name to the Association for the Future of Woman (Association pour l'avenir de la femme). The journal that Richer founded in 1869, *Le Droit des femmes*, elicited the same objection, forcing it too to appear throughout most of the next decade as *L'Avenir des femmes (The Future of Women)*. In 1875 the Association joined the International Woman's League, based in New York, and altered its name once more, emerging as the Society for the Amelioration of Woman's Condition. Regardless of the name, however, the Amelioration Society and *L'Avenir des femmes* together provided Deraismes and Richer with the means to control the organization and propaganda of the movement in its early years. No one challenged Richer's paper, due in part to press laws prohibiting women from directing journals until 1881. The Amelioration Society had two rivals in addition to André Léo's education-oriented group, but Julie Daubié's Association for Woman's Emancipation collapsed with its founder's death in 1874, and Hubertine Auclert's maverick suffrage group, established in 1876, did not come into its own until the 1880s.

Richer served as president of the Amelioration Society until shortly after the Women's Rights Congress of 1878. Deraismes then occupied the post until her death in 1894, followed by her sister, Anna Féresse-Deraismes. Only on the eve of World War I did the Society's leadership pass outside the "family." Despite the wealth of the Deraismes sisters, the Society was not well off financially until the early 1880s, when it merged with André Léo's group. The fusion of the two organizations brought nearly 20,000 francs into the Society's coffers, giving it a degree of security unprecedented within the movement. It also brought about a lengthening of the Society's name, which became the Society for the Amelioration of Woman's Condition and the Demand of her Rights (Société pour l'amélioration du sort de la femme et la revendication de ses droits).[70]

Fearing that women voters would undermine the republic, the Amelioration Society excluded political rights from its program in the 1870s, stressing instead the "complete identification of man and woman from the point of view of legal possession and the exercise of civil rights." Specifically its platform called for equality within marriage, one morality for all, reestablishment of divorce, and the "progressive initiation of woman into civic life." In the name of liberal individualism, it also demanded complete parity in education "without other limits than aptitudes and will," open access to all careers and professions, and equal pay for equal work.[71] Its original charter emphasized that in light of advances made by women in other countries, "particularly in England and America," France could afford to "remain behind the times no longer" and that, consistent with Pascal's words, if the strong could not be made just, then "let us at least make that which is just, strong." "Woman must be considered, if not identical to man," the charter ambiguously announced, "at least his equal in humanity; that is equality in dissimilarity." Woman's duties, although no less valuable than man's, might also be distinct; "it is equality in diversity." But in moral responsibility the same held for woman as for man; "it is equality in morality," and "therefore there is good reason to proclaim loudly the equality of the sexes before the law and with reference to morality.''[72]

The greatest crisis in the Amelioration Society's early years occurred in December 1875, when monarchist Interior Minister Buffet outlawed the group, citing its republican and anticlerical tendencies as a threat to public order. Richer, who suddenly found himself president of an illegal organization, denied the charge. In a series of editorials for *L'Avenir* and in an open letter to the press, he defended the Society as a force for ''moral order'' whose sole purpose was to improve woman's lot. Foreign newspapers wondered how a group devoted to stamping out prostitution, ''that most hideous expression of debauchery,'' could be considered a threat, Richer reported, but *L'Avenir* dared not print their comments for fear of also being outlawed. Richer speculated that Victor Hugo's obvious sympathy for the group, as well as Garibaldi's adherence, had prompted Buffet's action, and he accused the interior minister of disliking anyone who was not Bonapartist or clerical. But for the moment nothing could be done about it. He advised patience to Amelioration Society members and urged them to carry on the group's work as individuals. Buffet could not last long, Richer predicted; soon the current ministry would give way to one more liberal. Moreover, the ban on the Society had brought many new subscribers to *L'Avenir*. ''And that is how, in wanting to weaken us, the minister of the interior has fortified us,'' Richer observed. ''Thank you! A thousand times thank you!''[73]

Subsequent events proved Richer correct. The Amelioration Society began to regroup clandestinely in March 1877. Two months later, on 16 May, a serious constitutional crisis erupted, when President Mac-Mahon dismissed his prime minister without consulting the parliament and called for dissolution of the Chamber of Deputies. Republicans rallied in opposition to this ''coup'' and swept to victory at the polls, forcing the president to accept parliamentary sovereignty. The Amelioration Society benefited from the republican upsurge but did not immediately recover offical sanction. Richer complained a year later that the authorization his group deserved had gone to another worthy but less-elevated cause, the Animal Protection Society. The Amelioration Society nonetheless renewed its campaign for women's rights. Finally, on 3 August 1878, shortly after the Women's Rights Congress of that year, it once again acquired legal authorization. Several months later, Richer took advantage of the liberal trend to restore his journal's original name, *Le Droit des femmes*.[74]

At the time of the ban, Richer cited smallness as a point in the Amelioration Society's favor, implying that regardless of political orientation it hardly constituted a threat. He estimated its membership at 150 to 160, including foreigners, but its meetings drew only 10 to 12 of the more militant.[75] An 1894 *Bulletin* of the Amelioration Society listed 17 individuals and a group named Solidarity (*Solidarité*) of Geneva as founders. Seven of the original 17 were men, including 1 departmental councilor and 3 who became deputies. Among the men the most militant by far was Joseph de Gasté, a deputy from Finistère. All of the women but 2, Deraismes and Charlotte Duval, had married, although several had been widowed by 1870. By 1894, 9 of the 17 had died, including Deraismes.[76] Absent from the list of founders were Richer, Victor Hugo, and Garibaldi. Also absent were militants like Auclert, Aline Valette, Eugénie Potonié-Pierre, and Madame Vincent, each of whom joined after the 1870–1871 interregnum and later drifted away to found their own journals or groups.

Although president of the Amelioration Society throughout most of its first decade, Richer's primary concern was propaganda. He therefore turned the group's daily operation over to the Deraismes sisters and Griess-Traut and devoted himself to convincing doubters that a feminist newspaper could succeed. He viewed the effort as a further extension of what the Saint-Simonians and Laboulaye's *Histoire morale des femmes* (*Moral History of Women*) had begun. His previous journalistic experience, as well as his moderation, brought him the support of influential men of letters, including Émile de Girardin, Camille Flammarion, Ernest Legouvé, Frédéric Passy, Adolphe Guéroult, Jules Claretie, Francisque Sarcey, Victor Hugo, and Louis Blanc.[77] It also brought him letters of appreciation from the Englishmen John Stuart Mill and John Bright.[78]

To announce the reappearance of *L'Avenir* after the interruption of the Franco–Prussian War and the Paris Commune, Richer staged a sumptuous banquet in July 1872. One hundred fifty people packed the Corazza restaurant at the Palais Royal to hear Victor Hugo endorse the struggle for women's rights. Louis Blanc covered the event in a series of articles, and in general the press raised a great noise about it. But by then financial pressures had already turned *L'Avenir* from a weekly into a monthly, and for a brief period in 1873 it appeared only every other month. To cut contributors' expenses Richer wrote under the pseudonyms of Georges Bath and Jeanne Mercoeur, and to increase circulation he sent out costly complimentary copies while reducing subscription rates for second- and third-year renewals from ten to seven and five francs, respectively. Donations provided some relief—the Deraismes sisters regularly gave forty francs per issue—but not enough. By March 1877 *L'Avenir* had accumulated a debt of 1,200 francs, forcing Richer to salvage it by incorporating. Poor health led him to suspend publication indefinitely in December 1891.[79] At twenty-two years of age, Richer's journal had achieved a longevity unequalled by any of its pre-World War I rivals— and shortly thereafter a group of second-generation feminists resurrected it.

L'Avenir's finances suffered in part from Richer's program. His support of divorce proved particularly costly. Protests of an "extreme violence" inundated the journal's headquarters at Clermont (Oise). A reader from Nantes engaged Richer in a protracted exchange of published letters, and sixty or seventy women at Lyon pledged no longer to read *L'Avenir*. Richer estimated that altogether over 200 divorce opponents canceled their subscriptions at a "dead loss" of 2,000 francs per year. His support of woman's right to file a paternity suit likewise excited opposition, although the monetary impact is unclear. Jeanne Deroin, the utopian socialist feminist who fled France in 1851, wrote from England that the most certain effect of such a law would be an increase in infanticides. More unpopular than either proposal was Richer's call for legitimizing incestuous unions rather than leaving the parties in a state of public concubinage. He recommended limiting approval to "certain exceptional cases" and recognized that it would take fifteen or twenty years, "perhaps less," to secure the measure. He also anticipated renewed vilification for sapping the "sacred base of the family." But always, he proudly confessed, "my greatest wrong has been to be right too soon."[80]

Richer subtitled *L'Avenir* a "Political, Literary, and Social Economy Review." He hoped not only to promote feminist reforms but also to interest women in issues such as disarmament and an end to conscription, separation of church and state, tax cuts, abolition of capital punishment, and peace through international arbitration. After the crisis of 16 May 1877, he warned continually against the clerical threat and accused Louis Veuillot's *L'Univers* of attempting to involve France in a war with Italy on behalf of the Pope. He also warned against the reactionary tendencies of *Le Gaulois*, citing as evidence its attacks on the republicanism of the Deraismes sisters. The time had not yet come for woman suffrage, he maintained, but loyal democrats should do whatever they could to secure the support of woman's influence.[81]

Richer made a bid for the Chamber of Deputies in February 1876 at Troyes. He lost, as he did again in 1881, but what disturbed him more was that only two other candidates, Émile Acollas and Alfred Naquet, had campaigned on *L'Avenir*'s feminist program. Soon after his electoral defeat, Richer turned his attention to expanding feminism's organizational base. In 1876 he applauded Auclert's new group, despite its suffrage orientation, and served on its committee of initiative. The following year he urged each community throughout the land to establish a group of its own and published the statutes of a Parisian organization called Equality (*Egalité*) as a model. However, when in late 1876 Céleste Hardouin created the French League for the Amelioration of Women's Condition (Ligue française pour l'amélioration du sort des femmes) to improve the lot of working women, Richer endorsed the goal but objected to the use of a name so similar to that of his own recently banned feminist group. Then, stymied by Hardouin's refusal to change the name, Richer dashed off a letter to the press explaining that the new group should not be confused with his own.[82] Nothing more came of the incident, and presumably Hardouin's League soon collapsed. At least it played no official role in the grandest of Richer's designs for expanding feminism's organizational base, the Women's Rights Congress of 1878.

THE WOMEN'S RIGHTS CONGRESS OF 1878

Richer and Deraismes had begun to plan for a women's rights congress in the early 1870s, but the election of Marshall Mac-Mahon as president of the republic in 1873 signalled the frightening possibility of a monarchist coup. In March of that year, Interior Minister Goulard prohibited Olympe Audouard from lecturing on "La Question des femmes," citing her prospective audience as a bunch of "*over-emancipated* women" and branding her ideas as "subversive, dangerous, and immoral."[83] The brand no doubt suited Jenny d'Héricourt's ideas as well, and just a few weeks before she had addressed the first monthly dinner meeting of Richer's Association. In July 1873, Richer announced that, because "we no longer know where we are heading nor under what form of government we shall be living by the [time of the projected congress in the] month of September," and because "we are in a state of siege," the congress would have to be canceled.[84] Soon too the government canceled Richer's Association, but after the crisis of 16 May 1877, he and Deraismes returned to their plan. Paris was about to host an international exposition, and although time was short they decided to go ahead. In late July 1878, the first French Congress for Women's Rights (Congrès international du droit des femmes) opened at the Masonic Grand Orient, the scene of Deraismes's speaking debut twelve years before. It ended two weeks later with a grand, six-franc banquet in the family room of the Maurice restaurant.

Eight representatives from four foreign countries served on the congress's twenty-seven-member Committee of Initiative: three Italians, three Americans (Julia Ward Howe, Theodore Stanton, Mary A. Livermore), and one each from Switzerland and Holland. The nineteen French members included two senators (Victor Schoelcher and Eugène Pelletan), five deputies (Louis Codet, Tiersot, Charles Boudeville, Émile Deschanel, and Charles Laisant), three municipal councilors from Paris (Antide Martin, Georges Martin, and Severiano de Hérédia), Richer, and eight women. The planning of details fell to the all-French fifteen-member Committee of Organization. Richer served as the general superintendent of the congress, de Hérédia and Anna Féresse-Deraismes shared the treasury, and Eugénie Pierre took on the secretarial duties. The remaining eleven included Maria Deraismes, Hubertine Auclert, and Virginie Griess-Traut.[85]

The congress operated on a budget of 3,350 francs, donated by 81 individuals and 3 groups. Eighty percent of the contributions fell into the 2- to- 20-franc range, leaving to wealthy donors the task of supplying most of the money. The Deraismes sisters gave 80 francs, the Griess-Trauts 50, and the Henri Krohns 100; 250 came from the New York-based Association for Women's Suffrage, and the Count and Countess Malliani provided 2,000 francs. Two-thirds of the total went into printing the final report. The remainder provided 400 francs for additional printed matter, 500 francs for rent, 90 for meals for 15 newspapermen at the closing banquet, and 25 francs for the Grand Orient's *concierge* (building manager).

The official roster of delegates named 220 people and 16 groups from 11 nations. Women held a slight overall majority, 113 to 107, but represented only 45 percent of the French contingent, 77 of 168. The British and American delegations, reflecting perhaps a more advanced stage of organized militancy, included 88 percent women (24 of 29). Of the 16 groups only 2 came from France, compared with 9 from the United States and Britain. France in fact had 3, but without governmental authorization the Amelioration Society could not figure on the official roster.

One of the French groups was the Society of United Ladies (Société des dames réuniés) of Lyon. The other was the Trade Union Chamber of Women Lingerie Makers, Needleworkers, Embroiderers, and Dressmakers (Chambre syndicale des ouvrières lingères, couturières, brodeuses et confectionneuses) of Paris, which along with a similar group from London gave working women a small voice at the congress. Only two organizations, both from the United States, emphasized woman suffrage. Three of the six British associations existed to combat governmental regulation of prostitution. One of Italy's three groups was the Masonic Lodge Concordia of Florence, and Richer served as the delegate of the Naples Committee for the Emancipation of Italian Women. From Geneva came Solidarity, represented by Virginie Griess-Traut and Charles Lemonnier, and Lemonnier's League of Peace and Liberty.

The fact that only two groups represented working women underscored the bourgeois character of the congress—an impression reinforced by the large number of professionals among the French male delegates. French men constituted 88 percent of all the men who officially attended, and nearly half of them (42 of 91) came from politics, law, and letters. French women went undesignated for the most part, but their presence implied two things rarely found in proletarian circles, some money and more time. Finally, the figure of 220 delegates included 25 family units, so that the official roster listed only 188 different surnames. In addition to the official delegates, the public also attended the congress, with the first session drawing over 600 people.

The work of the congress fell to five sections, each dealing with an aspect of woman's situation. The History Section, which reported first, assumed the task of examining woman's role and influence, for good or evil, everywhere and at all times. The discussion centered on groups and individuals who had promoted women's rights in the past and the reasons for their failure. It also surveyed developments in countries that had strong feminist movements, hoping to unearth the determinants that made for success. The history report ended with affirmative answers to two rather rhetorical questions, both of which reflected liberal confidence in "right" inevitably replacing "might": Is this movement a fatal, inexorable law of the historical development of humanity? Is it a logical consequence of the moral, social, and political progress accomplished until now?

The Education Section reported next, and like the three subsequent sections it proposed a series of resolutions. It operated on the somewhat contradictory premise that both sexes partook of the same humanity but that the care of children constituted a unique feminine charge. Citing the higher mortality rate among infants farmed out to wet nurses, it called for mothers to breast-feed their own children. Where poverty made this difficult, it demanded that municipalities provide aid to women during the first eighteen months of their infants' lives. For preschoolers, the Education Section urged the establishment of kindergartens that would subscribe to "the *système Froebel* or better yet the *méthode naturelle.*" Children of all ages should attend sexually integrated classes, which, as American coeducation showed, served as "a powerful stimulant for the progress of studies and of moralization." Lastly, "considering that the essential vices of education are the result of social inequities that separate into distinct classes the citizens of the same country . . . [and] that integral education will be established only when schools will be absolutely distinct from churches," the Education Section demanded that all instruction be free, lay, and obligatory.

Richer chaired the Economic Section, which stressed that women deserved the same freedom and right to work as men. The question of whether or not women should work, however, raised the issue of woman's sphere and provoked one of the few angry exchanges at the congress. In opposition to Richer's claim that woman's dignity required her to work, two women countered that woman had no other mission than mothering and housekeeping and that she lost none of her dignity by living off the labor of her husband. Quickly, though, the section sidestepped the controversy with a consensual but contradictory resolution:

Inasmuch as the dignity, the independence of woman can only be safeguarded by work; that any woman who depends on man for the means to live is not free; the congress demands for woman a freedom to work equal to that of man, and affirms the value and merit of household or domestic work.[86]

That settled, the section also called for equal pay for equal work and open access to all professions; for working women it urged the creation of women's unions and the admission of women to the *conseils de prud'hommes* —elected boards charged with regulating industrial disputes. To improve the competitive position of women workers, it affirmed the strict supervision of convent and prison factories and the enactment of a special tax to equalize the cost of free and "compulsory" production. It also recommended women's cooperatives and factory associations, and once again the link between low wages and prostitution received an airing. Liberty should be the essential base of republics, the Economic Section concluded, and liberty required "the suppression of all laws restrictive of the right of assembly and the right of association."

Prostitution headed the agenda of the Morality Section, presided over by Deraismes. The section demanded a single standard for both sexes in order to bring human laws into line with moral precepts. Maintaining that state regulation of "public women" had no hygienic justification, it accused the government of sanctioning "the immoral prejudice that debauchery is a necessity for men." It urged ordinary hospitals, rather than prison infirmaries, to accept "women of the street" for treatment, and called for the establishment of half-way houses under lay direction to help women exconvicts adjust to freedom without falling victim to male lust. Citing "celibacy as one of the great causes of prostitution," it also demanded the progressive disappearance of all laws that impede or prevent marriage. The section concluded its work by passing resolutions in favor of woman's right to file a paternity suit and stiffer laws to protect minors from seduction.

The two-week congress ended with a presentation by the Legislation Section, chaired by Antide Martin. Richer delivered a "remarkable report" detailing the "flagrant iniquity" of the many laws that placed woman in an inferior position. Two of its resolutions reiterated the stands taken by the Morality Section in opposition to the morals police and in support of a paternity suit law. In a related action, the Legislation Section called for eliminating the distinction between legitimate and illegitimate children, making all offspring equally eligible to share in legacies. Other resolutions called for marriage promises to assume contractual status, enabling the jilted party to sue for damages, and for both sexes to suffer identical penalties for adultery, regardless of where the act occurred. The latter, proposed by Richer, sparked another minor flare-up. Constantin Calligari, a delegate from Rumania, argued that the threat of divorce alone would suffice to keep husbands in line. But most saw that as insufficient, whereupon Calligari returned his registration card and quit the congress. Nonetheless, because "the indissolubility of marriage is contrary to the principle of individual liberty," the congress emphatically endorsed the reestablishment of divorce. The section asked the legislature to specify the details, perhaps due to an inability to agree on them itself, but its intention left no room for doubt: "Divorce is necessary from the point of view of humanity, of morality, and in a word, of the social future."

Although the 1878 congress passed four printed pages of resolutions under twenty-six major headings, its foremost significance as an event was ordinal: it constituted not only the first international women's rights congress but also, as a later analyst reflected, "the first important act of feminism in France."[87] Richer claimed more, seeing in it proof that "the sentiment of right, of justice penetrates everywhere."[88] Prior to the congress he noted politically that the republican journals had expressed sympathetic support, whereas the reactionary press, especially the Bonapartist sheets, had bantered and laughed. "We are not at all surprised" that the reactionaries would ridicule an assembly of honest women and mothers, he added, "but their mocking proves nothing: the last laugh will be the best."[89] Afterward, exulting in the unanimity accorded to most of the resolutions, Richer pronounced that "the question of women is no longer a narrow question, the utopia of some EMPTY MINDS; IT IS A UNIVERSAL QUESTION."[90] Eugénie Pierre echoed Richer's opinion in pointing out that, despite initial fears, "the results of the propaganda obtained [at the congress] surpassed all hopes."[91] But in the opinion of another participant the congress proved only that the majority of French women were indifferent to their rights.[92] Moreover, although many leading feminists attended, no permanent association emerged. Indeed, disorder so marred the movement's subsequent growth that eleven years passed before a second congress took place in 1889.

CONCLUSION

Nonetheless, the Women's Rights Congress of 1878 marked the triumph of its organizers' special brand of feminism, the *politique de la brèche*. In the hands of Deraismes and Richer, this strategy, which accorded priority to the political objective of securing a liberal Third Republic while limiting the call for women's emancipation to civil rights, served the movement well in the crisis atmosphere of the 1870s. Liberal republicans generally welcomed feminist political support and in return raised little objection, as distinct from active endorsement, to the limited program of reforms. Once the republic consolidated itself in the 1880s, though, many of the movement's younger militants grew restive. Those who accepted the civil rights priority but wished to broaden the movement's popular base attacked the politics of Richer and especially of Deraismes as narrow and self-defeating. Others who desired a broader reform program, particularly the inclusion of woman suffrage, rejected the feminism of Deraismes and especially of Richer as too conservative and opportunistic. The divisive effect of the former appeared in the confusion that characterized the movement for a decade after Richer's retirement in 1891 and Deraismes's death in 1894. The divisive effect of the latter appeared immediately. Deraismes and Richer, anxious to avoid political immoderation, refused to allow Hubertine Auclert to "use" the 1878 congress as a forum from which to call for her favorite reform, woman suffrage. Angered and frustrated, Auclert quit the congress's Initiation Commission and Organization Committee and assumed leadership of a suffrage wing within the movement. She also publicly denounced the "gag rule," with the result that popular opinion—so very crucial to the plans of Deraismes and Richer and other liberals who sought peaceful reform from below—found itself immediately subjected to divergent feminist appeals.

CONFLICT:
HUBERTINE AUCLERT AND THE
STRATEGY OF *L'ASSAUT*

CHAPTER

4

If people were paid to bring children into the
world, I truly believe that men would find a
way to monopolize the job.

Hubertine Auclert, 1883

Life would be good if I were alone by myself!
But I am alone everywhere, alone in public life
as in private life! Alone at home, alone at the
Suffrage Society, alone at the journal, always alone,
everywhere alone.

Hubertine Auclert, 1884

Hubertine Auclert's embittering experience at the Women's Rights
Congress of 1878 coincided with political developments that perplexed
the founders of the liberal feminist movement throughout the 1880s. Until
then the feminists had marched in lockstep with liberal republicans.
Together they had fought against Napoleon III's personal rule, and, during
the first seven years of the Third Republic, the movement's founders had
deemphasized the struggle to emancipate women in order to concentrate
their energy against resurgent clericalism and monarchism. Success came
quickly. Republican victories in the wake of the crisis of 16 May 1877
lessened the immediate political danger, and with the resignation of
President Mac-Mahon in December 1878, and further republican gains in
the Senate elections of 1879, the siege that had so frightened Richer in
1873 lifted. Turmoil continued to track the new regime, but the Third
Republic had at last established itself.

Had their strategy been correct, therefore, the *brèchistes* who dominated the 1878 congress should have achieved rapid implementation of their reform program. Instead, victory over reaction revealed within republican ranks a fissured spectrum of radicals, moderates, and conservatives, none of whom possesed sufficient strength to govern alone. As a result, power fell to a shifting coalition of moderates and a few radicals who called themselves "Opportunists." Their motto was "*sérier les questions*"—take up questions one at a time—which resembled the "breach" strategy of Deraismes and Richer. Unfortunately for the founders of the feminist movement, though, the Opportunists proved very reluctant to take up the woman question.

Government by the Opportunists in the 1880s brought reforms in only two areas of concern to the founders of the French feminist movement, education and divorce. Even then, the expanded system of girls' schools, with its special curriculum and inferior degrees, simply institutionalized woman's subordination on a larger scale, whereas the 1884 divorce law, although it permitted wives to escape legally from brutal husbands and partly eliminated the double standard for adultery, completely sidestepped the problem of woman's servitude within marriage. Consequently, feminism and republicanism reached a fork in the road in the 1880s. Throughout the decade, although many feminists were slow to realize it, the republic itself increasingly became the chief obstacle to women's emancipation.

One of the first to recognize the limits of mutual interest between feminism and the new republic was Hubertine Auclert. Like Deraismes and Richer, with whom she had worked closely in the 1870s, Auclert held strong republican convictions. Well in advance of most of her feminist colleagues, however, Auclert perceived that the young regime had become a bastion of male domination. To storm this new bastion of *masculinisme*, she devised the *politique de l'assaut* (strategy of assault), a plan of attack that reversed the *brèchiste* strategy by placing "the political emancipation of woman ahead of her civil emancipation."[1] Unless France's 17 million women shared power they would forever remain enslaved to an equal number of men, Auclert exclaimed in 1881: "Therefore, it follows from all evidence that political rights are for women the keystone (*clef de voûte*) that will give them all other rights."[2]

HUBERTINE AUCLERT

Thirty years old at the time of the 1878 congress, Auclert was born at Tilly in the commune of Saint-Priest-en-Murat, 150 miles south of Paris in the Department of Allier. The fifth of seven children, she spent her early youth in relative ease and displayed contemporary signs of "feminine" precocity.[3] Although financially secure throughout her lifetime, her later youth proved tragic. Left homeless upon the premature death of her parents, she spent the remainder of her minority in a convent orphanage.

There, under the tutelage of local nuns, Auclert acquired an awareness of social injustice and perhaps the martyr-like attitude that characterized her campaign for woman suffrage. But the Church itself held no lasting appeal for her, and like the other founders of the liberal feminist movement she eventually became a rabid anticlerical. The stay in the convent also limited her access to a broader education. Neither philosophy nor literature attracted her, so that in comparison to Deraismes she possessed only an "average culture."[4] She spoke and wrote well enough, but polemics were her forte, impulsiveness her style. Although the precise circumstances are unclear, Auclert interpreted her youthful experiences as disastrously formative. "I have been a rebel against female oppression almost since birth," she later recalled; "so much brutality of man toward woman, which terrified my childhood; prepared me at an early age to demand independence and consideration for my sex."[5]

Auclert's exit from the convent orphanage coincided with two events of crucial significance to her subsequent career. First, while caring for the victims of smallpox during the Franco-Prussian War, news reached her home town of the Second Empire's collapse, sending her into transports of joy. The prospect of a republican France filled her with hope, and, although her devotion to woman's emancipation eventually brought her into conflict with the Third Republic, she never abandoned faith in the twin idols of "my country and my republic." "Oh my country," Auclert later exclaimed, "you must be incomparable because I prefer to live here in slavery than elsewhere in freedom."[6]

The second event brought her into direct contact with the feminist movement. Accounts of the first feminist banquets had begun to reach the provinces in the early 1870s. When Auclert heard of them she immediately set out for Paris to meet their organizers. Upon arriving in the capital, she joined a "feminist committee," probably Deraismes's Amelioration Society or Daubié's Association for the Emancipation of Woman.[7] Whichever, she came to know Deraismes well (Daubié died in 1874), and Richer took her on as secretary of *L'Avenir des femmes*. At about that time, she also heard from Victor Hugo, the most famous of the feminist banquet luminaries, the words that guided her campaign to the end: "In our legislation, woman is without political rights; she does not vote, she does not exist, she does not count. There are male citizens; there are no female citizens. This is a violent condition; it must cease."[8]

From then until her death on the eve of World War I, Auclert labored incessantly to effect a cessation of this violence. Indeed, on only one occasion during the movement's formative years did she suspend her campaign for woman suffrage. At the height of the 1877 political crisis, she called on feminists to concentrate their energies against the danger of reaction. "The republican ideal excludes the aristocracy of sex as it excludes the aristocracy of caste, she exclaimed, "but we would be wrong to speak of social questions in the face of the dominant necessity of the present."[9] With the return of republican stability, however, she redoubled her efforts to obtain the franchise for women.

Accordingly, Auclert intended to raise the issue of woman suffrage at the 1878 Women's Rights Congress, and she served on the congress's Initiation Commission and Organization Committee. But when Deraismes and Richer gagged her she quit both committees and blasted the congress in a pamphlet, *Le Droit politique des femmes: question qui n'est pas traitée au congrès international des femmes* (*Women's Political Rights; Question Not Dealt with at the International Congress of Women*).[10] In January 1879, she exacerbated the growing rift within the feminist movement by repeating the pamphlet's theme in a press release. The time has come for women to seize their liberty, Auclert announced: "Man makes the laws to his advantage and we are obliged to bow our heads in silence. Enough of resignation. Pariahs of society, stand up!"[11]

THE WOMEN'S SUFFRAGE SOCIETY AND *LA CITOYENNE*

In attempting to raise the politically supine through woman suffrage, Auclert, like the *brèchistes*, first formed a group and then founded a newspaper. The group, initially called the Women's Rights Society (Société le droit des femmes), took shape in 1876. Richer, whose Amelioration Society had been outlawed the previous year, publicly applauded the effort and served on its Initiation Committee. But his support was less than wholehearted. Auclert's program considered "the political emancipation of woman as the sole means of arriving at the economic and civil emancipation of woman."[12] It was an organization bent on *l'assaut*. Richer could hardly disavow the group because he had just urged all communities to establish feminist organizations. But six years later he founded the French League for Women's Rights (Ligue française pour le droit des femmes), one of whose purposes was to offset the radical image of Auclert's Society.[13] The following year, in 1883, Auclert brought the name of her group into line with its objective. From then until World War I it was known as the Women's Suffrage Society (Société le suffrage des femmes).

In addition to political rights, the program of Auclert's Society stressed common feminist themes such as equal pay for equal work, coeducation, the right to file a paternity suit, and divorce—in a phrase, "equality of both sexes before the law." The group also professed neutrality in matters of politics and religion, but words could not disguise its obvious republican and anticlerical orientation. The same conservative government that outlawed the Amerlioration Society rejected Auclert's request for authorization in 1877 and ordered her group dissolved. The Women's Rights Society obeyed publicly but continued to meet in private until the political situation improved after the crisis of 16 May 1877. Finally, on 28 September 1879, it received official approval.[14]

According to its statutes, either sex could join Auclert's Society, although all members had to support the goal of women's suffrage and eligibility. Dues were three francs per year, and an annually chosen three-member Control Committee oversaw the group's finances. Administration fell to a ten-member Executive Committee, elected each year along with a general secretary, corresponding secretary, and a treasurer. The group had no permanent president, and each assembly chose its presiding officer by a show of hands.[15] Its headquarters were at 21 rue Cail in the tenth *arrondissement*, the home of its perennial general secretary, Hubertine Auclert.

Auclert's initial appeal for members, carried in October 1876 by *Le Rappel, La Tribune,* and *Les Droits de l'homme* among others, emphasized the similarity between workers and women. "Women of France," Auclert wrote, "despite the benefits of our revolution of 1789, two kinds of individuals are still enslaved, proletarians and women." Male workers contribute luster and richness to the nation, she maintained, only to die of misery. Working women are worse off; for the same tasks they receive less than half the wage of men. And regardless of income, all women suffer from "vexations and injustices in a legislation that restricts the circle of activity in which they move, that exploits and atrophies them." The proletariat has begun to free itself, Auclert concluded, and women must follow its example: "It is time to abandon indifference and inertia in order to protest against the prejudices and laws that humiliate us. Let us unite our efforts, let us associate; the example of the proletariat invites us; let us learn from it how to emancipate ourselves."[16]

Prospective members could find Auclert at home every Tuesday and Friday afternoon. Twenty joined the first week, some others later. By February 1877, enough had enrolled to convene a private meeting at the Sax Hall in the Saint-Georges quarter of Paris. Armand Duportal, deputy from Toulouse, presided, assisted by Deputy Charles Laisant (Loire-Inférieure) and Municipal Councilor Ferdinand Buisson. Discussion centered on woman's civil condition, especially the right to file a paternity suit. Whether suffrage came up is unclear. Also unclear is the status of the three men; were they members or simply guests? Buisson at least may have joined inasmuch as he eventually emerged as the chief parliamentary sponsor of woman suffrage in the decade before World War I.[17] At the time, however, the question of membership quickly became moot. Shortly after the meeting the government refused to authorize the new Society, which probably caused some resignations. In any case, when the group openly reemerged two years later, it embarked on a campaign that appealed only to the most ardent feminists.

In 1881, Auclert founded *La Citoyenne* (*The Woman Citizen*) with the aid of two attorneys, Léon Giraud and Antonin Lévrier. Giraud had a doctorate in law and a prolific pen, which he employed in his own name and under two pseudonyms, Camille and Draigu.[18] Lévrier possessed a *license* in law and an interest in journalism. Both men had participated in the 1878 Women's Rights Congress. Of the two Auclert worked more closely with Lévrier, who served as her legal counsel in the tax strike appeals of 1880 and 1881. Their long association also evoked a personal attachment, and in 1888 they married. The timing of the nuptials coincided with Lévrier's appointment to a judgeship in Algeria. Auclert accompanied her husband to his new post, leaving one of her associates in charge of *La Citoyenne*. Four years later, after Lévrier's death, she returned to

Paris, but by then *La Citoyenne* had passed out of her hands and changed its name. Its last issue appeared in November 1891.

In founding *La Citoyenne*, Auclert capitalized on one of France's most liberal press laws. Promulgated in July 1881, the new regulation permitted almost anyone to direct a newspaper—Maria Deraismes, for example, took advantage of it to acquire *Le Républicain de Seine-et-Oise*. But more important to Auclert was the decriminalization of *délits d'opinion*, printed statements inciting hatred or contempt of the government. Thus freed to attack with impunity the constitution, laws, and beliefs that subordinated women to men, Auclert set forth a case for woman suffrage that echoed, often without attribution, within French suffragism until full enfranchisement came at the end of World War II.

La Citoyenne began as a weekly, and nearly one-third of its 187 issues appeared the first year. Lack of money, the scourge of the French feminist press, forced it to switch to monthly publication in April 1882. Auclert tried to forestall the cutback by raising the subscription rate to ten francs from the original six and by offering inducements. Semi-annual subscribers could receive a bottle of Pinaud perfume for five francs, half the regular price, and those willing to sign up for a full year could purchase a "superb revolver" for a nominal eight francs. Purchasers of the Christmas edition of 1881 got a free copy of *L'Historique de la société le droit des femmes (History of the Women's Rights Society)*. When contributors began to ask for pay, Auclert reminded them that their articles represented an act of devotion, not a source of financial gain. She also doubled her own output, as had Richer when faced with the same problem, by writing under the pseudonym Jeanne Voitout. But nothing, not even incorporation in February 1882, solved the money squeeze. The next 108 issues appeared monthly at an annual subscription rate of one and a half francs. Only in July 1889, when her successor devoted three editions to the second Women's Rights Congress, and in 1891, when the new management brought it out fortnightly, did the publication tempo increase.[19]

La Citoyenne might not have survived the first year, let alone a decade, had it not been for an elderly politician named Joseph de Gasté. Auclert early created a special fund "for the propagation of the journal," but donations came infrequently and in small amounts. Then in May 1881 Auclert sent a questionnaire on women's rights to each deputy. De Gasté, who had just introduced Deraismes's proposal for the *commerçante* vote in the Chamber, responded affirmatively with the first of a series of fifty- and one hundred-franc gifts. Altogether, during *La Citoyenne*'s ten-year life, he gave close to ten thousand francs, a boon Auclert attempted to repay by repeatedly supporting his reelection. Others also gave, but in 1889, for example, de Gasté donated 1,200 francs of the 1,358 collected in the special fund. Little wonder that Auclert's successor dubbed him the John Stuart Mill of France.[20]

De Gasté's generosity, which earned him a reputation for eccentricity in the Chamber, contrasted sharply to the apathy and hostility that Auclert sensed all around her. Auclert could count on her group to support *La Citoyenne*, particularly after she raised yearly dues from three to five francs to include the monthly subscription cost. She also found some support in the provinces. A speaking engagement at Nîmes in the spring of 1884, for example, netted 220 francs in donations and 100 new readers. But most women remained indifferent, lacking in courage and paralyzed by fear of ridicule. John Brown died in 1859 because blacks failed to follow him, Auclert complained upon her return from Nîmes; how many French women were making the same mistake? Liberty required financial sacrifice, she asserted later in the year, drawing attention to the death of a millionnaire who had subscribed to *La Citoyenne* but left no money to the cause.[21]

Auclert attached several mottos to *La Citoyenne*'s masthead during its decade. The first, lifted from positivist Émile Littré, defined the woman citizen as a person who possessed ''full rights'' within the state. Another, taken from Dumas *fils*, optimistically forecast that within ''ten years women will be electors like men.'' A third described the emancipated woman as one ''who enjoys the integrality of her rights and is irreproachable in the accomplishment of her duties.'' Throughout *La Citoyenne*'s lifetime, Auclert urged sympathizers ''to dare and to resist''—to dare to claim woman's rights and to resist unjust laws. Respecting legality, she explained, meant submission to the arbitrary whims of *masculinisme*. Except for violence, which man's superior physical strength rendered useless, all means were legitimate. With freedom at stake, slaves could not afford to observe traditional loyalties.[22] But perhaps the best expression of Auclert's objective relied more on visual effect. For years *La Citoyenne* ran a cartoon depicting a man and a woman standing beside a ballot box. The man held a vote marked ''WAR.'' The woman held a ballot marked ''PEACE.'' The caption stated what sight made obvious:

peace, social harmony, and humanity's well-being would exist only when women helped men make the laws.[23]

In spite of detractors like Richer and despite in theory aspiring to print all things of interest to women, in practice *La Citoyenne* relentlessly and singlemindedly pressed for woman's political rights. When less sweeping proposals found their way into its pages, Auclert hastened to point out that piecemeal efforts would no longer be necessary once women had the vote. In contrast to the "old school" of the *brèchistes*, which restricted its program to "partial rights," Auclert designed *La Citoyenne* as the voice of the *assautistes*, the "young school," whose goal was "full rights." In the past, she explained, feminists had waited for male legislators to grant their demands, but now the time had come for women to capture power for themselves. The age of beggars pleading for alms had given way to that of creditors claiming their legitimate due.[24]

In an effort to strengthen the creditors' bargaining position, Auclert repeatedly advanced new organizational schemes. Only through unity, which she saw as the key to the success of both foreign feminists and domestic masculinists, could French women move toward freedom. "Let us do as the men do," she urged. Consistent with this objective, Auclert first proposed in 1882 a George Sand Circle, which would provide Parisian women with a place to meet and give France a counterpart to London's Sommerville Club—a thousand-strong women's group whose name honored a woman who belonged to the Royal Society. When that failed, she suggested in the following year an even larger undertaking, a National Women's Suffrage Society with its own monthly journal entitled *Franco*.[25]

When the National Society also failed, Auclert proposed an ambitious scheme for women's parliaments. In response to Susan B. Anthony, who in 1888 invited her to attend the inaugural meeting of the International Council of Women in Washington, D.C., Auclert explained that "the women's movement of all countries is presently too platonic." The theoretical phase has lasted too long; now is the time to put ideas into practice. Women's parliaments would demonstrate women's political ability and give feminists everywhere the status and activity they needed. Each parliament should follow the calendar of its male counterpart and use the national agenda to avoid wandering. Such parliaments would have no legal authority, Auclert recognized, but their moral influence would be great—much like that of Paris's "conference of lawyers"—and feminists of both sexes could signal their devotion to the cause by footing the bill. Regardless of details, Auclert concluded, fortune would favor the audacious.[26] Fortune did not favor the proposal, however, and, although French feminists organized several Women's Estates General along similar lines forty years later, Auclert's parliaments never got beyond the idea stage.

Indeed, on only two occasions in the 1880s did Auclert succeed in expanding the organizational base of French suffragism. The first success occurred in 1884 when, as the internationally recognized "head of the agitation in favor of woman's political rights" in France, she entered into a formal relationship with American suffragists by becoming a corresponding secretary in the National Woman Suffrage Association, founded by Susan B. Anthony and Elizabeth Cady Stanton in 1869.[27] The second success came in the same year when, soon after the collapse of the proposed National Society, she created a group called the Women's Suffrage Circle (Cercle le suffrage des femmes). Similar in name to her other group, which the year before had become the Women's Suffrage Society, the Suffrage Circle included Deputy de Gasté and had as its prime mover a wealthy young Russian woman, Mademoiselle Marie de Kapcevitch. The Suffrage Circle initially met at 31 rue Paradis-Poissonière, a few blocks from Auclert's residence, but ran afoul of an unsympathetic landlord who tore down its posters and ordered it to move. Finally, in November 1885, thanks to Kapcevitch, it found new quarters at 8 Galerie Bergère in the southeastern corner of the ninth *arrondissement*. Soon thereafter the Women's Suffrage Society began to meet there as well.[28]

Even with the Suffrage Circle, though, Auclert's cadre remained small. Her total following throughout the 1880s, combining the staff of *La Citoyenne* with the membership of the Suffrage Society and the Suffrage Circle, barely exceeded a hundred, with many fewer than that available at any particular moment. Deraismes's Amelioration Society and Richer's 1882 French League for Women's Rights were only slightly larger if counted separately, but taken together they outnumbered Auclert's supporters by more than three to one. As a result, strength became more a matter of doctrine than numbers, which meant that Auclert's case for woman suffrage sprang as much from the internal dynamic of the feminist movement than from the all too obvious necessity to swing around public opinion.

THE CASE FOR WOMAN SUFFRAGE

Auclert's defense of woman suffrage drew on two interrelated themes. As citizens, she argued with the title of her newspaper, women should enjoy equality as a matter of right; whereas, as a special segment of the citizenry, women should have the opportunity to express their virtues as a matter of progress. Unless women shared power, she maintained, the republican ideal would forever remain an empty abstraction. Sovereignty was indivisible; the strength of the nation depended on the total participation of all citizens. Until all adults possessed the right to vote, French democracy could never function properly. The time had come to put an end to elections that were little more than "public comedies" in which "the feudal noblemen of the nineteenth century" chose "557 monarchs" to sit in the Chamber of Deputies. If France refused to jettison its male "royalty of sex," Auclert predicted, revolution would once again stalk the land.[29]

The demoralizing effects of a truncated electorate had already begun to appear, Auclert argued. Women paid little attention to politics because they lacked the ballot, and as a result men often refused to vote or to take elections seriously. Wives also wanted their husbands with them on Sundays, the traditional French election day, which further discouraged men from voting. Deputy Letellier of Algiers had proposed the obligatory vote, Auclert acknowledged, but that reform would not alone improve the republic because suffrage, the machine of progress, required two motors: the male and the female. The only certain cure for political apathy was to enfranchise women, which would eliminate abstentions by making politics a subject of family discussion. When in the fall of 1881 a retired chief engineer proposed enfranchising the family by giving male heads of households additional votes for their wives and children, Auclert objected to the idea but conceded that in contrast to the obligatory male vote the so-called family vote at least recognized the nonrepresentation of women.[30]

Additional evidence of political demoralization could be seen in the continuing controversy over electoral procedures. Radical republicans, led by Léon Gambetta, hoped to replace single-member constituencies (*scrutins d'arrondissement*) with larger districts composed of several deputies (*scrutins de liste*). Auclert endorsed this reform on the grounds that it would subordinate personalities to issues and permit male feminists to protest against woman's disenfranchisement by writing in women's names for all available seats. She did not, however, expect it to repair the body politic; no amount of tinkering could compensate for the exclusion of half the population. When France tried the system in the election of 1885, Auclert noted that not only did the *scrutin de liste* cost women more—an extra 303,008 francs for twenty-seven additional deputies—but defenders of the republic nearly lost their majority. Had reactionaries attracted another 337,000 votes, *La Citoyenne* charged, they would have killed democracy without the consent of half the nation.[31]

As with electoral reform, so too for constitutional reform. Suffrage restricted to males, not the limited electoral base of the Senate, against which Richer persistently inveighed, or the lack of Parisian autonomy, caused France's problems. In their present masculine form, Auclert maintained, both Senate and Chamber violated the spirit of true republicanism. Order required either despotism or universal suffrage, and as long as only men voted there would always be "too many or not enough kings." Man's sense of superiority had raised him to such lofty heights, Auclert charged, that he had lost sight of the realities of life. An enfranchised womanhood would restore honesty, hard work, and dignity to the nation. Woman suffrage would ensure that fundamental decisions emanated from the sane atmosphere of the home, not from the alcoholic vapors of the cabaret.[32]

Auclert urged republicans to transfer to the cause of women the same sense of injustice that had led them to demand the vote for men. Duty imposed a variety of roles on people, she observed, but no duty should entail the loss of inherent rights. To deny the vote to women for keeping house and raising children made no more sense than to disenfranchise bakers for kneading dough, cobblers for making shoes, or lawyers for pleading cases. Except for childbirth, all aptitudes existed independent of sex; women could develop a taste for legislating just as men could develop a taste for cooking. Indeed, woman's acknowledged superiority in the home and the importance of home and family life to French society raised the possibility that women might become better politicians than men. Women and men frequently engaged in the same tasks, such as writing and farming, and when their jobs differed society benefited from the resultant specialization. No one, in short, performed a duty so low as to jeopardize inherent rights. Nor would women become ugly if they exercised such rights. Happiness, not slavery, produced beauty, Auclert contended, and with the vote women could only become more attractive.[33]

In stressing a beneficent link between the general good and woman suffrage, Auclert mixed the notions of equality and equivalence into combinations that lent an air of contradiction, evasion, and expediency to her rationale for women's emancipation. A typical contradiction, provoked in part by the inconsistencies in the antisuffrage position, ran through Auclert's response to the militarist stand that women should not vote because they did not fight. Women could fight, Auclert maintained, citing Joan of Arc in the fifteenth century and the Fernay sisters in 1789, but they should not have to because a civilized right should not depend on barbarous conduct. Men paid a blood tax for their right to vote, she admitted, but what of woman's maternity tax? Were wars to cease, as Auclert confidently predicted, women would still confront the risks of procreation. Moreover, adding the blood tax to woman's already heavy burden would unnecessarily aggravate France's depopulation problem. No, Auclert cried, women should no more have to fight in order to vote than men should have to give birth.

Besides, Auclert continued, many men displayed a marked reluctance to serve in the military. In the Seine Department alone, she pointed out in 1883, exemptions let off 60 percent of the young men. Yet, regardless of whether they served or not, all men—except for those on active duty—enjoyed the right to vote. In the absence of woman suffrage, this practice could effect no other result than the perpetuation of domestic and international strife. Accordingly, Auclert claimed, women in the Chamber of Deputies would have prevented the 1882 invasion of Tunisia—so reminiscent of the Second Empire's "criminal chauvinism" that provoked the War of 1870—because, unlike the ordinary male politician, their dreams do not rest on mountains of dead. Similarly, when shortly thereafter France intervened in Indochina, Auclert, citing the precedent set by a former Chinese empress, maintained that an enfranchised womanhood would have stopped the war by ordering imperialist premier Jules Ferry into the front line.

Yet, during the Franco-German war scare of 1887, Auclert altered tack completely, urging woman's enfranchisement in the name of patriotism rather than pacifism. Not only would woman suffrage permit French men to show war-minded Germans that sex discrimination no longer disunited the nation, but it would also enable women to offset the influence of the

"Schwartzs," expatriate Prussian males of dubious loyalty whose sex alone qualified them for the French ballot. Possessed of the vote, women would rekindle French national spirit just as women teachers kept French culture alive in Alsace, a province seized by the Prussians in the War of 1870. Once granted full citizenship, women would also prevent repetitions of "immorality" like the 1891 Paris performance of Wagner's *Lohengrin*, whose composer, Auclert recalled, had earlier spit in the face of a vanquished France.[34]

Evasion characterized a critical aspect of Auclert's response to the anticlericals who charged that woman suffrage would strengthen the forces of reaction in France. Men deserved blame for having turned France into a "vast monastery," Auclert fumed with exasperation. Men let priests vote and voted for priests; men also opened each legislative session with an obligatory prayer and appropriated funds for the Church. Men even sent ambassadors to the Pope. When the anticlerical Jules Ferry visited Leo XIII in 1885, Auclert wrote that she could hear the Holy Pontiff excusing his errant parishioner for having married a Protestant in a lay ceremony:

I know, my son, that you have been badly counselled by your concubine; the devil haunts the spirit of this woman who lives with you without having gone before our holy altars; calm yourself, it is against this free thinker, who has badly advised you, that are directed the thunderbolts of the Church.

If, despite culpably abetting reaction, men could practice religion and still vote, then why should women forfeit their political rights for worshipping? "All these illogisms are stupefying to human reason," Auclert snorted, especially when universal suffrage would cure women's addiction to clericalism. Once enfranchised, Auclert predicted, women would involve themselves in public affairs and adopt scientific and rational ideas. Freed from endless domestic routine, they would abandon religious escapism and devote themselves to civic duties. Armed with the vote, women would no longer resort to prayer.[35]

But what of the interim? How would the Third Republic survive the transition from "woman as reactionary," a danger which Auclert acknowledged, to "woman as rationalist"? Her answer, typically, obscured the present in prophecy. To prohibit woman suffrage on the grounds that women neither wanted nor had the capacity to vote was absurd, Auclert maintained. Not all males wanted the vote when manhood suffrage became law in 1848, nor were they all well educated or politically experienced at the time. Once enacted, however, manhood suffrage had acquired legitimacy through practice, a legitimacy that woman suffrage would likewise acquire. Men made it difficult for women to overcome their political backwardness, especially because girls' schools lacked funds and adult women could not legally attend party rallies. But all that was beside the point. Suffrage should be viewed as the means, not the reward, for obtaining public knowledge. Serious contact with administrative and legislative matters constituted the best political pedagogy. In short, Auclert again stressed, "women must vote in order to be able to educate themselves."[36]

The expediency dimension of Auclert's case for woman suffrage juxtaposed the alleged superior traits of women as a group to the presumably obvious faults of individual men. For every potential misfortune forecast by the opponents of woman suffrage, Auclert asserted, dozens of actual disasters resulted from its absence. Male negligence, for example, had caused the deaths of twenty people when a bullfight arena collapsed near Marseilles in 1881, and the loss of ten times that number in the 1887 fire at Paris's Opéra-Comique. Detached from practical problems familiar to women, men had also permitted the Seine to become polluted, which caused an outbreak of typhoid fever in the late 1880s. Prior to the divorce law of 1884, Auclert blamed "criminal senators" for murders and maimings born of marital passions and infidelities. And throughout *La Citoyenne's* decade, down to the paternity suit law of 1912, she held male lawgivers responsible for infanticides:

The culpable one is the legislator who, in order to keep his seducer's passport, much prefers to preserve infanticide, rather than permit a paternity search. It is with justice that a philosopher has said that one must attribute daily, to each deputy, the death of a hundred new born or about-to-be-born infants.[37]

As in civilian life, so too in the French army, where individual males regularly committed acts of "criminal chauvinism." Shortly after the new year 1882, Auclert reported, a suicide occurred near the garrison of Vosges. The victim, a seventeen-year-old girl, had taken her life after the officer who seduced her refused marriage. The officer "suffered" forced retirement, but what irked Auclert more was that the marriage could not have taken place because the girl's parents were too poor to pay the dowry required by army regulations—28,000 francs in the case of a second lieutenant. Low salaries kept officers from supporting penniless wives, Auclert recognized, but the solution to the problem was simple: the military should enroll women for duties like nursing, accounting, sewing, and cooking. Officers could then marry their auxiliaries in arms, whose wages would supplement their husbands' salaries. With the ranks open to women, Auclert concluded, recruitment would become easier, military costs would drop by eliminating middlemen, and above all army morality would improve through reducing recourse to seduction.[38]

Men possessed great expertise in applying principles selectively whenever it suited their ends, Auclert charged. They used woman's testimony to send criminals to the guillotine but refused to permit her to witness certificates of birth or marriage. They prized woman's maternal instinct but reserved the administration of public assistance, welfare, and childcare to themselves. "If people were paid for bringing children into the world," Auclert wrote in 1883, "I truly believe that men would find a way to monopolize the job." When the Municipal Council of Paris censured the prefect of police in 1881 for misuse of city money, it never considered the fact that women had no control over the taxes they paid. When five years later the government expelled a group of royalists for attempting to usurp power, it paid no heed at all to how all men had become usurpers in relationship to women. Men could even enlarge the electorate, as in 1889 when they reenfranchised wine and food merchants previously convicted of fraud, but never see that women needed the vote as much as ex-criminals. Indeed, from Auclert's point of view, no man could style himself a democrat unless he stood for woman suffrage. He who opposed the rights of woman, Auclert pronounced, would sooner or later attack the rights of man.[39]

The particulars of Auclert's case came together in a sweeping assessment connecting woman suffrage to France's historic destiny. One part of this assessment sharply contrasted the status of women in France to that of women elsewhere. By the time *La Citoyenne* appeared in 1881, for example, women had acquired local suffrage, usually dependent on property qualifications and sometimes subject to proxy regulations, in parts of Germany (first enacted in Westphalia in 1856); Austria–Hungary, Sweden, Australia, and Finland (1862); and England (1869). Even Russian women voted in municipal elections, although men had to drop their ballots into the voting urn. By 1891, the year *La Citoyenne* folded, women had received the local franchise in Scotland (1881); Canada and Iceland (1882); Madras (1885); and New Zealand (1886). Within the United States, only Kansas (1887) had followed suit, but the territories of Wyoming and Utah had given full political rights to women in 1869 and 1870 respectively. Outside North America, with the exception of exotic places like Pitcairn Island, only the Isle of Man had enfranchised women on an equal basis with men.[40] Compared to France, however, where the only enfranchised women were schoolteachers whose right to vote applied only to the education hierarchy, the rest of the Western world had begun to move ahead.

The other part of this assessment reemphasized Auclert's two interrelated themes: "right" required woman's full participation in liberal society, and progress depended on the full public expression of woman's virtues. France had not completely lost its prominent position in the struggle for progress, Auclert felt, but signs of slippage had become abundant. For example, the British Parliament had stolen a march on France in 1883 by abolishing the official regulation of prostitution and by debating and only narrowly defeating a bill to enfranchise single women. Britain had also permitted municipal woman suffrage in Canada, which was French at heart according to Auclert, giving the lie to antifeminist claims that women's emancipation would violate Latin traditions. What the French government failed to see, Auclert maintained, was not only that Britain had supplanted France in North America but that the British also ruled more justly. Furthermore, if Britain could enact wise legislation, so could other countries. Would Germany, she asked, also surpass France? Utah and Wyoming had already begun to reap the benefits of woman suffrage, Auclert announced in 1881. Women there had abandoned the "futilities of coquetry," and wifely virtues had increased "to a surprising degree." "In France, woman's vote will have the same moralizing influence." Without it, she warned, the French would surely fall behind their Anglo-Saxon neighbors.[41]

LAUNCHING THE ASSAULT

While elaborating the case in theory for woman suffrage, mere mention of which rankled the *brèchistes*, Auclert launched a series of protests that further offended the feminist movement's moderate majority. Through a variety of attention-grabbing actions, which the *brèchistes* thought would not only pose risks to the republic but also provoke doubts about women's capacity for full citizenship, Auclert sought to swing and, occasionally, shock public opinion into supporting votes for women and, at the same time, convert, or isolate if necessary, her opponents within the movement. These actions ranged from relatively inoffensive public meetings, petitions, letters, and editorials to flamboyant "media events" such as public demonstrations, a tax strike, a census boycott, and "shadow" electoral campaigns. In addition, Auclert's assault included a constant campaign of "clarification," a campaign directed at maintaining orthodoxy within her own ranks, avoiding too close an identification with more radical women, pointing out antisuffrage feminists, and exposing antifeminist politicians and political parties.

With the politically successful crisis of 16 May 1877 and the highly unsuccessful Women's Rights Congress of 1878 behind her, Auclert commenced the assault with several public meetings and, spread out over the decade, dozens of written protests. Her Society, upon receiving official authorization, sponsored open forums first at the Petrelle Hall in March and July 1879, then at the Oberkampf Theater in March 1880, and finally at the Levis Hall and the Rivoli Hall in May and July 1880. Her petitions, letters, and editorials, covering a gamut of issues, called on legislators and ministers to enact a paternity suit law, grant equal visiting privileges to women teachers at the 1878 National Exposition, look into the plight of abandoned children, set up an extraparliamentary watchdog commission composed of both sexes to oversee government spending, include women in the process of constitutional revision, create centers for unemployed women, reserve public halls for women to instruct men in civic virtue, post a Declaration of Women's Rights in all girls' schools, and require men who took women's jobs—dubbed *hommes-filles* by Auclert—to pay a tax of one hundred francs per year.[42]

Auclert also petitioned the Chamber of Deputies on behalf of woman's right to petition. In reaction to a republican proposal to strike women's signatures from Catholic complaints against the government's education reforms, Auclert, while disclaiming any sympathy for the Church's position, declared: "If one did not continually deny the rights of women, if one gave them knowledge and power, one would not find so many female clericals." The petition represented the only legal means of political protest available to women, Auclert pointed out: "We who are not, we protest equally against the ideas that have guided the [clerical] petitioners and against the injustices of men, who deny to women their right to petition."[43]

Of the many petitions that specifically demanded woman suffrage, two had special significance. In 1882, after months of patient effort, including weekly attendance at *La Citoyenne*'s headquarters where every Tuesday from noon to 5 P.M. was set aside for petition signing, Auclert managed to collect a thousand signatures. "Never has a more important manifestation been produced in France in favor of women's political rights," she wrote at the time, but never again in the decade did so many publicly commit themselves. Moreover, when the Chamber's petition committee blocked further action, even the motion's sympathetic sponsor, socialist-feminist Clovis Hugues, despaired of making a direct appeal to the floor.[44]

The other petition, initially filed in 1884, spent a year in committee and then sparked the Chamber's first debate on woman suffrage when Deputy Adolphe Pieyre (one of Auclert's monarchist "friends" according to Richer) put the issue on the agenda. As important as this "first," however, was the petition's substance; it expressly called for enfranchising only single women. The origin of this demand dated back to *La Citoyenne*'s birth. In its thirteenth issue, consistent with the view that women as a group possessed special qualities, Auclert asserted that if only fifty women sat in the Chamber their sex solidarity would protect the interests of all women. Limited woman suffrage violated her avowed integralism, she admitted, but some power would be better than none. In defense of the *célibataire* (single-woman) vote, she argued that unmarried women lacked even the indirect representation afforded to wives by husbands—a central claim of the antisuffragists. Later she whittled her demand even more. On the assumption that inequality in liberty was preferable to equality in servitude, she proposed enfranchising women who could pass an examination or had actively claimed the vote for more than one year. But when the Chamber greeted the idea with indifference, she reverted to the single-woman proposal. As in war and in games, she explained, one must devise a strategy to win. Deputy Vicomte Levis-Mirepoix took the same view but from the opponent's camp, warning that the single-woman vote would open the door to broader woman suffrage and lead to demands for eligibility. Men alone should sit in the legislature, he countered; women, the guardians of morality, should stay at home.[45]

Well before then, however, much to the chagrin of the *brèchistes*, Auclert had concluded that public morality required woman's public participation, even if at first such participation could only take the form of demonstrations. In 1885, for instance, just months before Levis-Mirepoix's remark, she and her followers, carrying a rose-and-blue suffrage banner, took their campaign against *masculinisme* into the midst of the million-strong cortege that bore Victor Hugo's casket from the Arc de Triomphe to the Panthéon. Furious public protests also greeted every Bastille Day, which Auclert viewed as woman's "Day of Dupes," the forerunner of the paper Bastille known as the Napoleonic Code. "The fourteenth of July is not a national festival," she announced, "it is the apotheosis of masculinity." A typical counter demonstration occurred in 1881. Under a banner wreathed in the black of mourning, Auclert and a handful of supporters marched the two and one-half miles from *La Citoyenne*'s headquarters to the Place de la Bastille, where, amid taunts and jeers, they denounced the revolution. Rather than the 14th of July, Auclert asserted, France should celebrate the 30th day of May, the date of Joan of Arc's death. She had once saved the nation, and her female descendants, if enfranchised, would likewise save the Third Republic. To dramatize her stand, Auclert led her cadre to the Place des Pyramides in 1885, where she laid a wreath on Joan of Arc's monument.[46]

Even more a source of chagrin to the *brèchistes* than the public demonstrations were Auclert's tax strike and census boycott. The strike developed out of an attempt by Auclert and a few other women to register to vote in February 1880. They argued that legally and constitutionally the term *les français* (the French) should apply to all citizens regardless of sex. Women had to obey the laws and pay taxes under that designation; it should therefore entitle them to the franchise. But the mayor of Paris's tenth *arrondissement* disagreed, pointing out that every judicial and administrative decision since 1789 had reserved political rights exclusively to men and that, in addition, he had no authority to intervene in a matter requiring legislative action. Auclert lashed back by comparing the mayor's ruling to the doctrine of original sin and the pretensions of the French nobility, both of which had assigned all or part of humanity to hereditary ignominy. Then she informed the prefect of the Seine that, having been denied representation, she would no longer submit to taxation:

Having wished to exercise my rights as a French citizen, having demanded during the revision period my inscription on the electoral lists, [the authorities] have told me that "the law confers rights only on men and not on women."

I do not admit this exclusion en masse of 10 million women, who have not been deprived of their civic rights by any judgment. In consequence, I leave to men, who arrogate to themselves the privilege of governing, arranging, and alloting the budgets, I leave to men the privilege of paying the taxes that they vote and divide to their liking.

Since I have no right to control the use of my money, I no longer wish to give it. I do not wish to be an accomplice, by my acquiescence, in the vast exploitation that the masculine autocracy believes is its right to exercise in regard to women. I have no rights, therefore I have no obligations; I do not vote, I do not pay.[47]

Twenty women joined Auclert's tax strike, at least eight of whom were widows. Presumably the rest were single like Auclert because husbands had legal control over family finances. Most lived in Paris, although a few resided in Marseilles, Lyon, and Pont-Lieu. All backed down when the authorities demanded payment, except Auclert and the widows Bonnaire and Leprou, who held out and appealed first to the Conseil de Prefecture and then to the Conseil d'État. Although neither appeal succeeded, Auclert continued the strike until an officer of the court attempted to seize her furniture. Whereupon, having made her point, she abandoned the protest.[48]

"It would take too long to recall here," Auclert remarked of the media reaction, "the noise that the demand for the inscription of women on the electoral lists made in the great Parisian press." Another feminist later confirmed that Auclert's "refusal to pay taxes particularly caused waves of ink to flow." Predictably, hostility characterized much of the reaction, with the conservative *Le Figaro* caustically inquiring if, after women, cattle would vote. Yet, several journalists, including Auguste Vacquerie, Albert Delpit, and Henri Fouquier, expressed qualified support. Fouquier praised the tax strike as courageous and indicated agreement in principle with woman suffrage, for instance, but warned against hasty enfranchisement due to woman's lack of education. Most surprising of all, however, was the response of Alexandre Dumas *fils*, who reversed his earlier stand and endorsed woman suffrage in *Les Femmes qui tuent et les femmes qui votent (The Women Who Kill and the Women Who Vote).*[49]

Dumas's about-face stemmed in part from Auclert's campaign and in part from another *cause célèbre*—the trial and eventual acquittal of

Madame du Tilly, who had bathed her husband's mistress in acid. The vote would enable women to bring laws into line with changing values, Dumas felt, thus stabilizing marriage. Once enfranchised, women would no longer have to resort to illegal or disruptive acts in order to protect their homes. With the ballot, they could perfect their roles as wives and mothers and provide society with a reinvigorated domestic base. However, because family life constituted their "natural" sphere, Dumas added, women would betray both themselves and society if they also aspired to hold office. Men alone should govern, he concluded, because they alone defended France with their blood.

Despite Dumas's hedging, Auclert welcomed his support and later offered him the leadership of her Society. Dumas declined, declaring, "I would aid you more by remaining independent; if I accepted the presidency that you offer me, they would say to me: 'You are with Hubertine Auclert,'...and I would no longer be heard at the Académie." What Dumas probably meant by "with Hubertine Auclert" occurred in April 1880. In that month, Auclert accompanied a wedding party to the town hall of the tenth *arrondissement*, the place where she had attempted to register two months before. Upon completion of the vows, she complimented the newlyweds for marrying in a civil ceremony and urged them to disregard the Napoleonic Code's subordination of the wife just as they had thrown off the shackles of the Church. Much ado followed until the prefect of the Seine, critical of Auclert's lack of respect for the law, barred her for four years from speaking at the town hall.[50]

The census boycott flowed out of the tax strike. Shortly after Auclert's last suffrage appeal failed, the legislature discarded the *scrutin d'arrondissement* in favor of a departmental *scrutin de liste*. Under the reform, political parties ran slates of candidates, each of whom represented an equal number of citizens. Auclert supported the change in principle but demanded that only males should figure in the apportionment process. This would reduce the size of the Chamber by fifty-five seats, she calculated, thus lessening women's tax burden. When the legislature rejected a petition to that effect, Auclert and twenty-four others signed an appeal urging all French women to boycott the census. Married women should report only male members of their households, and single women should withhold name, age, civil status, religion, and profession. Do not fear reprisals, Auclert counseled; the state would never call out the military against women as it had against the residents of Toulouse for resisting a door and window census in 1838. No arrests resulted, due undoubtedly to the small number of boycotters. But Richer, who ridiculed so many of Auclert's actions, found the census tactic especially objectionable. "Deputies are not only the representatives of those who name them," he responded, "they are the representatives of all [the people]." "This is the principle," he argued, but "*Eh! bien*, what have the women who obey Mlle. Auclert done? They have pronounced against the republican principle, against the democratic base. . . . They are sacrificing, without doubt, the Republic to their rancor."[51]

As the assault on public opinion escalated in word and deed, Auclert paid increasing attention to "clarifying" her position vis-à-vis other suffragists, radical women, other feminists, and the French political world. Within her own ranks the problem of suffrage orthodoxy came to a head in August 1881 when her Society expelled two members, Commandant Claude-Célestin Épailly and Marie-Jeanne Drouin, a writer who employed the pseudonym Louise de Lasserre. Épailly was the chief culprit. He edited *Le Libérateur* (*The Liberator*), organ of the 200-member Society of the Friends of Divorce (Société des amis du divorce), whose fourth issue had lightheartedly ridiculed Auclert's Bastille Day demonstration of the previous month. Such ridicule had no place within a movement whose opponents all too often resorted to sarcasm, so that Épailly's less than serious reportage represented the public reason for his and Drouin's expulsion. The other reason involved a complex disagreement between Épailly, Auclert, and Lévrier over who should run against divorce opponent Henri Brisson in the 1881 elections. Épailly suggested Auclert's candidacy or his own. Auclert declined the honor, but Lévrier, who also wanted to run, objected to Épailly's candidacy. Épailly discounted the objection, ran, and lost. The purge occurred the day after the balloting, 22 August 1881, and provoked a series of suits and countersuits, each side accusing the other of character defamation. Nothing came of the legal actions with one exception: Lévrier received a ten-franc fine for calling Drouin an *entremetteuse* (pimp).[52] Thereafter, within Auclert's group at least, the "correct line" went unchallenged.

More troublesome than internal dissent was the possibility that radical reformers and revolutionaries would tarnish the "respectable" image that Auclert hoped to project. Shortly after *La Citoyenne's* founding, for example, Auclert felt compelled to defend herself against the charge that she advocated free love. Marriage constituted woman's "supreme desire,'' she countered, but new laws were necessary to ensure family sanctity. Neither traditional matrimony nor *mariages parisiens* (Parisian marriages, a euphemism for free love) met woman's need for security and independence, because men exploited both situations. Therefore, she concluded, to criticize marriage in its contemporary form implied no approval of free love.[53]

Another problem arose when the Communards finally received amnesty. Auclert had urged that step throughout the 1870s, petitioning the president of the republic on their behalf and organizing a committee to aid their return. Once back in France, however, they included within their ranks the indomitable personality of Louise Michel. Michel and Auclert had much in common. Both opposed the prevailing ''Opportunism'' and felt a devotion to the oppressed. Auclert often linked woman's plight to that of the working class, whereas Michel, a convinced anarchist, displayed a decided interest in feminism and founded upon her return to France a Women's League (Ligue des femmes) to enlist women of all nations in a struggle against war and prostitution.

But they did not agree on either goals or means. Woman suffrage struck Michel as stupid. Each must choose her own weapon, Michel responded in rejecting a symbolic candidacy in 1885, ''but the ballot is less than ever mine.'' ''I believe,'' she explained, ''that women in the Chamber would not prevent the absurdly low pay of women's work and that the prison and the pavement would continue no less to vomit, one onto the other, legions of unfortunates.''[54] The prospect of violence provoked a similar response from Auclert, whose sympathy for the Communards never included their destructive conduct, and, except for the breaking of a ballot box toward the end of her career, she eschewed force absolutely. Nonetheless, Michel persisted in the behavior that had earned her a decade of deportation, and three times during *La Citoyenne's* life she suffered imprisonment. In the spring of 1883, alarmed and fearful, Auclert accused the press of confusing Michel's violent acts with the peaceful transformation envisaged by the proponents of woman suffrage. She also reprinted a letter, originally published in *Le Soir*, in which Lévrier inveighed against anarchism and excused his presence alongside Michel at a demonstration as purely accidental. As for the notorious woman herself, *La Citoyenne* took an indulgent tact. Michel was old and devoid of new ideas, an extreme representative of an unrepresented sex, wrote one of Auclert's collaborators during Michel's

1883 trial. Fault lay not in her person but in a society which forbade legislative careers to women. Denied a seat in the Chamber, where reality would have mellowed her theories, Michel had rejected the republic as it had rejected her. Regardless of her ideas, society must bear the blame for having deprived her of legitimate means of expression.[55]

Auclert hoped that women like Michel and Séverine, a well-known socialist journalist who stood aloof from the movement until 1913, would one day rally to woman suffrage. But until that day there was still much to do, particularly within the feminist movement itself. "Old school" civil rightists, advocates of " *le droit fractionné*" (partial rights), subscribed to a strategy of stagnation in Auclert's opinion, while far too many women outside the movement rejected feminism, expecting others to pull their chestnuts out of the fire. "Young school" proponents of "*le droit integral*" (integral, or full rights) had, therefore, to combat the platonic, wasteful dreams of the "*féministes opportunistes*" (opportunist feminists) and point them down the more practical path of woman's political rights.[56]

In pursuit of this goal Auclert reevaluated the careers of old and new feminists alike. When Eugénie Niboyet died at the age of eighty-five in 1883, for example, *La Citoyenne* recounted her lengthy career, particularly her role in the woman's rights movement of 1848, and concluded that she had been only a weak feminist. She had once declined the presidency of a woman's club and had persistently avoided the issue of divorce. But above all, *La Citoyenne* charged, she had opposed woman suffrage. Even Isabelle Bogelot received equivocal praise when in 1888, as the representative of a group devoted to helping former inmates of the Saint-Lazare women's prison (l'Oeuvre des libérées de Saint-Lazare), she became the first Frenchwoman to attend an American feminist congress. "Let us render thanks to Madame Bogelot," *La Citoyenne* wrote of her trip to Washington, D.C., "who has not feared to carry out a long journey to represent her sisters; although she is not, properly speaking, one of us and she limits herself to works of rehabilitation and charity, we are united by a community of pity for numerous unfortunates."[57] But in Auclert's eyes, Niboyet's and Bogelot's mistaken orientation paled in comparison with that of the decade's two most prominent feminists, Deraismes and Richer.

Shortly after *La Citoyenne*'s birth, Auclert's Society passed a resolution condemning Deraismes for rejecting a symbolic candidacy in the

1881 election. "One ought to know how to do one's duty," remarked tax-strike participant Leprou; "she [Deraismes] has not done it." But a year later, after Deraismes had delivered a speech in favor of suffrage, Auclert commented on how far the Amelioration Society's president had come since the congress of 1878. And in 1885 Deraismes actually stood for office, although in Auclert's opinion she refused to invest sufficient time and money. Instead of campaigning, Auclert lamented, Deraismes had waited at home for Prince Charming the elector to call. When he did not, the fault lay first of all with masculine prejudice but secondly with Deraismes's attitude. Between 1881 and 1885, while she edited *Le Républicain de Seine-et-Oise*, Deraismes had made and unmade deputies, but, according to Auclert, she had refused to exert her full influence on behalf of woman suffrage. Deraismes had also spread herself too thin, with the campaign against vivisection being especially tangential. *Masculinisme* had already deprived women of heart and reason, Auclert exclaimed, and it would continue to do so until women had the power to prevent their own vivisection.

Although insufficient in Auclert's eyes, Deraismes's hesitant support of suffrage contrasted sharply with Richer's persistent opposition. Richer accorded an absolute priority to civil rights, arguing that any other orientation would delay woman's enfranchisement and endanger the republic. He acknowledged Auclert's "good intentions" but castigated her for playing into the hands of royalists and clericals: "Given at this time the general state of women's mentality in France, their upbringing, their tendencies, if tomorrow women voted, the day after tomorrow monarchy would be reestablished." Richer accused Auclert of alienating thousands of excellent republicans by her haughty manner, thus detaching "from the cause of women most of those who were prepared to sustain it." "You compromise coldly, wittingly the goal, the just cause you pretend to defend," Richer fumed: "I wash my hands of your imprudences and your faults."[58]

In turn, Auclert and her followers accused him of legalism, opportunism, and bad faith. Does Richer really want woman suffrage? asked Joanny Rama in an 1885 article for *La Citoyenne*. He claims so but then argues that to demand it would compromise and retard its chances of enactment. Instead of invoking the principle of justice, Rama maintained, Richer relies on legal texts and reveals himself as an impractical reformer. He also confuses civil with penal rights, Giraud added four years later.

In asserting that women cannot vote until they enjoy full civil rights, Richer illogically lumps the many who have done nothing illegal into a category of the few who have suffered criminal convictions.[59]

The world of French politics excited a dual interest in Auclert. On the one hand, like the *brèchistes*, she believed that women's emancipation depended on prior realization of the liberal-political precondition. On the other hand, unlike the *brèchistes*, she maintained that only the immediate enactment of woman suffrage could stabilize that precondition. Hence, in trying to clarify her position vis-à-vis the French political scene, she employed a standard that reversed in detail the priority of the feminist movement's moderate majority. Rather than focusing foremost on the liberal-republican "political question," which the *brèchistes* preferred, she emphasized the "woman question" in determining her relationship to individual politicians and political parties.

Throughout the movement's formative years, however, Auclert found little support within the French political world. Except for de Gasté, her 1881 Chamber questionnaire on women's rights turned up only one other sympathetic deputy, Alfred Talandier. Shortly thereafter the national elections of 1881 returned a third, Clovis Hugues, but by mid-decade Auclert could count at most on no more than a dozen deputies. Of these, Yves Guyot, author of *La Prostitution (Prostitution)*, particularly endeared himself to Auclert because he alone of Paris's Radical-Socialist candidates in 1881 included sex equality in his platform. He lost that year, as did several "secret" advocates of women's rights, but it seems unlikely that antifeminists caused his defeat. Indeed, on only one occasion during the 1880s did a candidate attribute his loss to a stand on women's rights. Auclert's companion Lévrier charged early in 1881 that the press refused to endorse his bid in the sixth *arrondissement* due to his support for *La Citoyenne*'s program, and on election eve a virulent poster attacked his views. However, as the nominee of the minor Parti de l'autonomie communale (Communal Autonomy Party), Lévrier probably had no chance of success in any case.[60]

The feminist contingent was even smaller in the Senate, where only Victor Hugo, Alfred Naquet, Victor Schoelcher, Émile Deschanel, and Jean Macé evinced regular interest in women's rights, and all five preferred the Deraismes-Richer line to that of Auclert. More promising than either national body were local councils. An original member of *La Citoyenne*'s committee, Pierre Leroux's son-in-law Auguste Desmoulins, who had been proscribed in 1851 like Talandier, won a seat on Paris's Municipal Council in late 1881, and by the end of the decade nine incumbent councilors had endorsed women's rights. At the departmental level, the General Council of the Seine also included a relatively large number of sympathizers. In 1885 Auclert petitioned the council for a resolution in favor of woman suffrage. Thirty-seven voted against the proposal after its *rapporteur*, Georges Berry, vehemently attacked it, but eleven cast their ballots in favor.[61] More important than the outcome, however, was the fact that at last an elected group had brought the issue to a vote, something the Chamber and Senate studiously avoided. As a result, although Auclert never gave up on the national legislature, she increasingly turned to local political bodies. Through them she hoped to pressure senators and deputies into taking suffrage seriously. In 1907, twenty-two years after her initial request, the General Council of the Seine reversed its 1885 decision and endorsed woman's municipal suffrage. After that the precedent gained ground, and in the years immediately preceding World War I fifty-odd councils at the departmental, municipal, and *arrondissement* level passed resolutions in support of the reform.

Despite the eventual conversion of many politicians to woman suffrage, opponents continued to outnumber supporters. Auclert was more than willing to employ *La Citoyenne* on behalf of any feminist candidate, but avowed advocates of woman's rights were scarce. Much easier to identify were the outright opponents and, in some cases, the backsliders. The latter were few in number, but Auclert's warning to de Hérédia against "platonic feminism" illustrates the problem. Not until 1885, four years after *La Citoyenne*'s founding, did the Chamber hold its first debate on woman suffrage. Its initiator, Deputy Pieyre (Gard) performed a "brave act," but where, Auclert asked, had the other suffrage advocates been all these years? Even Deputy Henri Michelin, an honorary member of Auclert's Suffrage Circle, had betrayed the cause. He first failed to press for woman's right to vote for the *conseils de prud'hommes*, elected committees that oversaw labor disputes, and then, in 1888, he proposed constitutional revision without providing for woman's participation.[62]

Among outright opponents cited by *La Citoyenne* in 1881, two had earlier shown sympathy for woman's plight. Eugène Pelletan, an ardent republican adversary of the Second Empire and a vice-president of the Senate until his death in 1885, refused to take a stand on woman suffrage despite the liberal attitude of his essay *La Mère* (*The Mother*). Jules Simon, whose *L'Ouvrière* (*The Woman Worker*) had revealed the misery of working women, drew criticism for asserting the need for masculine dominance within the family. Simon also exercised a decisive and deleterious influence on education reform. The wholly inadequate law creating girls' secondary schools bore the name of Camille Sée, Auclert pointed out, but Sée had entered the Chamber under Simon's protection and could hardly have ideas larger than his mentor's.[63]

The Sée reform especially angered Auclert because, given the importance that she and other liberals attached to education reform, it created a false impression of progress. To believe, Auclert charged, that this "sterile law" represented a new level of equality in France was a "profound error: before, as after the law's promulgation, the status quo continues for women." Women will obtain upon graduation a useless "honorary diploma," which will stifle their aspirations to higher education and profitable careers. The worthless diploma will also alienate parents:

Those who are rich will prefer to give their daughters, through private tutors, the knowledge required by the University for a bachelor's degree. Those who are less fortunate will not bother to assume the sacrifice.... [Instead] they will make sacrifices in order to provide a dowry for them.

Moreover, the new law placed too heavy a financial burden on departments. If its sponsors had sincerely wished to improve women's education they would have voted 2 billion francs immediately or, preferably, opened boys' schools to girls. In a coeducational system, Auclert contended, "the children, receiving the same substantial education from infancy, would have shared their mutual qualities: the rude nature of man would have taken on something of the soft character of woman, the woman would have acquired from man the energy that her nature lacks." Seated alongside each other, the two sexes would have become comrades, "respectful of each other and no longer the two enemies who they are today."[64]

Of all the high office holders during *La Citoyenne*'s decade, the most disappointing to Auclert was Léon Gambetta. Auclert credited Gambetta with saving France in 1870 and the republic during the crisis of 16 May 1877. But once in power he had done nothing to prevent the exclusion of half the citizenry from politics, thus "besmirching his system with sterility." He had failed to recognize, despite high-flown rhetoric to the contrary, that the French nation consisted of both men and women. *La Citoyenne* had frequently supported him, Auclert recalled, but in return Gambetta had "opportunistically" betrayed women by blocking their demands in the Chamber and by dragging his feet on divorce. During his brief premiership he had also rejected Auclert's advice to appoint women to the ministries of agriculture and fine arts. Instead of full human representation, all the more necessary because women comprised a numerical majority, he had turned the republic over to a masculine coterie, making politics a game and retarding the day of social well-being. Only in death, which struck prematurely in 1883, had he lent support to Auclert's cause. Ignorant men had long reinforced their sexist prejudices with false criteria, *La Citoyenne* noted, but an autopsy revealed that Gambetta, whose intelligence was universally acknowledged, possessed a brain no larger than a woman's.[65]

Among political parties, the socialists proved the most disappointing. In 1879, one year after Deraismes and Richer "gagged" her at the first Women's Rights Congress, Auclert attended the first French Socialist Congress at Marseilles and inspired a sweeping resolution in favor of women's social and political equality. Then, upon her return to the capital, she played an instrumental role in founding a Paris section of the party, and one of her Society's lieutenants, *Citoyenne* Keva, became its treasurer. Keva then helped organize the second French Socialist Congress, held at Havre in 1880, but during its proceedings she inexplicably sided with the mutualists (reformist Proudhonians) in opposition to the dominant Guesdists. As a result, the party's branch in the Paris region (L'Union fédérative du centre) expelled Auclert's Society, isolating its eighteen dues-paying members from further direct participation in the workers' movement. Auclert managed to maintain her ties with several prominent socialist feminists, particularly Léonie Rouzade and Eugénie Pierre (later Eugénie Potonié-Pierre after her marriage to Edmond Potonié), but the gulf proved unbridgeable. Auclert or her followers occasionally attended subsequent regional or national socialist congresses as delegates of *La Citoyenne*, but the profound difference in orientation between socialists and feminists, as well as internecine rivalries, prevented anything but momentary cooperation. The stand adopted at Marseilles remained unique: "The socialists," as Charles Sowerwine observed, "never again produced a bill of women's rights to equal this in its breadth and profundity.'' In its place, they substituted a workers-first, women-second resolution adopted at the Paris Regional Congress of July 1880: ''The Congress, while proclaiming the equality of the sexes, declare: 'That the question of women's rights will be resolved and will only be resolved with that of labor, by the collective appropriation of all instruments of production.' ''[66]

Hence, although initially attracting ''numerous sympathetic working women'' to the cause and succeeding at Marseilles in ''the first effort to bring the working-class movement to adopt a more progressive view of the role of women,'' Auclert quickly found herself at odds with those who accorded more importance to the class struggle than to the sex struggle.[67] More flexible than the *brèchistes* in exploring possible alignments with the French Left and Right, she nonetheless shared their fundamental attachment to liberalism. Like Richer, who applauded the Marseilles congress for discarding the Proudhonian perspective on women but rejected the collectivist ideal as contrary to human nature and inimical to individual liberty, Auclert recognized the gulf between classes but maintained that an even greater gulf separated women from men.[68] Neither women nor workers had benefited from the Great Revolution of 1789, Auclert observed, but the problem of sex oppression ran deeper than that of class:

Those who go off to war against the monopolies of capitalism forget that men are like the rich.... Men exercise monopolies over lucrative work, public functions, employment, rights and sovereignty.... The question of women is the new Gordian knot that, once severed, would permit resolution of the social question, but, so long as women have their hands tied by civil laws and are, from a political point of view, gagged, the economic transformation advocated by collectivists will only operate to the profit of men.[69]

In contrast, therefore, to the position of socialist-feminists like Louise Saumoneau, who at the turn of the century exclaimed that ''the general interests of the female bourgeoisie, being attached to the interests of their parasitic class, are in profound antagonism to those of the female proletariat, attached equally to the interests of their exploited class,'' Auclert remained steadfastly liberal in her quest for women's rights.[70] Although at odds with the *brèchistes* over the issue of woman suffrage, she was at one with them politically, a stance made clear by the title of chapter 28 of her posthumously published *Les Femmes au gouvernail*, "Le socialisme n'aurait pas pour résultat l'affranchisement de la femme" ("Socialism Will Not Bring About Woman's Emancipation").[71]

THE SHADOW CAMPAIGN OF 1885

The most vexing *assautiste* incident in Richer's career—as well as the single most important woman suffrage demonstration during the feminist movement's formative years—was the large-scale shadow campaign of 1885. In running a slate of symbolic candidates, suffragists sought through pressuring public opinion to obtain a political reversal of the administrative and judicial decisions that had denied women the right to vote. As a pressure tactic, shadow campaigns offered three advantages. First, because elections occurred frequently and predictably, suffragists had many occasions to use the tactic and plenty of time to prepare. Second, inasmuch as the electoral procedure involved several stages, suffragists could publicize their cause by attempting to register to vote, by challenging male candidates at party rallies, by running themselves as symbolic office seekers, and by filing protests against officials who refused to count the votes cast for women. Finally, unlike tax strikes and census boycotts, which needed widespread support to succeed, shadow campaigns required only a handful of determined women.

Several years of shadow campaign experience went into the 1885 demonstration. In 1881, enthused by the press coverage of the previous year's registration attempt, Auclert and thirteen others repeated the drive. Also in 1881, when Léonie Rouzade polled fifty-seven votes in Paris's twelfth *arrondissement*, three women received five votes at Thorey (Meurthe-et-Moselle), Madame Jules Lefebvre garnered a few at Grandpré (Ardennes), and Madame Augustine Debouis nearly won a seat on the municipal council of Nièvre. Three years later, women polled majorities in local elections at Houquetot (Seine-Inférieure) and Vornay (Cher), and, although their victories were immediately annulled, Auclert interpreted the results as a promise of better times. Citing *Le Figaro's* endorsement of the idea that women should serve as municipal councilors, she predicted the likelihood of at least acquiring eligibility, if not the vote itself. With legislative elections only one year away, she urged in 1884, proponents of woman suffrage must rally for an all-out effort.[72]

Although Auclert inspired the year-long effort and issued the initial call for the campaign, she refused to pose her own candidacy, a refusal that Richer mocked by pointing out that "a brave officer is not content to push his soldiers into battle, he marches at their head." At the outset of the demonstration, she participated in the registration phase in both the ninth and eleventh *arrondissements* and later protested against the refusal of officials to tally votes cast for women. She also drew up petitions to exclude women from the electoral census and to obtain the single-woman's vote. But when asked by the campaign's slate makers to become a candidate herself, she declined. "I am profoundly touched by the honor you do me and I thank you ever so much," Auclert responded:

But you understand that having these last ten years put so much determination into resuscitating the question of woman's political rights, that having, for seven or eight [years] especially, seized all occasions to protest against masculine autocracy and to demand that taxpaying and responsible women participate in the government of the country, it would be completely out of place for me to claim for myself the benefits of my campaign.[73]

Selflessness aside, Auclert also opposed the scale of the tactic, warning that too many candidates would dilute the suffrage vote and provide the authorities with an excuse for discounting favorable ballots. Her plan had called for running only one candidate, the rich and influential Maria Deraismes. But others in her Circle wished to run as well, with the result that organization and direction quickly passed out of Auclert's hands and into those of Louise Barberousse and Jules Allix.[74] Both had close ties to the Amelioration Society, which accounts perhaps for Deraismes's half-hearted participation in the campaign.

Barberousse (1836-1900) was a life-long teacher. An ardent free thinker and devotee of science, she first taught at Nièvre, the place of her birth, and, after a sojourn in Britain, arrived in Paris in time for the seige of 1870-1871. It was probably then, while serving as a nurse, that she met Allix, who founded a women's committee in the fifth *arrondissement* and displayed a passionate interest in education reform. In 1883 she resigned the directorship of the Free School of the rue Jean-Lantier and joined him in a new venture, the rue Saint-Honoré school for girls. In December of the following year, Barberousse and Allix founded the Women's Protection League (Ligue de la protection des femmes), through which they attempted to implement Auclert's call for electoral action. To Auclert, however, Barberousse lacked the originality of Deraismes and Rouzade, and the League to which she belonged represented a group of "noisy nonentities, of adventuresses lacking merit and intelligence." It might have a hundred members, but "not one single *serious* woman."[75]

In the career of Jules Allix (1818-1897) the Women's Protection League represented only one in a series of fantastic enterprises. Sixty-six years old at the time, he had spent a third of his adult life in forced exile, prison, and insane asylums. Born at Fontenay-le-Comte (Vendée) of bourgeois parents (his brother once served as Victor Hugo's personal physician), he became a *licencié en droit* but preferred the titles of professor of gymnastics and professor of sciences. His militant, mystical socialism and cooperativism brought him seven years of banishment under the Second Empire and eight years of incarceration at the beginning of the Third Republic. During the siege and Commune, he held several important positions and won notoriety for two unique ideas. To protect Frenchwomen from Prussian rapists, he proposed the *doigt prussique* (prussic finger), an elongated rubber tube designed to discharge acid on impact; and to improve communications, he suggested telepathic snails. Freed by the amnesty of 1879, Allix turned increasingly to feminism and education as means of social and moral improvement. In addition to belonging to Auclert's Suffrage Circle, he founded a short-lived women's committee in 1880 and served as the Amelioration Society's secretary for over a decade. In 1881, he and Barberousse represented the women's committee at the Universal Congress of Free Thinking (Congrès universel de la libre pensée). In education he rejected rote memorization and mechanical exercises. With new methods, he claimed, students could master reading in fifteen hours and definitive French in six months. These goals underlay the Saint-Honoré girls' school, which also served as the headquarters of the Women's Protection League.[76]

The opening phase of the 1885 campaign focused once again on registration. Under the auspices of the Women's Protection League, Barberousse, Marie Picot, the widow Jeannot, and Auclert demanded inscription on the voting lists. Immediately repulsed at the administrative level, all except Auclert appealed to the courts. Barberousse's case drew the most attention. On 6 February 1885, Léon Giraud, one of *La Citoyenne*'s cofounders, and Jules Allix presented her plea before Justice of the Peace Carré in the first *arrondissement*. Giraud spoke first:

Whence do women derive the right that they demand? From the very texts of the law which have never made a distinction between the sexes. What a strange pretension it is, in fact, on the part of men to attribute sovereignty and political power to themselves alone, and is this not a veritable criminal outrage on the part of one group of citizens against another? If they persist in maintaining the exclusion of which women have been the object until now, they will create thereby a sort of caste, similar to that of India's pariahs, and they will render legitimate certain opposition to the law that they have witnessed in times past.

Allix then asked, after a brief historical review, "By what right is the legislator the legislator if woman does not vote? By what right is the law the law?"[77]

In response, Carré cited numerous constitutional and legislative texts, dating back to 1791, that omitted specific mention of woman's political rights. He then summarized the law of 7 July 1874 which required voters to possess full civil and political rights. Enumerating the areas in which women lacked these rights, including the Chamber's rejection of the *commerçante* vote in 1883, Carré concluded:

If women, repudiating the privileges of their sex and inspired by certain modern theories, believe the hour has come for them to break the tutelar bonds with which traditions, mores, and the law have encompassed them, it is not before the courts, but before the legislative power, that they should present their demands.

Thus, he ruled, "there is no reason to register démoiselle Barberousse on the electoral lists." Carré's lengthy ruling also applied to Madame Picot, Barberousse's co-plaintiff. The widow Jeannot's appeal, pursued in the Faubourg-Montmartre quarter of Paris (ninth *arrondissement*), elicited a shorter but equally negative reply.[78]

Denied judicial redress—a second appeal failed before the Cour de cassation in March—Barberousse and Allix resolved to run a full slate of candidates in the upcoming election. The political vehicle they chose was the Socialist Republican Federation (Fédération républicaine socialiste), created in the fall of 1884, to which Auclert also belonged. One of the many new parties that hoped to take advantage of the *scrutin de liste*, the Federation shared the League's headquarters at the girls' school and wrote political equality for women into its platform in October 1884. After several months of infighting, the Federation agreed in February 1885 to add women to its candidate list. Those who opposed the step quit the party, the socialist *La Bataille* reported, leaving "Allix, Barberousse and Co." in command of "the wreckage of the old Federation."[79]

Altogether the Socialist Republican Federation invited twenty-seven women to become candidates. Fifteen accepted, ten refused, and two were dropped, actress Sarah Bernhardt and Mademoiselle Rousseil, the latter, according to Richer, "notoriously known for her clericalism and her faith at Sacre-Coeur."[80] Those who refused included Magdeleine Godard, concert violinist; Caroline de Barrau, director of l'Oeuvre des libérées de Saint-Lazare; and Eugénie Pierre, one of Richer's collaborators who, like Auclert, objected to the excessive number of candidates. Three women on the left also balked, primarily for ideological reasons. Communard Paule Mink wrote from Algeria that illness had compelled her to retire from public life, but in any case her candidacy was out of the question "because I do not believe that women will have their situation ameliorated by the conquest of their political rights, but only by the social transformation of our old world." Séverine, director of the socialist *Le Cri du peuple (The People's Cry)*, declined because she felt too feminine, objected to joining any group, and preferred the "social struggle."[81] And anarchist Louise Michel, whose attitude was already well known, persisted in her conviction that woman suffrage represented a mirage "that we shall be offered because it means nothing. . . . It is in the struggle for progress, for universal peace, that we must take our place."[82]

Less expected, judging from Auclert's vehement reaction, were the refusals of two staunch republicans, Céleste Hardouin and Madame Adam. Hardouin, a teacher who had led a petition drive to secure amnesty for Louise Michel in 1879, at first figured on the acceptance list. But in August 1885 she corrected the error:

To Monsieur Jules Allix, who came to make me a rather ridiculous proposition a week ago, I responded that I had enough occasions to prove my devotion to the cause of the people in giving to the girls who are confided to me an education conforming to the republican spirit, without searching elsewhere for another outlet for my activity.[83]

Madame Adam, director of the chauvinist *La Nouvelle Revue*, had helped launch the feminist movement a generation earlier. By 1885, however, she had acquired a rather dim view of French womanhood:

If I were English or American, I could accept a candidacy, because in England and America most men admit that one can, without danger, make a place for women in the administration of public affairs. Also the women of those two countries work with the laudable goal of being, when the time comes, worthy of sharing [responsibility].

It seems to me that, here in France, ambition comes to women before the search for merit. My principle of reform is that it is necessary first to require of those who one emancipates the proof that demands for their rights rest on knowledge of their capacity, that is to say, their duties.[84]

The tenth refusal represented a unique case, an outgrowth of the Morin affair. In 1883 Dame Lenormand, who had a reputation for beauty under the Second Empire, sought grounds for separation from her second husband. Convinced that Monsieur Lenormand had a mistress, she hired a private detective, Monsieur Morin, to uncover the correspondent. Unfortunately, he singled out the wrong woman, the wife of Deputy Clovis Hugues. Hugues and his wife immediately sued for defamation of character, and Morin lost. Faced with 2,500 francs in fines and two years in prison, Morin launched a series of appeals in the courts and a flurry of poison-pen letters at Madame Hugues. In November 1884, nearly a year after the original verdict and five minutes after Morin won another stay, Madame Hugues did what Richer thought any honest woman might. She emptied six shots into Morin, killing him instantly in the middle of the Palais de Justice. Tried for murder, she secured an acquittal in January 1885, although a civil trial awarded 2,000 francs in damages to Morin's father. Shortly thereafter came a bid from the Socialist Republican Federation, which, despite her husband's feminist sympathies, Madame Hugues rejected. "I regret to announce to you," she informed Jules Allix, "that it is impossible for me to accept this candidacy, which I hardly expected in the first place, because I have never accomplished any political act that would call me to the attention of my fellow citizens."[85]

Of the fifteen who undertook to run, Maria Deraismes equivocated the most. She agreed to fulfill the duties of office if elected but declined to do more than lend her name to the campaign. "I do not refuse," she told Barberousse, "but I do not propose." French women had as much right to vote in 1885 as men had in 1848, she believed, but the electorate must decide. If women could obtain suffrage without soliciting it, she felt, their cause would be strengthened. According to Richer's report, "Mademoiselle Deraismes made known that she would take no part in the electoral battle, that she would attend no public meetings, that she would put up no posters, distribute no leaflets, in a word that she would abstain from all initiative."[86]

Six other candidates appeared only as names in Auclert's and Richer's extensive coverage of the campaign: Augustine Bouhin, Louise Martane, Marie Schacre, Angèle Charrier, Amelina Olivier, and Clara Rougier. The remaining seven included Adéle Esquiros, whose *L'Amour* (1860) had enhanced the movement's literary phase, and Léonine Rouzade, the 1881 candidate in Paris's twelfth *arrondissement*. Granddaughter of a deputy to the Third Estate in 1789, disciple of Cabet and Fourier, Rouzade was born at Paris in 1839. Raised by a brother after her parents' death, she worked as an embroiderer until her marriage to Auguste Rouzade at the age of twenty-two. Forty-one years of happiness followed, due, according to Auclert, to Auguste's immunity to "the stupid pride of sex." Encouraged by her husband, Rouzade wrote several books on social questions— *Le Voyage de Théodose à l'île de l'Utopie, Le Roi Johanne, Le Monde renversé*—and stumped France on behalf of socialism and feminism. She informed Jules Allix:

I am a socialist without revolutionary or other adjective because the means to arrive at the goal are necessarily variable according to events, circumstances, whereas the goal is not; I am content therefore to march there with all my strength, without preoccupying myself with what manner one will arrive. That is all there is to say; I am with you.[87]

Five years younger than Rouzade, candidate Madame Vincent (née Eliska Girard) ranked as one of the founders of French feminism. Born at Mézières (Eure-et-Loir), she arrived in Paris in time to help André Léo and Deraismes establish the Society for the Demand of Woman's Rights. Her role in the 1885 campaign represented one of many actions on behalf of women's emancipation, the most important of which were yet to come.[88] Both Rouzade and Vincent were neophytes next to Léonie Manière. Described by Auclert as an "old battler" and "well known," Manière was born at Marey-sur-Tille (Côte d'Or) in 1826. Widowed and left with a large family, she earned a teaching certificate at the age of forty. She sympathized with the Paris Commune of 1871 and openly criticized the republic. Nevertheless, with the help of a friend at the

Banque de France, she had secured a public subsidy by the time she joined the Federation's ticket in 1885. Youngest of the candidates was Lara Marcel, whose poetry, written under the male pseudonym of René Marcil, included *Les Satires marciliennes* and *La Féodalité littéraire*. Marcel, like several of the others, belonged to Auclert's Suffrage Society. Newest of the candidates was the widow Jeannot, whose feminist career began with her registration bid in the ninth *arrondissement* earlier that same year. In contrast to Rouzade's marriage, Jeannot's had failed. Her husband, a notary, had squandered her dowry before his death. Forced to work, she was a seamstress in 1885.[89]

Rounding out the Federation's slate was Emilie Saint-Hilaire, whose birth at Naillat (Creuse) in 1818 made her sixty-seven at the time of the election. Prior to the Commune of 1871 she had apparently lived the quiet life of a Parisian boardinghouse keeper and wine seller. Once the insurrection began, however, she embraced the revolution with ardor. Her son, who served in a Communard artillery unit, died during the fighting, and Emilie herself was subsequently deported, like Louise Michel, to New Caledonia. Amnestied in 1879, she returned to Paris and immediately joined Auclert. She also took up writing under the pseudonym Madame Godot. When offered a candidacy in 1885, she remarked pluckily, ''I want my share of the ridicule.'' That she got. As the October election approached, the Federation's list aroused a storm of vituperative comment. Later feminists interpreted the decline of ridicule as an indication of growing public sympathy, but in 1885, with ridicule coming from all sides, Auclert drew a different conclusion. Citing hostile articles in *Gil Blas, Le National,* and *Le Figaro* (which ran favorable notices as well), she claimed that men had begun to panic. Male cynicism, sarcasm, and the boycott of feminist news, she felt, was a sure sign of progress.[90] If so, Auclert must have been pleased with the announcement by *Le Voltaire*'s anonymous ''Dame Voilée'' that ''definitely the feminine candidates are very sick'':

After successive refusals by all women having some intelligence, some good sense and some celebrity, the famous committee presided over by the sympathetic friend of snails, Monsieur Jules Allix, has had to show little discrimination in its choices and to take at random, to help itself, to the first women who came by. . . .

There is one especially, much ignored by the public, but well known in the offices of newspapers and the bureaus of publishers that she besieges, and whose comic physiognomy will deliver the last blow to Mademoiselle Barberousse's attempt and kill it under ridicule. . . .

She is Madame Saint-Hilaire, her true name Madame Godot [*sic*].

Oh! she is a type, a curious type, amusing as possible.

You must often have seen, descending in small steps from the heights of Montmartre to the rue du Croissant, a small wizened old lady carrying under her arm a packet wrapped in newspaper—those are her works—and followed by a hideous dog, always horribly dirty, a kind of seeing-eye dog belonging to no known species. . . .

One would spontaneously take her, thanks to her get-up and gait, for one of the quadrupeds of the Corvi circus. . . .

Absolutely illiterate. . . and of an ignorance that exceeds all limits, she has dreamed for ten years of living by her pen and she rails against Monsieur Zola, Monsieur Daudet, and the others who congest the paths of celebrity; against editors and journalists who do not understand her or who envy the originality of her talent. . . .

She will ask you seriously if you have heard of someone named Mirabeau. . . .

She believes that Raphael is a nineteenth-century painter, takes Rembrandt for one of our contemporaries. . . .

Nearly twenty years ago she was thrown in with Victor Hugo at Guernsey; she calls him with pride *mon confrère*.[91]

As candidates the shadow campaigners fared poorly. Not all ran in Paris, and at least some may have run on the nine-woman slate offered by the Independent Women of Versailles. But from nowhere in France came any women's vote returns. In the Paris region, the Federation's 6 candidates, who vied with nearly 500 competitors for 38 Chamber seats, quit after the first round of balloting and in any case failed to crack the ranks of the top 147 vote getters.[92] Allix, the much mocked ex-inmate of the Charenton mental hospital, went down to an ignominious defeat with only 171 votes.[93] Whether *La Citoyenne*'s call to support profeminist men in the run-off balloting had any effect is impossible to tell. In fact, only the village of Saint-Sever (Landes) produced a concrete shadow campaign statistic. Two women cast ballots there on 4 October 1885, bringing its mayor, Monsieur de Dubedout, a 200-franc fine.[94]

The poor showing immediately provoked recriminations within the feminist movement. Auclert and others of like mind repeated their objection to so many symbolic candidacies, which accounted for why "the most determined suffragists abstained from taking part in the demonstration."[95] Unfortunately, Auclert implied, some women had put personal ambition ahead of women's emancipation. If fewer had run, their votes would have been counted like Rouzade's in 1881, she charged, and the Federation further blundered by neglecting to send a delegate to the worker's party that had sponsored Rouzade's earlier electoral bid.[96]

The difference in strategy between *assautistes* and *brèchistes* also flared up again in the campaign's immediate aftermath. Republicans fared badly at the first turn, but, recovering in the run-off, they secured 56 percent of the vote and 367 seats in the new Chamber of Deputies, as against the Right's 202. But, in the opinion of Auclert and other *assautistes*, the outcome simply sanctioned the most scandalous of royalties, that of sex. The strong showing of the Right revealed that men lacked political education, despite having possessed the ballot for years. Only woman suffrage, Auclert repeated, could correct that fault and make men conscious of their duty.[97] In contrast, Richer, speaking on behalf of the *brèchistes*, accused the Federation of siphoning off republican votes and alienating feminism's natural supporters:

I have no intention of dwelling anew on the disastrous consequences of the electoral campaign so maladroitly provoked by Mlles. Barberousse and Hubertine Auclert. . . . [But] the cause that we have to defend meets enough hostility already and includes enough adversaries that we must have the prudence not to divide ourselves.

Many people misunderstand our demands, Richer implored, so we must "unite our efforts, *o femmes*! in order that it can no longer be said that you are your own worst enemies."[98]

Despite the recriminations, however, subsequent activists looked back on the shadow campaign as a turning point for woman suffrage and feminism. Before the year was out the campaign helped provoke the General Council of the Seine into recording the first vote on woman's political rights by an elected assembly in France, and between 1885 and the outbreak of World War I at least four doctoral dissertations in law gave close and favorable scrutiny to Barberousse's registration claims.[99] Twelve years after the event, the Amelioration Society's *Bulletin* asserted that the shadow campaign of 1885 had produced "such a reverberation that we can say that since that time the feminist movement, which before had lain dormant, has openly taken a new upward direction."[100]

AN ISOLATED LIFE: EVERYDAY EXPERIENCES AND EPILOGUE

As an advocate of a minority point of view within a minority movement that at first had little else to draw on except enthusiasm, Auclert
frequently despaired. In the first of twenty-five diary entries covering the
period from June 1883 to March 1886, she wrote:

I work harder than a mercenary but I am not rewarded like one. The mercenary
finds instant satisfaction in the results of his labor, and, after a hard day of toil, the
supreme relaxation: affection! love!

As for me! Nothing! but. . . suspicion, envy, ridicule, hate!

All along the line negative results. I stand alone against the prejudiced and
when I sense the goal close at hand, having overcome the greatest difficulties, I
am hurled back to the starting point. What I do would seem sublime if I were rich
[but] being poor it is only ridiculous.

I fight exclusively for women. I exert myself to liberate them, to exalt their
qualities, to conceal their faults, and these vile slaves would repay me for
defending them so ardently by spitting in my face if they could.

Those who understand me have no faith in me. People like me reject a place in
the world and wish to make the most extensive changes that have yet occurred in
the social order.

However much I may seem reckless to all, I am sensitive and small. Rather
than make excuses for my audacity, I would better disarm my enemies perhaps if I
knew how to make the most of myself.

However hopeless the struggle may seem and as I have been created equal, I
have an unquenchable faith. One of this Christian belief must toil hard and long to
quell the beasts. [101]

The diary also offers an unusual insight into the problems that plagued
the daily operations of groups like Auclert's. In an entry on the difficulties of finding vendors for *La Citoyenne*, she noted a day spent going "up
and down the exterior boulevard in front of benches filled with human
brutes, dandies, bums, etc." Finally, she discovered "a figure slightly
less repulsive than the others," whom she approached "timidly and with
a suppliant's air" amid "jeers and dirty jokes." He agreed to the work,
which meant showing up the next day at Auclert's apartment. Others also
agreed, but out of more than a hundred "hooligans" who tramped to her
door to pick up their newspapers not one returned with the proceeds. "So
much time, so much pain, so much suffering uselessly wasted," Auclert

reflected after the "sale." Occasionally her vendors came back, Auclert wrote a few months later, which required her "to wait sometimes until ten o'clock." And then, they returned "reeling, insolent," and, instead of turning over the proceeds, they demanded additional "bottle money." Refused, they left "cursing all the while as they descended the stairs," while the "building reverberated from the vulgar insults."

Auclert's friends worried for her safety in dealing with so many street people, but she discounted the danger. More bothersome were the constant interruptions. A typical day found her finalizing *La Citoyenne*'s copy for the printers and receiving a request from *Le Matin* for an article that had to be in by midnight. Then a vendor stopped in and, after a few minutes of chit-chat, left without his newspapers. Tired and hungry, Auclert quickly threw a cutlet on the grill. Three more vendors came by, asking about prices, and the cutlet burned while Auclert answered their questions. One bite later, a subscriber rang, and, fearful of making a bad impression, Auclert left her meal for yet another conversation. When at last she returned to her table, the meal was cold, and she was so hungry that she could not eat.

Auclert's difficulties stemmed in part from a lack of able assistants. "Jesus in the Garden of Olives had faithful apostles," she bitterly complained; "as for me I feel that I have truly no one with me; the end of each meeting, seeing that it has been useless, is my Calvary, my Garden of Olives." "I am always at the same point," she repeated on another occasion, "much hated and little heard. These brave imbeciles, after whom I chase for help, rely on me to do [everything] and believe themselves destined to play the role of critic." Difficulties also grew out of crossed signals and unanticipated developments. A week's preparation for a meeting at the Capucines's Hall went for naught, for example, when Auclert found out at the last minute that the hall had mistakenly been let to another party. "These things only happen to me," she recorded. "My life is a continuity of wasted efforts." Two months earlier, in April 1884, a similar problem arose when, with a hall secured, the principal speaker attempted to bow out. "In truth I am a singular imbecile," Auclert wrote disparagingly, and then despairingly: "What is the best thing in life? It is death!"

Auclert lived in terror of having to speak before large audiences. She lacked confidence in her ability to reach listeners, and she feared the cutting remarks that her words so often provoked. A brief entry on one of her forays during the 1885 shadow campaign reflected both concerns:

At an electoral meeting at the Molière Hall for the feminine candidates, I was forced to mount the rostrum. Certainly the listeners were much deceived in seeing me so ineloquent; much applause and I finished with a blunder in proposing a collection for posters and for these women. Not a hand went up in support of my proposal.

As I climbed down from the rostrum to leave the hall, I heard three women say: "That Hubertine Auclert, what gall she has to mount the rostrum to pick men's pockets."

The principal speaker who attempted to avoid the meeting of April 1884 was Doctor Eugène Verrier, a utopian socialist who published a pamphlet the following month on *La Femme devant la science* (*Woman Before Science*).[102] His reluctance to attend, however, fell far short of the searing disappointment that others induced in Auclert. These others included Paule Mink and Louise Barberousse. In 1883 a frightful English woman had insulted Auclert; in 1884 the insults had come from Barberousse. "Why?" asked Auclert, "because as small as I make myself I still annoy the ambitious." Most disappointing of all was Victor Hugo, who, like Dumas *fils*, declined to assume a position in Auclert's Society:

Victor Hugo, who refused the honorary presidency of the Suffrage Society, has just accepted the presidency of the Society against Vivisection. Why this difference? Because those who asked him to join the suffrage society of progress were poor, while those who urged him to join the antiscientific antivivisection society were rich.

Yet Auclert mourned Hugo's death in 1885 with characteristic fatalism: "Ah, why stupid death did you not take me, the lonely, the sad, the hopeless, in place of this god of the earth so loved and adored?" She and other members of her Circle also marched in Hugo's magnificent funeral cortege, where, despite ten hours without anything to eat or drink and placement by reactionaries at the rear of the procession, their suffrage banner elicited numerous tippings of hats and wavings of handkerchiefs.

The individual who engendered the most profound ambivalence in Auclert was Antonin Lévrier, the man she married in 1888. Their working relationship covered at least the previous decade, and one of the earliest entries in Auclert's diary reveals a personal attachment of long standing. In August 1883, after a separation of nine months, Auclert traveled to the coast to meet him. Strangeness born of absence provoked a coolness between them at first, and they talked of "indifferent things" until they rediscovered each other over dinner. However, separation continued to plague their relationship. In March 1885, Auclert wrote:

How my character has changed! I now [experience] more than anyone else the anxiety of love. I am indifferent to life and death, but not yet indifferent to politics. I passionately attend the meetings of the Socialist Republican Federation.

I think that A[ntonin] will not return to Paris. What effect time has on the liveliest of emotions. We write letters as strangers, which is funny as well as sad.

Auclert prefaced these observations with a typical lament: "Life would be good if I were alone by myself! But I am alone everywhere, alone in public life as in private life! Alone at home, alone at the Suffrage Society, alone at the journal, always alone, everywhere alone."

A year later, the tension between the cause she loved and the man she loved reached a peak. On 12 March 1885, Auclert noted the dilemma:

I sensed a feeling of well-being, I was happy for several days. Then this morning I received a letter from Antonin that turned my joy to tears; it announced that he was about to be sent to Tahiti to replace the imperial procurator at a salary of 4,500 [francs]. I cried, cried, cried, rummaged through an atlas. Marie tried to comfort me, but everything has become bleak for me. This will pass and if I went with Antonin to the end of the world, I would never forgive myself for having sacrificed Marie, my liberty, the cause, my quasi well-being to a man who has always brought me more pain than joy. Love was always thus, so fragile, so easily broken! How much I have sacrificed as I have loved to be loved so little. Beautiful women have the joys and triumphs of love. Ugly me has had only its sorrows and sacrifices. Is nature so cruel as to put into the bodies least made for love the hearts most avid for love?

At month's end, Lévrier confirmed Auclert's worst fears. "Despite all my prayers and supplications Antonin is leaving. He told me coldly without hesitation: 'I have no choice but to stab you to the heart.' "

Three years after the shadow campaign of 1885 and two years after the Tahiti crisis, Auclert married Lévrier. They immediately embarked for Algeria, settling at Frendah where Lévrier had accepted an appointment as justice of the peace. How much Auclert felt the distance would affect her cause is unclear. Nor is it clear how long she intended to remain in North Africa. She designated Maria Martin, whose name first appeared on *La Citoyenne*'s masthead in June 1888, as the journal's new director. From across the Mediterranean she kept in touch with metropolitan events and continued to write for *La Citoyenne*. She also drew on the North African situation to develop new charges against *masculinisme*, such as, for example, the complicity of Frenchmen in permitting polygamy to thrive among their Muslim subjects. As the months passed, however, Auclert's influence declined. The new director gradually assumed complete control of the journal, and by the time Lévrier died and Auclert returned to Paris in 1892, *La Citoyenne* had disappeared. Its last issue, number 187, bore the date 15 November 1891. Back in the capital, Auclert took an apartment at 151 rue de la Roquette, near Lévrier's tomb in Père-Lachaise.

Under Maria Martin's direction, *La Citoyenne* reappeared as *Le Journal des femmes* (*The Women's Journal*), which survived from December 1891 until Martin's death in January 1911. The *Journal*'s program differed from its predecessor's in only one respect: it slightly deemphasized woman suffrage in favor of other feminist objectives. Bitterness from the takeover lingered on, however, and even after a lapse of seventeen years Auclert could do no better than refer to her former colleague as "that woman." The "indelicate proceedings" provoked a single satisfaction: Deputy de Gasté completely dissociated himself from the new venture and withdrew his subsidies.[103] Auclert never attempted to found another newspaper. She regrouped her Society as best she could—Martin had also created a new group called Women's Solidarity (Groupe de la solidarité des femmes)—but confined her writings to selected journals, pamphlets, and books. Between 1896 and 1909, she contributed at least fifty-four articles to *Le Radical*, as well as others to *Le Matin, La Libre Parole*, and the feminist daily *La Fronde* (1897-1905). In addition to her 1878 *Le Droit politique des femmes* (*Women's Political Rights*) and in 1926 her posthumous *Les Femmes au gouvernail* (*Women at the Helm*), she published in 1900 *Les Femmes arabes en Algérie* (*The Arab Women of Algeria*), in 1908 *Le Vote des femmes* (*Women's Vote*), and three pamphlets—the 1879 *L'Égalité sociale et politique de l'homme et de la femme* (*The Social and Political Equality of Man and Woman*), the 1904 *L'Argent de la femme* (*Woman's Money*), and the 1905 *Le Nom de la femme* (*Woman's Name*).[104]

The milieu that confronted Auclert upon her return from Algeria was singularly hostile to woman suffrage. In her absence, Deraismes and

Richer had staged a second Women's Rights Congress during the 1889 revolutionary centennial, which, like the congress of 1878, banned the discussion of woman's political rights. A third major congress in 1900 followed suit, and it was not until 1908 that a feminist congress accorded woman suffrage an official airing. Nevertheless, Auclert persisted in her attempt to convert both feminists and the public at large. Petitions continued to flow from her pen. In 1910, for instance, she induced Clovis Hugues to submit 3,000 signatures to the Chamber on behalf of the *célibataire* vote, and in 1904 she urged Premier Émile Combes simply to decree woman suffrage in order to enlist republican women, his "best auxiliaries," in the struggle to separate church and state. Demonstrations also proliferated. In 1904 Auclert and several supporters protested against the centenary of the Napoleonic Code by ripping a copy to shreds at the base of the Vendôme column. Four years later she invaded a polling booth in the fourth *arrondissement* and smashed a ballot box. A few months after that she led a band of twenty suffragists into the Chamber, button-holed Deputy Charles Benoist, and flung suffrage flyers onto the floor from the gallery. She also introduced two new forms of protest. In 1901 her Society issued suffrage stamps designed to appear alongside regular letter postage—a technique that American feminists and the French Radical-Socialist Party later adopted. A short time afterward she devised a series of pro-vote postcards.

The net effect of Auclert's persistence brought her little personal support. During the first decade of the twentieth century, large segments of the feminist movement rallied to woman suffrage, but Auclert offended many of the converts. They chose to concentrate on the municipal vote, whereas Auclert, who had often advanced restricted proposals in the past, pressed increasingly for full political suffrage. Most new suffragists also subscribed to *"le suffragisme réformist"* (reform suffragism), which attempted to adapt the tactic of *la brèche* to the new priority. Auclert, in contrast, represented *"le suffragisme révolutionnaire"* (revolutionary suffragism), which stood for repeated frontal assaults on all male bastions.[105] Their differences came to a head in 1908. The Women's Rights Congress of that year finally placed suffrage on its agenda, but Auclert felt that the time for talk had passed: "After having employed all legal means to obtain their political rights, feminists are forced to resort to revolutionary means."[106] Few feminists agreed, however, and two years later Auclert lashed back. She accused newcomers of self-seeking and protested their attempts to stifle the initiators of the movement. Thanks to them, she spat, "the discord of suffrage claimants, more than the indifference of women, retards feminine emancipation."[107]

Auclert's opponents within the movement came to identify her with the violent tactics of the Women's Social and Political Union, founded in Britain by Emmeline Pankhurst in 1903. With this identification in mind, they made a distinction between peaceful, law-abiding "suffragists" and disruptive "suffragettes" like Auclert, "whose temperament," according to the feminist historian Léon Abensour, "was that of English or American militants and who was a suffragette before the word [came into existence]."[108] They also chastised her for imitating the feminist radicals of the French Revolution, for "not taking into consideration that," as her contemporary Jeanne Schmahl put it, "the recollection of the uproarious proceedings of those women was perhaps uppermost in the minds of the men who reelaborated the laws that will—until they are abolished—prove an insurmountable obstacle to the admission of women to the franchise."[109] Consequently, Auclert found it very difficult to play a part in the expanding suffrage movement. She refused to represent the National Council of French Women, founded in 1901, at an international suffrage conference in 1906. Shortly after, she accepted the chair of the Council's suffrage section, but resigned a few months later. When Schmahl, one of her most persistent critics, helped to create the French Union for Women's Suffrage in 1909, Auclert declined to participate.[110]

Despite the criticism, provoked in part by her own uncompromising attitude, Auclert inspired several advances. Municipal and national suffrage eluded her, but working women secured the vote for *conseils de prud'hommes* in 1907 and eligibility in 1908. Auclert also helped secure the "seat law" of 1900, which required employers to provide chairs for sales personnel. In addition, Auclert had a lasting, although largely unacknowledged, impact on the movement itself. Aside from introducing the word *feminism* to the French public through an open letter to the prefect of the Seine, published in *Le Temps* in 1882, she elaborated a case for woman suffrage that remained essentially unchanged for years and developed protest tactics that made most subsequent feminists her imitators. Also, her testing of the administrative and judicial channels clarified woman's subordinate position and awakened the advocates of women's rights to the need for legislative action. Finally, her devotion to the cause provided a model of determination that even her severest critics could not deny. On 13 March 1914, she presided over a suffrage meeting in the eleventh *arrondissement*. Twenty-two days later, at the age of sixty-six, Hubertine Auclert died.

CONCLUSION

As much as any other, the word *paradox* fits the career of Hubertine Auclert. By juxtaposing the "strategy of assault" to the "strategy of the breach," the "young school" to the "old school," the pursuit of full women's rights to the quest for partial women's rights, Auclert imparted to liberal feminism an appearance of dissension that bore little relation to the outlook shared in common by her and all of the other founders of the movement.

None of the *brèchistes* objected to woman suffrage in principle, as a goal; at most, therefore, the angry exchanges between prosuffrage and antisuffrage feminists revolved around the question of timing. Tactically, given the atmosphere of political crisis in which the movement developed, this was a substantive question, but its substance had everything to do with the means requisite to creating a liberal society rather than any fundamental disagreement about liberalism itself. Hence, although Auclert appeared to be calling for a new departure in the struggle to emancipate women, she essentially reinforced the movement's two outstanding characteristics.

First, by demanding the immediate extension of liberal political rights to women, she not only directly accentuated the movement's liberal orientation but also, due to the reaction that she provoked within the movement, indirectly reaccentuated the *brèchistes'* commitment to accord the political question priority over the woman question. Second, by asserting that suffrage would enable women as a group publicly to display their special equivalent qualities and, simultaneously, by engaging publicly in what many considered to be "unfeminine" behavior, she not only directly intensified the movement's attachment to the mother-teacher ideal but also, due again to the reaction that she provoked within the movement, indirectly intensified the *brèchistes'* determination to keep power out of the hands of reactionary and, as in their view of Auclert, irresponsible women.

In short, just as the *brechistes* within the French feminist movement partook of Auclert's faith in the twin idols of country and republic, so too, despite appearances, did the *assautistes* partake of the movement's belief in the twin idols of liberalism and equivalence.

COUNTERATTACK: THE FRENCH LEAGUE FOR WOMEN'S RIGHTS AND THE CONGRESS OF 1889

CHAPTER

5

I believe that at the present time, it would be dangerous—in France—to give women the political ballot. They are, in great majority, reactionaries and clericals. If they voted today, the Republic would not last six months.

Léon Richer, 1888

Yes, I shall go to the end. I accept the fight. But by God! by unjustifiable blunders, by inexcusable impediments, we must not continually compromise the great cause of equality and justice that I have defended, in my modest sphere, for more than thirty years.

Léon Richer, 1890

Despite basic agreement between the *assautistes* and the *brèchistes* on the need for a liberal republican solution to the political question and for a liberal equal opportunity solution to the woman question, Auclert and her small band of suffragists nonetheless provoked consternation within the French feminist movement in the 1880s. Convinced that only disaster could result from the immediate enactment of woman suffrage, many of those whom Auclert dubbed the "old school" rallied around Léon Richer, who in 1882 founded the French League for Women's Rights

A version of the material presented in this chapter appeared earlier as "The Politics of French Feminism: Léon Richer and the Ligue française pour le droit des femmes, 1882-1891," *Historical Reflections/Réflexions historiques* 3, no. 1 (Summer 1976), 93-120. Reprinted by permission of *Historical Reflections/Réflexions historiques*.

(Ligue française pour le droit des femmes). Almost overnight the League became the largest of the feminist groups in France, and, although it suffered alarming membership losses in the last half of the decade, it succeeded in preserving within the movement the dominance of *la brèche* over *l'assaut*. In 1889, with Auclert in Algeria, Richer and Deraismes cohosted the second French Congress for Women's Rights, which once again forbade discussion of the vote issue. Yet, by the time Richer retired in 1891, followed three years later by Deraismes's death, liberal feminism had slipped well into the disarray that the founders bequeathed to their successors.

THE FRENCH LEAGUE FOR WOMEN'S RIGHTS

Richer had little desire to create a new group. He preferred the role of propagandist to that of organizer, and soon after the 1878 congress he resigned as president of Deraismes's Amelioration Society in order to devote full attention to his monthly, *Le Droit des femmes*. His program of civil reforms remained intact but largely unaccomplished. A law permitting divorce seemed close at hand, but only in education had significant breakthroughs occurred. Yet, as a convinced proponent of *la brèche*, Richer viewed the two developments as portents of better times. Cautious, patient determination during the 1870s had sown the seeds of reform, he thought, and barring major mishaps the new decade promised a rich harvest.

Auclert's aggressive campaign threatened Richer's easy optimism. In short order, she had denounced the 1878 Women's Rights Congress; appealed successfully to the 1879 Socialist Congress; caused waves of newspaper ink to flow in reaction to her registration drive, tax strike, and census boycott; and in 1881 created *La Citoyenne*. The next year, in October 1882, Auclert applauded a speech by Deraismes in favor of woman suffrage and approvingly noted how far the Amelioration Society's leader had come since the 1878 congress.[1] Richer responded quickly. Within weeks of Deraismes's speech, he announced the founding of the French League for Women's Rights. The names of its initial sixty-six members appeared in the December 1882 issue of *Le Droit des femmes*, and the League held its first general assembly the following month. For a moment the new organization and its rival had nearly identical titles, but soon into the new year Auclert relinquished the word *droit* to Richer by appropriately renaming her group the Women's Suffrage Society.

Shortly after the League's birth, Richer published *Le Code des femmes (The Women's Code)*, a handbook spelling out "the most urgent reforms" and "the easiest to realize *immediately*." Designed as a legislator's guide, *Le Code des femmes* demanded revision or elimination of sixty-five provisions in the Civil Code and Article 339 of the Penal Code, the statute stipulating the double criminal standard for adultery.[2] As in his 1873 *Le Divorce*, Richer supplemented his critique with model laws, hoping to find others like Alfred Naquet, the "father of divorce," who would press within parliament for women's civil rights. Consistent with *la brèche*, Richer excluded woman suffrage from his program. He also eschewed tactics of confrontation, so clearly identified with Auclert's campaign. Even legal confrontation might alienate potential allies, Richer felt, whereas he intended to respond "to the preoccupations of those—a large number I am sure—who do not much believe in the efficacy of petitions addressed to the chambers. We shall therefore proceed less by way of petition than by the introduction of laws. Will they [our detractors] say now that we are not practical people?"[3]

Richer initially imagined his League as the progenitor of a mass movement. He looked to the Education League founded by the Freemason Jean Macé in 1866 as a model. It "had done so much so well" to promote free, lay, obligatory education, Richer noted, and had additionally leaped to fifty-nine circles comprising seventeen thousand members in its first four years. Richer may also have hoped to replicate the feat of Léo Taxil, yet another Mason, who had federated yet another seventeen thousand men and women into an Anticlerical League in the early 1880s. Auclert's premature campaign might require only a small band of hardcore activists, Richer observed in November 1882, "but for a group that desires to be reformist, it is certain that a large number of adherents means success."[4] The League's most influential members had so far come from the "most advanced groups" in Parliament, he acknowledged the next month, but recruitment should not stop there. "For my part," he announced, "I am going to force myself—and I intend to succeed—to recruit members from among the diverse nuances of the republican majority; our legal projects will then have defenders on all benches." Reform should then come rather easily, he forecast, because, in contrast to Macé's objectives, the League's program would cost nothing:

We can do so much better because to achieve the program of the Education League the State had to spend millions; whereas to give us satisfaction neither the State, nor the departments, nor the communes will have to disburse a cent. . . . I do not say that this [the elimination of woman's civil disabilities] can be done in a day, but we shall succeed with perseverance—and time. Be patient, and success, I predict, will crown our efforts.[5]

The League's composition was overwhelmingly bourgeois. Richer designated 31 December 1882 as the cutoff date for founding members but granted a month's extension to accommodate latecomers.[6] In the end 142 enrolled as "founders," and an additional 52 joined by the end of 1883. Males comprised nearly half the total, 96 of 194, and included 21 politicians: 2 senators, 13 deputies, 3 Paris municipal councilors, 2 general councilors, and a mayor, Charles Riveau of Grenouille (Charente-Inférieure), who also served as the local cantonal delegate for school surveillance. Fifteen men, including several of the politicians, lived by the pen as journalists, authors, or general "men of letters." Education contributed three professors (mathematics, physics, and music), a secondary teacher, and two students, one in law and the other in pharmacy. Two lawyers, an architect, and a doctor represented the professions; two merchants, a broker, and a distiller, business. From the ranks of white collar workers the League drew a lithographer, a bookseller, a practicing accountant, a retired accountant, an inspector of weights and measures, and six clerks. From skilled labor came two tailors, a sculptor, a barber, and a mechanic. The only male member with a lower class occupation was Jules Poisson, a cab driver (*cocher*) at Nantes.

Of the ninety-eight women only fourteen worked for a wage. Eight, including a Swiss professor, were educators: two teachers, one adjunct teacher, a director of a girls' school, and three other professors (piano, singing, and German). Two considered themselves "women of letters," two more engaged in Danish painting (*peintre danoise*), and another performed as a lyric and dramatic artist. Only one professional woman joined, Doctor Guenot of Paris. At least three others simply managed their wealth, one as a *rentière* and two as *propriétaires*. None worked in commerce or industry, according to Richer's list. More than two-thirds had married, of whom at least four were widows. One of the latter, Madame Marie Moret, lived at the utopian Familistère de Guise and married its founder, J.-B.-A. Godin, in 1886. Three women and four men refused to permit Richer to publish their full names.

From outside France, the most important of the League's fifteen foreign members was Mademoiselle Mary Vincent of Vernox-Montreux in Switzerland. Vincent had followed the French feminist movement for over a dozen years, and Richer described her as "the true founder of the French League," possibly because she donated eleven hundred francs to the fledgling organization. From within France, the League drew members from twenty-five of the nation's eighty-eight departments. Outside the capital, Richer's greatest success was at Nantes, whose sixty-odd members represented nearly a third of the League's total. Led by a retired infantry captain, Pierre-Louis Goron, the Nantes group held its first meeting in February 1883. A month later a second meeting chose Deputy Charles Laisant as honorary president. As with the League as a whole, almost half of the Nantes group's members were men and two-thirds of the women had married. Richer hoped that other towns would follow Nantes's example, but in April 1883 he observed that "after Paris it is the only city in France where we count enough adherents to form a local group."[7] Nevertheless, considering the predominantly Parisian makeup of Deraismes's and Auclert's organizations, the League's branch at Nantes represented a significant achievement. For the first time in France a feminist association with headquarters in Paris had established a solid following in a provincial city.

The League's strength and focus nonetheless lay in its Parisian cadre, which reflected the moderate and influential clientele that Richer hoped to recruit. Fewer than half of the League's members came from the capital, but many of them held positions within "the diverse nuances of the republican majority" that Richer prized so highly. The League's eleven-member Executive Committee, elected by the first general assembly on 21 January 1883, was entirely Parisian. Its six women included Amélie Germance, the lyric and dramatic artist, and the wives of Georges Martin, a physics professor who served in the Senate from 1885 to 1891, and Lucien-Victor Meunier, a man of letters. In addition to Richer, its five males included two writers, Paul Bonnetain and Charles Gérard, and two deputies, Laisant and Guillot. The first general assembly also elected two honorary vice-presidents, Maria Deraismes and Auguste Vacquerie, editor-in-chief of *Le Rappel*. Victor Hugo served as honorary president. Richer drew on Hugo's acceptance conditions to emphasize the League's moderation. "You yourself promise me not to throw in exaggerations, to maintain your program intact?" the illustrious poet and senator asked, "then I accept. I have known you for a long time. Moreover it is you who directs [the League], is it not?" "Most certainly," responded Richer. "Then use my name," Hugo concluded with a cordial handshake.[8]

The size of the League fell far short of Richer's expectations. Its nearly two hundred recruits initially surpassed the combined memberships of Deraismes's Amelioration Society and Auclert's Women's Suffrage Society, but Richer had anticipated more. The Education League had grown spectacularly after its first year, whereas throughout the 1880s Richer's League never exceeded its original total. Alexandre Dumas *fils* eventually joined, as did Jean Macé, and its delegation in the Senate increased from two to five. But its representation in the Chamber decreased from thirteen to six, mirroring the overall decline in membership. A decade after its creation the League numbered only ninety-five individuals, fifty-five of whom resided in or around Paris. Of those who joined the first year only forty remained in 1892.[9]

Among potential recruits, subscribers to *Le Droit des femmes* proved the most disappointing to Richer. Senators, deputies, and municipal councilors had joined the League, Richer wrote in December 1882, "but it is especially to our subscribers that we address ourselves." If dues stand in the way, he said, "once again we repeat that this point is secondary":

Without doubt in such a venture money is not to be scorned; we need much of it—a great deal even—especially if we wish to act effectively on public opinion, to expand our propaganda, to organize conferences, meetings, to hold numerous gatherings in Paris as well as in the departments; but we need numbers above all.

Therefore let dues stop no one.

We have received contributions of 25 francs, 15 francs, 10 francs. But we have also received those of 50 centimes, 25 centimes—and even less.

Consequently one would be wrong to permit oneself to lag due to this detail.

The lag never closed. After 128 founding members had enrolled, a disappointed Richer averred that he was "the first to recognize that the largest number of male and female subscribers to our journal still have not responded to the appeal."[10]

The response of Richer's fellow Freemasons also proved disappointing. Both Macé's Education League and Taxil's Anticlerical League had elicited enthusiastic Masonic support. In its first two years, for example, Macé's organization had attracted fifteen entire lodges, a large number of individual Masons, and the endorsement of the 1868 International Masonic Congress. Individual Masons joined Richer as well, and in 1892 at least a third of Richer's truncated male following held Masonic rank. But, as Mildred Headings observed, whereas lay education and anticlericalism received overwhelming support from the various lodges, "the few societies concerned with women's rights, such as the League for the Protection of Women [of Allix and Barberousse] and [Richer's] The Right of Women, although encouraged by individual Masons, were not supported by Masonry as a whole."[11]

Without a steady influx of new recruits, the League began to shrink. Deaths, including Victor Hugo's in 1885, took a small toll. Two other names vanished from the roster when Richer stopped listing his pseudonyms, Georges Bath and Jeanne Mercoeur, as separate members. Others simply quit, some out of defeatism, a few out of optimism. In 1887, Richer assessed the situation in an address to the League's general assembly:

A certain number of adherents have retired giving the pretext of business stagnation, and for the determining motive, for the same reason, that we are attaining nothing. They no longer want to accept useless sacrifices. Others—and the fact needs to be stressed—write that the goal sought being obtained, there is no longer any reason to maintain the League.

Members must judge for themselves "these two contradictory allegations," Richer concluded, but "the truth is that the spirit wanes and that devotion grows weary."[12]

The decline also sprang from internal disorder. Expulsions and angry defections sapped the League's strength throughout the 1880s. One of the first to be ousted was Paul Bonnetain (1858–1899), a prominent man of letters who had helped edit *Le Droit des femmes* and served as the League's secretary. His "crime," committed within months of the League's creation, consisted of publishing a book on women that violated the League's sense of propriety. With him went his wife and parents, all of whom had enrolled as founding members. A second major expulsion came three years later when Deputy Maurice Vergoin (Seine-et-Oise), a member of the League's Executive Committee, turned up as one of the principals in the de Sombreuil affair. The messy business, which involved the shuttling of Mademoiselle Schneider de Sombreuil in and out of Paris and ended in Vergoin's divorce, threatened the League's public image. Richer eventually had misgivings about the deputy's "guilt," but when the scandal broke he executed the League's unanimous verdict to demand Vergoin's resignation.[13]

Most crippling of all was the defection of the Nantes group, which announced its withdrawal from the League in September 1885. Richer conceded that it had every right to become autonomous, but the group's hostility left him puzzled. "The rupture is today complete," he informed the 1886 general assembly, but the origins of the split "remain and will truly always remain an enigma for us." On at least five occasions, according to Richer's reports, Nantes had censured the parent organization. It first accused Richer of "financial operations" and failure to publish the League's accounts. Richer denied the charge and, referring "the defamatory group" to several specific issues of *Le Droit des femmes*, pointed out that the League had barely enough income to meet fixed expenses let alone engage in speculation. Then the Nantes group shifted its attack, accusing the League of spending too little. "That is the highest comedy," Richer countered, citing the League's meager 1,514-franc reserve. Indeed, pronounced an exasperated Richer, "the proof of the inanity of the reasons invoked to justify this strange attitude stems from the contradictory resolutions voted by the Nantes group." However, unable to prevent the defection, he could only urge his followers to look beyond it: "Let us not attach, mesdames and messieurs, to this incident, however regrettable it may be, more importance than it warrants."[14]

Perhaps the growing dependence of *Le Droit des femmes* on League subsidies angered the Nantes group. Like other feminist newspapers, Richer's constantly flirted with bankruptcy. Costs always outran subscription income, despite attempts to improve circulation through reduced rates for extra copies, free oil portraits painted from photographs, and complimentary issues of the *Journal du magnétisme*, monthly organ of the French Hypnosis Society. Richer repeatedly pleaded with subscribers to pay on time and urged recipients of free copies to subscribe, for at ten francs per year "the sacrifice is not of a nature to burden a budget very heavily." In February 1885 he attempted to boost revenues by shifting from monthly to fortnightly publication. To attract more purchasers he lowered the price from eight to forty centimes, and to cut costs he reduced the pages from sixteen to twelve. The maneuver failed, leaving *Le Droit des femmes* dependent on gifts and subsidies. The Deraismes sisters donated several hundred francs each year and others gave smaller amounts, but the crucial difference came from the League's coffers. Beginning with an initial gift of four hundred francs in 1885, its annual general assemblies regularly appropriated six hundred francs to the enterprise. That amount represented nearly 50 percent of the League's limited receipts. Richer claimed that the Nantes group contributed only fifty francs in dues to the yearly budget, for which it received the newspaper free of charge. Whatever the amount forwarded by the branch, though, the subsidy may have prompted the split.[15]

Richer tried to take the sting out of the Nantes group's defection by attributing it to natural law. All new organizations suffer losses, he asserted, as time winnows those lacking in enthusiasm and conviction. New recruits would take their place. In the past year, he informed the League's 1886 general assembly, Deputy Michelin had joined as well as President Abel-Alexandre Hovelacque of Paris's municipal council, General Secretary Tommy Fallot of the League for the Improvement of Public Morality (Ligue pour le relèvement de la moralité publique), and Doctor Henri Thulié, author of the "beautiful book entitled *La Femme* [*Woman*]." A new branch had also come into existence, the Gironde group, which centered on Bordeaux and called itself the Louis Blanc Circle. But the Gironde group had too few members to offset the net effect of deaths, expulsions, and defections.[16]

As a result, Richer gradually shifted from his original emphasis on size to a stance worthy of his rival Auclert. "Besides," he added in reference to Nante's defection. "these losses are for us so much less sensitive because indifferent [participants] in a League such as ours are a cause of weakness rather than a real source of strength." By the following year, 1887, he had completely discarded the stress on numbers:

Indifference has invaded hearts. And I maintain that it manifests itself everywhere, even in politics.

However, a faithful nucleus remains with us, and these I hope will not weaken, will not abandon us. I estimate our number at one hundred. That is few. But above the quantity of numbers, I place firmness of convictions. . . . The best are still with us. . . . Perseverance is strength; let us persevere.[17]

Richer blamed much of the League's decline on women. He contrasted his dwindling cadre to that of the expanding feminist groups in the United States and Britain. Even in France, he pointed out, Madame Koechlin-Schwartz's Union of French Women, the national Red Cross affiliate, had doubled its size to twelve thousand members in the course of a single year, 1887. In 1888 he claimed that men outnumbered women in his organization two to one. But that seems unlikely. Although no membership list appeared for that year, the 1892 roster named sixty-two women and thirty-three men—the reverse of Richer's assertion.

Perhaps he did not see them. As he lamented in 1877:

Women for the most part do not worry about these matters!. . . The Code abuses them; the Code dishonors them; the Code inflicts outrage upon outrage on them; the Code throws them back to the class of imbeciles and rogues; the Code throws into suspicion their loyalty, their integrity, their morals; the Code declares that it has no confidence in their testimony—and all of this does not move them!

"They remain indifferent in the face of this social inequity," he charged, and "I am convinced that most of them are ignorant of the degrading position in which the law holds them."[18] Or, although other feminists shared Richer's view, perhaps potential recruits saw in him too much patriarchal disdain for women.

In any case, once the League failed to spark a mass movement, its relative smallness had little effect on its daily operations. Without doubt, more women might have helped, just as more members of either sex might have boosted morale, increased income, and enhanced the prospects of success. A larger following would also have lent greater weight to petitions and street demonstrations, if Richer had employed such Auclert-like tactics. But the League publicly turned out in force on only one occasion, to grace Hugo's 1885 funeral cortege with "a magnificent wreath of natural flowers" costing 150 francs. Hence, although thousands of additional recruits might have transformed the League into a popular movement, a few dozen more could not have made much difference. Despite Richer's criticism, the League remained at the end of the decade what it had always been, a pressure group.

THE POLITICS OF *LA BRÈCHE*

As a pressure group, the League in its day-to-day activity relied almost exclusively on its male contingent, although women represented nearly

70 percent of the new recruits between 1882 and 1892. Richer complained in June 1891 that League women had refused to have their names published, but when an updated roster appeared the following year a footnote emphasized that "the preceeding list contains the names of":

Two members of the Institute: M. Alexandre Dumas, member of the Académie Française, and M. Frédéric Passy, member of the Académie des Inscriptions et Belles-Lettres;
Two former ministers: MM. Yves Guyot and de Hérédia;
Five senators: MM. Frédéric Petit, H. Couturier, Émile Deschanel, Jean Macé, and Victor Schoelcher;
Six deputies: MM. Barodet, Ch. Boudeville, Yves Guyot, Hovelacque, Laisant, and Victor Poupin.

"One sees by this simple enumeration," the note concluded, "that the men and women who come to us are in good company."[19] The good company that Richer accented, however, was entirely male.

Richer's reliance on the League's male contingent stemmed in large part from tactical and political considerations. Although he demanded reforms, such as abolishing restrictions on incest and legalizing "free love" marriages, that placed him in advance of many of his feminist colleagues, he in effect accepted the constraints that limited women's opportunities for effective action. They could—and should—lend financial and propaganda assistance to the League, but as long as men dominated French institutions necessity dictated a subordinate role to women. Furthermore, while convinced that no program of reform could succeed without male support, he also believed that no amount of male support could ever improve women's lot if the republic were to succumb to monarchical or clerical reaction.

Richer thus found himself in an unenviable and somewhat contradictory position. Women's emancipation depended on rights that men alone could grant, but in order to grant them men had first of all to see to the safety of the republic. Among national legislators, however, less than 3 percent endorsed women's rights in the 1880s, whereas some legislators and many men outside the Parliament opposed the Third Republic. Precisely how many stood in opposition is beside the point because, in a psychopolitical sense, Richer perceived the republic as always on the brink of disaster. It followed therefore that, as Richer constantly urged, feminist republicans had above all to band together with anitfeminist republicans to protect the institutions of reform. The predictable result also followed: the institutions of reform remained in the hands of men who consistently opposed women's emancipation.

Yet Richer could see no viable alternative to this strategy. Reforms would come either slowly or not at all. The campaign to reestablish divorce took years, he noted, and resulted in a "very bad" law when the Senate forbade suits based on mutual consent. But the 1884 bill also represented a "brilliant victory" inasmuch as it struck at the ultraclerical tradition of the Restoration. "In all things," Richer adjured the partisans of *l'assaut* in 1885, "order and method are necessary":

All progress is measured, linked, coordinated. Never would it occur to an architect to begin construction of a house with the roof; he would commence with the foundation. This is elementary. . . . How often have I cried out to the impatient: "for pity's sake! in your own interest do not put the cart before the horse."[20]

Hence, whenever conflicts arose between the political question and the woman question, Richer implored feminists to give priority to the former.

This priority also reflected Richer's personal "connections." Other feminists emphasized the political question, particularly Deraismes, and most, like Auclert, had at least one or two "friends" in the legislature. But, as a man possessed of full civil rights with untrammeled access to party rallies and the Chamber's "males-only" press gallery, Richer had much closer ties to the political establishment than did women feminists. While partisans of *l'assaut* waged their shadow campaign in 1885, for example, Richer sat on an extraparliamentary committee that drew up a legislative proposal to grant full civil rights to unmarried women. Richer had hoped to extend the same rights to wives, but others on the committee feared that too broad a bill would invite defeat. Even the restricted version failed, but Richer exulted that the committee had at last moved "the question of women's rights from the domain of pure theory into the domain of parliamentary discussions and public discussions."[21]

Indicative of how "connections" influenced Richer's strategy was the banquet sponsored by the League for its parliamentary delegation on 6 December 1885. Held at the Grand Hotel, the guests of honor included Senators Victor Schoelcher and Alfred Naquet and Deputies Ernest Lefèvre and Yves Guyot, all of whom had worked on the committee with

Richer. At twelve francs per head the cost of the celebration came to nearly two hundred francs, about one-sixth of the year's expenditures. Perhaps in response to criticism of the expense, Richer informed the next general assembly:

If in organizing the banquet we have burdened the League with an exceptional and relatively heavy expense given the meagerness of our resources, you will recognize that it was a productive expense. Let me repeat, mesdames and messieurs, were we to obtain only this result [parliamentary discussion of the civil rights proposal] we would lose neither our money nor our labor.[22]

Experiences like his 1885 committee assignment provided Richer with an insider's perspective and a sense of progress shared by few outside the League. Not until 1904 did a woman, Zhenia Avril de Saint-Croix, sit on an extraparliamentary committee. Richer recognized that much remained unaccomplished, but rather than disparage the past he viewed it with measured satisfaction. Before the same general assembly that listened to his banquet explanation, for instance, he recalled some of the reforms that had won approval since the founding of *Le Droit des femmes* seventeen years earlier: "the admission of women to the *baccalauréats*, their admission to *lycées* and *collèges féminins* as well as *écoles d'enseignement supérieur*, the reestablishment of divorce, and so on."[23] He also predicted passage of the committee's civil rights bill.

When things went wrong, Richer sometimes blamed structural defects in the political system itself. In 1883, for example, he made constitutional revision "the first article of our program," throwing the League into the struggle to suppress or at least to modify the conservative Senate. "It is beyond doubt," he wrote at the time, "that revision of the constitution alone can lead to the emancipation of women." When the amendment campaign failed, though, Richer emphasized the positive by shifting to other developments. The League had partly offset its losses by entering into an informal alliance with Tommy Fallot's League for the Improvement of Public Morality, he proudly informed the members in 1886, and League stalwart Camille de Chancel had opened the Credit Foncier's bureau of central administration to women employees.[24]

The assumptions that dictated the League's moderate reformism also provided the grounds for Richer's opposition to radical feminism. Partisans of *l'assaut* stood for an "absolutely irrefutable" position in theory, he repeated again and again, but in practice they "gravely compromise the cause that they claim to defend." "No one is more in favor of woman's right to vote than I," Richer exclaimed at the time of the 1885 shadow campaign. "Since the year 1869, well before Mlle. Barberousse, Mme. Picot and Mme. Jeannot dreamed of it, when Mlle. Hubertine Auclert was still in a convent, I proclaimed this right":

Yes, woman should possess the vote. She is human; she has her own interests; she is in business, industry and [subject to] licensing; she participates in the maintenance of the State; she pays, like us, direct and indirect taxes, that is to say the personal assessment, the real estate levy, the tax on bread, meat and drinks; she is judged in our courts; she pays her blood—the blood of her son (is not this blood hers?)—on battlefields; she shares our miseries, as she would share our triumphs and joys. All that we touch touches her. Her exclusion from common rights is not only a denial of justice, an act of individual oppression, it is a social crime.

The fault of *l'assaut* lay not in its goal but in its means, Richer stressed: "One point alone divides us: how to proceed."[25]

Only *la brèche* could bring success. Court decisions had made it perfectly clear that "no one could vote if he [or she] did not enjoy the plenitude of his [or her] civil rights," Richer wrote in the spring of 1885:

Woman is grouped with minors, convicts, habitual criminals and individuals struck by infamous condemnation. So long as this injurious analogy exists, woman cannot be inscribed on electoral lists.

What, from this, should be the path to follow? Good sense indicates it: first relieve woman of her legal incapacities.

Once in possession of all her civil rights, woman becomes the equal of man; the principal argument—the only one, I would dare say, that one can invoke to contest her electoral right—will disappear.

Conversely, he argued, if civil emancipation were not first obtained and "if in the state of [our current] legislation, we recognized women's right to suffrage, it would be necessary to recognize it equally for criminals."[26]

Other political realities also compelled prudence. Few within the republican majority acknowledged woman's capacity to deal with questions of government, foreign policy, and taxes. "This is inept," Richer admitted, but undeniable. Yet many of these same men expressed concern for woman's civil status, and, even though their concern lay in "the old prejudice'' that "woman is a being apart, having to fulfill special functions in the family, having distinct duties,'' their support or opposition would determine the fate of all reform efforts. "Unfortunately,'' Richer charged, "there are impatient among us, who, by their intemperate demands, detach from our cause a goodly number of those who had asked no more than to sustain it.'' Especially in the Chamber, where everything hinged on patience according to Richer, Auclert's extreme demands had hurt the cause by inviting defeat without debate.[27]

Graver still was the apparent indifference of the *assautistes* to the republic's well-being. Haunted by the specter of counterrevolution, Richer never tired of repeating that premature woman suffrage would destroy French democracy. "I believe that at the present time,'' he warned in 1888, "it would be dangerous—in France—to give to women the political ballot. They are, in great majority, reactionaries and clericals. If they voted today, the Republic would not last six months.''[28] The republican parties should encourage mixed attendance at their meetings, and business women should have the nonpolitical *commerçante* vote, Richer thought, but woman suffrage should await the advance of republican education. "The antechamber of the polling booth,'' echoed honorary League vice-president Auguste Vacquerie, "is not the church, it is the school.''[29] "Let us not repeat the sad experience of 1848,'' Richer added:

I am not of those (no one will doubt it) who regret the brusque enactment of universal [manhood] suffrage. I saluted with enthusiasm the decree initiated by Ledru-Rollin, affirming to the great astonishment of Europe, the principle too long misunderstood, of national sovereignty. To that decree I owe my political freedom. But I cannot forget that that reform, so equitable, so necessary, brought us the Second Empire. The ignorance of the peasants caused all the evil. Suddenly called upon to vote, without prior preparation, they raised to power the man who, three years later, executed the [coup of] 2 December [1851].[30]

Women had in particular to guard against self-seeking politicians, Richer warned. General Boulanger, who came close to toppling the republic in 1889, was a case in point. He "turns to women, not in order to say to them that he will work for their emancipation, but to adjure them, like Gambetta, to preoccupy themselves with the grand interest of the country.'' According to his *L'Invasion allemande* (The German Invasion) of 1881, Richer reported, Boulanger assigned women only one mission in life:"Give us a vigorous generation, solidly tempered morally and physically, and you will have worthily accomplished your task." "As for your personal interests, as for the restoration of your dignity, as for your rights," Richer exclaimed, "General Boulanger troubles himself no more than Gambetta did previously. Not even a discreet allusion. Not a word of hope for the future!" Perhaps Boulanger had since changed his mind, Richer granted out of ignorance, but whatever politicians might think of women's rights, "it does not prevent them, when they believe that the support of women can be useful to their ambitious aims, from appealing to them in warm and solemn terms."[31] Sincere democrats had thus to maintain constant vigilance: whether enfranchised legally or amassed emotionally, the vast majority of women could not be trusted to defend the republic against would-be despots.

The same was almost as true for men, Richer thought. Many men still opposed the republic, despite better education and previous voting experience. By Richer's count, for instance, 37 percent of the deputies elected in 1889 represented reaction, whereas half the rest, all of whom called themselves republicans, objected to further democratic reforms. For women the situation was worse. Of the 9 million who might have voted in 1877, according to Richer's estimate, only a few thousand had escaped from the confessional.[32] This was sex-role transference, the assigning to women of perspectives drawn from the beliefs and experiences of men. But rather than a transfer of *principle*, as Auclert demanded in urging an extension of men's rights to women, Richer applied the *practice* of men to the position of women.

Paradoxically, the logic implicit in Richer's pragmatic transference clashed even with his faith in *la brèche*. On the one side, he maintained that political equality between the sexes would follow without further struggle and as a matter of course once women obtained civil equality. On the other side, he maintained that women remained too reactionary to entrust with the vote. Hence, because he always accorded priority to preventing the latter, he in effect pinned the survival of the republic on prolonging the minor status of women. The way out of course was to create a new type of woman, one who would guarantee a democratic future through unwavering devotion to republican ideals. While waiting for the new type to multiply, however, he had not only to resist the political adventurism of the *assautistes* but also to guard against an overly hasty emancipation of women from the civil constraints of *masculinisme*. Only after women had undergone a complete transformation could they assume full republican citizenship. In short, women's emancipation depended on political rectitude, which meant in the interim that all right-thinking women had above all to lead exemplary republican lives.

Much in Auclert's behavior struck Richer as especially unexemplary. When she petitioned the Chamber to exclude women from the population-based apportionment process, for example, Richer detected a disdain for popular sovereignty, the essential base of any democratic polity. "Those who do not vote," Richer wrote, "even when they are unjustly excluded from balloting—soldiers on active duty for example—have interests that should be defended." Auclert and her *assautiste* colleagues had undoubtedly overlooked that point, he added, "but willfully or not, they nonetheless do much evil." Another of her petitions called for woman suffrage, which always engendered a negative "situational" reaction from Richer, but this one provoked extra ire because she had submitted it to the Congress of Versailles. Composed of Senate and Chamber sitting together as the National Assembly, the Congress of Versailles had the statutory right to alter the constitution—precisely the goal Auclert had in mind. But in Richer's eyes the Congress had no right to speak in the name of the people due to the unrepresentative character of the Senate. Sincere democratic women had therefore to avoid any act that might legitimize that institution. Political rights for women would invariably strengthen the clerical camp, Richer pointed out again, but "I especially regret that in claiming woman's right to vote before the Congress of Versailles, [Auclert] has committed a grave fault that will remain in everyone's memory as an argument against women's political capacity."[33]

Auclert also displayed a lack of rectitude in her actions and in her choice of associates. The 1885 shadow campaign constituted a perfect example of the former. Republican candidates will suffer, Richer warned two weeks before the balloting, because, as the reactionary *Le Figaro*'s endorsement of the campaign proves, "you will favor, by this ill-considered, useless, culpable displacement [of votes cast for women], the success of our enemies and yours." Auclert's indiscretion in choosing associates appeared on the petition to eliminate women from the apportionment count. Its fifteen signers included royalist Deputy Pieyre, and its Chamber sponsors numbered the reactionary and antinationalist Count de Roys and M. Ribot, "the friend of the princes of Orleans." Auclert's ultimate objective had merit, Richer repeated, "but when blunders succeed blunders, I cannot remain silent." "I understand when women unjustly deprived of the right to vote defend their cause, but not in this manner or by similar arguments," he pleaded: "If they wish to return to a restricted electorate, then let them say so; if, for republican principle, they wish to substitute the doctrines of the Second Empire, let them avow it. At least we shall know in whose company we are."[34]

In equating the *politique de l'assaut* with treachery, Richer provoked protests from friend and foe alike within the feminist movement. In April 1885, Joanny Rama, a founding member of the French League for Women's Rights, employed Auclert's *La Citoyenne* to brand Richer a "legalist" and a "fake republican." Rama questioned the genuineness of Richer's oft-repeated espousal of woman suffrage and accused him of sacrificing justice to a narrow interpretation of the statutes. Richer countered by charging Rama, Auclert, and others with following a "compromising course" whose "detestable effects" would soon be felt. As for the label "legalist," Richer snapped, "that signifies, in the thinking of M. Rama, that I put the law *above right*—which is inexact." "When a law exists, however bad it may be, even if unjust, I submit to it," Richer argued. "But in submitting, I do all that I can to reform it. Does not M. Rama himself obey existing laws? Willingly or by force, does he not submit?" As for being a "fake republican," Richer concluded, hardly anyone could avoid that label as long as true republicanism meant "the line of conduct traced by Mlle. Auclert and Mlle. Barberousse." In respect to what counts most, though, at least "I do not make alliances with royalist deputies."[35]

Perhaps the most frustrating proposal encountered by Richer was the "fantastic," "eccentric," and "bizarre" scheme advanced by Auclert's friend and financial backer, Deputy de Gasté. In reaction to the deputy's proposal for amending the constitution to guarantee women not only the vote but half the seats in the legislature, Richer commented: "I would not like to be unpleasant to M. de Gasté, but I ask myself if he has been truly sincere, or if he has wanted to play a dirty trick on women and to mock them." Why propose a constitutional amendment when a simple law would suffice? Moreover, what principle of democracy would sanction parliamentary sex quotas? "After having taken sides between the sexes, it would be necessary to take sides between the classes, so many [deputies] for the bourgeoisie, so many for the proletariat, so many for the liberal careers, so many for manual workers." The amendment also threatened passage of the *commerçante* vote, which had finally moved from the Chamber into the Senate. "Had M. de Gasté wished to defeat our law," Richer charged, "he could not have conducted himself otherwise." When a League member defended de Gasté on the grounds that he might obtain a little by demanding a lot, Richer threw up his hands in disgust: "Yes, I shall go to the end. I accept the fight. But by God! by unjustifiable blunders, by inexcusable impediments, one must not continually compromise the great cause of equality and justice that I have defended, in my modest sphere, for more than thirty years."[36]

Richer's pained outcry stemmed from a heightened sense of betrayal. Practical reforms moderately pursued constituted the essence of *la brèche*. Most women failed to see this, Richer felt, a majority out of indifference born of confinement in narrow family circles, a minority out of reckless disregard for political realities. During the bitter recriminations of the 1885 shadow campaign, Richer ruefully recalled the words of warning that he had heard from the lips of a "great [unnamed] publicist" at the time of the founding of *Le Droit des femmes* in 1869: "You are undertaking a very heavy task. It is not from the side of men that the greatest difficulties will come to you, it is from the side of women." "The prediction is fulfilled," Richer added as the campaign unfolded. Henceforth, as always, women's emancipation would depend on right-thinking, republican men, who realized the need "to proceed by successive reforms."[37] Outwardly, at least, de Gasté represented precisely that type of person—a male, a republican, a legislator, and a feminist. His advocacy of *l'assaut* therefore amounted to a kind of ultimate betrayal. At a moment when *la brèche* seemed on the verge of delivering a long-sought reform, his proposal could only arouse unnecessary opposition. Furthermore, the year was 1890, and, whatever the effect of de Gasté's behavior on the parliamentary front, his scheme jarringly contradicted the intent of the Women's Rights Congress organized by Richer and Deraismes the year before.

THE WOMEN'S RIGHTS CONGRESS OF 1889

The idea for a second women's rights congress originated indirectly with Monsieur R. Davenne, president of the League's Louis Blanc Circle at Bordeaux. Shortly after the 1885 shadow campaign, Davenne wrote a series of articles for *Le Droit des femmes* on how the League might expand its influence in the provinces. Richer's activities in the capital received almost no local press coverage, Davenne observed, and in any case Frenchmen tended to read little and remember less. A greater effort to provide outlying areas with speakers, tracts, and newspaper releases would help some, but regional congresses offered the best prospect for success. They would attract reasonable people who had no desire to join the League itself and guarantee publicity, inasmuch as local journals could hardly ignore an event lasting several days. In addition to his native Bordeaux, Davenne recommended seven key cities as sites for such congresses: Lyon, Marseilles, Toulouse, Bourges, Rennes, Lille, and Nancy. The campaign to reestablish divorce had successfully brought an issue and the masses together, Davenne recalled; regional congresses would do the same for women's rights.[38]

Richer endorsed Davenne's proposal and, characteristically, urged the League's parliamentary deputies to implement it. Before they could act, however, attention shifted back to the capital. In the fall of 1886, the government appointed a commission to organize the centennial celebration of the 1789 Revolution. Auclert immediately protested the commission's all-male composition and demanded the inclusion of seven women members.[39] The commission rejected the demand but eventually made a concession to the growing interest in woman's condition by sanctioning an official congress on "feminine works and institutions."

Two League members spearheaded the move for the official congress, Deputy Yves Guyot, who served on the centennial commission, and Madame Emilie de Morsier.[40] De Morsier (1844–1896), a Calvinist apostate to free thinking and Buddhism, became the general secretary of the resultant International Congress of Feminine Works and Institutions (Congrès international des oeuvres et institutions féminines). Her interests made her a logical choice for the post. She represented a point of view and a constituency that stood at a small distance from the partisans of *l'assaut* and the advocates of *la brèche*. With close ties to France's Protestant community, de Morsier stressed the need for moral reform and philanthropic alleviation of misery. Although she belonged to the League and supported the campaign for women's rights, she focused her efforts on the Oeuvre des libérées de Saint-Lazare and the crusade to abolish governmental regulation of prostitution, a cause she had championed since joining Josephine Butler's abolitionist campaign in 1875.[41] Isabelle

Bogelot, the director of the Oeuvre des libérées de Saint-Lazare and a self-proclaimed "philanthropic feminist," assumed a vice-presidency in the official congress.

When the congress convened at the town hall of Paris's sixth *arrondissement* in July 1889, it strictly forbade any discussion of "sect and dogma, militant politics, and class struggle." In his opening remarks, honorary president Jules Simon ruled the issue of woman suffrage out of order: "Very simply, having other things to do, we shall do other things. I hope that this is well understood."[42] Pledging to confine itself to the unique character of the French, the official congress worked through four sections: philanthropy and morality; arts, sciences, and letters; education; and civil legislation. Charitable activities and moral concerns dominated the proceedings, and in the course of the six-day event over 120 individuals delivered addresses on issues ranging from "Teaching through Music" to "The Vegetarian Diet and Growing Up." More than 550 individuals attended the congress, nearly 400 of whom lived in France. Within the French contingent, women outnumbered men by three to one, a ratio that reflected the traditional involvement of middle- and upper-class women in social missionary work.

Richer applauded the government's decision to sponsor the International Congress of Feminine Works and Institutions, but he refused to abandon plans for a congress of his own. This was due in small part to the orientation of the official congress, whose designation as "feminine" belied the emphasis on women's charitable and philanthropic endeavors. The larger part of his determination stemmed from a threefold set of interrelated objectives. First of all, and consistent with the purpose that had informed the League from the beginning, Richer wanted a congress of his own to ensure the preeminence of *la brèche* within the French feminist movement. Prospects in this area seemed especially promising in 1889 due to Auclert's marriage and departure for Algeria the year before. The second and third objectives were organizational. Through a congress under his personal control, Richer hoped both to place the League in the forefront of the domestic movement and to raise the French movement to a position of leadership on the international scene.

Only Deraismes remained as an obstacle. She and Richer had drifted apart during the 1880s as the dispute over strategy increasingly polarized the movement. She also distrusted the official congress and, by implication, the League's involvement in it. Her laissez-faire liberalism could not abide Alphonse Daudet, a proponent of protective legislation for working women and the centennial commission's initial choice to head the congress. Her anticlericalism could not abide Jules Simon, the commission's final choice. In the fall of 1888, therefore, she announced plans to host a congress of her own.[43]

The prospect of separate women's rights congresses competing with each other and with the official congress alarmed French feminists, who had neither the numbers nor the money to support three such events in the same year. French feminists also feared the effect of open disunity on foreign feminists, who made very little distinction between the movement's factions. In soliciting adherents to the 1888 American women's congress, for example, Susan B. Anthony sent invitations to Richer as well as Auclert, and the self-proclaimed "philanthropic feminist" who represented France in Washington, D.C., Isabelle Bogelot, belonged to both Richer's League and Deraismes's Amelioration Society. The 1888 American congress had also created the International Council of Women to encourage and coordinate national women's coalitions in all countries. French women failed to construct such a coalition until 1901, but on the eve of the centennial celebration these foreign developments interacted with the movement's meager resources to put considerable pressure on Richer and Deraismes for some kind of reconciliation.

Negotiations between the Amelioration Society and the League took place throughout November and December 1888. Mutual agreement on *la brèche* quickly eliminated wrangling over strategy, leaving a procedural issue as the main stumbling block. Consistent with the membership policy of the League, Richer wanted a congress open to all and free of charge for those who could not pay. Deraismes objected, conceding that anyone might attend but only the paying should vote. Unable to resolve the issue through informal talks, Richer and Deraismes agreed to hold a unity conference.

The conference met at Deraismes's home on 23 January 1889. Each group was entitled to fifteen delegates, but the League mustered only eight. With entente at stake, Richer's "minority bowed before the votes of the majority." Deraismes emerged as the congress's president and Amelioration Society members secured four of the six subordinate posts. Richer assumed an honorary presidency. Deraismes also prevailed on the procedural issue. "Contrary to our views," Richer reported soon afterward, "there have been established several categories of members for the

Congress." Each participating organization could send three voting delegates, and any individual could attend as a "sympathetic member." But only honorary members and ten-franc donors could vote. The ten-franc rule permitted two exceptions; foreigners living outside France and, as a concession to Richer, individuals enrolling prior to publication of the agreement. "All this is very complicated," Richer admitted, "but again the majority having thus decided, we are forced to accede."[44]

Upon learning of the agreement, League members passed along their "observations." Indeed, Richer wrote, "I would almost say recriminations." One member complained that "it is not democratic," and another added "and this, in 1889!" Richer agreed in principle with the complaints but maintained that "what is voted is voted." Deraismes and her friends might be protesting now if our full delegation had attended the unity conference, Richer pointed out. Should we have broken the alliance because we lost? Should we have tried to hold our own congress?

> We did not think so.
> To cause division at this moment, at this date, before foreign [opinion], would appear culpable.
> We have yielded.
> Patriotism, as well as the interest we share in the great cause about to be fought, would make it our duty [to submit].
> Union! Union! Union!!![45]

The second French International Congress for Women's Rights (Congrès français et international du droit des femmes) opened at the end of June 1889 in the Geography Hall—three weeks prior to the official congress. Richer's appeal for union apparently worked because the League enrolled the larger number of delegates. Both sponsoring groups solicited participants independently, with the names appearing in separate columns of *Le Droit des femmes*. The Amelioration Society signed up 66 individuals and 5 groups; the League, 110 and 8 respectively. A few like Clémence Royer, who joined Richer as an honorary president, figured on neither list. Only eight attended as official "sympathetic members," although dozens paid less than ten francs. The combined total of the various categories of individuals and groups came to almost two hundred—about one-third the size of the official congress and a 14 percent decline from the 1878 congress. Most of the latter decrease resulted from a dropoff in foreign participation; the French total actually increased by at least six and perhaps a dozen in 1889.[46]

The most striking difference in participants between the two feminist congresses appeared in the sex ratio. Women barely outnumbered men in 1878, and comprised only 45 percent of the French delegation. In 1889 they represented 70 percent overall, and Frenchwomen outnumbered their male colleagues by approximately 130 to 50. Comparatively, Frenchwomen nearly doubled their representation between 1878 and 1889, whereas males declined by half. A much higher percentage of women had also remained faithful to the movement, with women accounting for nineteen of the twenty-five holdovers from 1878. This increase in women's representation at the 1889 congress began to bring the French feminist movement into line with the sex ratio of the Anglo-Saxon and Scandinavian movements, a trend which marked Richer as the last of the major male feminists within the French movement. With his retirement after the 1889 congress, women consolidated their control over the movement's top positions by capturing the League's presidency as well. Ferdinand Buisson eventually emerged as a man of comparable stature, but the League of Male Voters for Women's Suffrage that he helped found in 1911 consisted entirely of men.[47]

Otherwise, the ten-franc rule guaranteed that the second Congress for Women's Rights would be at least as bourgeois in social composition as the first. Neither of the two workers' groups that attended in 1878 participated in 1889, and only eight women possessed obvious job credentials. All were professionals: six doctors, including Elizabeth Blackwell, the first nineteeth-century woman to receive a medical degree, and Blanche Edwards, who had pressured the director of public assistance to open internships to Frenchwomen in 1885; one practicing teacher, Madame Ferrand of La Rochelle; and one nonpracticing lawyer, Marie Popelin, whose life-long exclusion from the Belgian bar made her a feminist *cause célèbre*. Nearly half the male participants came from politics and the professions, as in 1878.

The ten-franc rule and the entente with the Amelioration Society also ensured solvency. Deraismes's contingent, representing 35 percent of the participants, contributed 57 percent of the proceeds. None of her enrollees paid less than the minimum; a third paid more. As a group, the Amelioration Society donated an additional 500 francs, a sum matched by the Municipal Council of Paris. In contrast, nearly half the participants on Richer's list slipped below the 10-franc standard, and only a sixth exceeded it. Receipts eventually totaled 4,794, 50 percent more than in 1878. When costs fell short of that amount, the congress ended with a 500-franc surplus, two-thirds of which went to the Amelioration Society for providing the seed money. Hence, without the society's participation, although the ten-franc rule angered Richer's followers, the League would have been hard pressed to finance the event by itself.

There was never any doubt about the strategic orientation of the congress. Auclert's marriage had removed the foremost partisan of *l'assaut* from Paris. Barberousse and Allix, the leaders of the 1885 shadow campaign, donated ten francs to the congress through their Women's Protection League, but Richer pointed out in November 1888 that they had played no role in planning the event.[48] To forestall any last minute disruptions, the congress decided to exclude the public from its sessions. The cosponsors of the congress had a slight overall majority, with half the League's members and about one-third of the Society's participating. Among the groups in attendance, Deraismes had close ties to the Seine-et-Oise Federation of Free-Thinking Groups, whereas Richer had close ties to the Paris and Marseilles branches of Fallot's French League for the Improvement of Public Morality. Both probably had ties to the Masonic Lodge Jerusalem écossaise. Women's groups included the Nantes Women's Rights Society (Société nantaise: les droits des femmes), socialist Astié de Valsayre's Group of Independent French Women (Groupe des femmes indépendantes de France), and the Future of Women Society (Société l'avenir des femmes) of Nîmes. Richer had helped create the Nîmes group and held honorary membership in it, but its local founder, widow Fabre, derived her initial inspiration from reading Auclert's 1888 letter to Susan B. Anthony. Moderate feminists of all persuasions might have received additional support from activists in the peace movement had not the peace congress chosen the same June dates for its convention.[49]

The format of the 1889 congress resembled that of its predecessor with one exception—advances in education since 1878 led the organizers to drop a special section on that subject. The four remaining sections, which met on consecutive days from 26 June to 29 June 1889, dealt with history, economics, morality, and legislation. Clémence Royer chaired the history section, Popelin the legislation section, and Deraismes the other two sections. Altogether the delegates listened to about fifty addresses, some of which exceeded the twenty-minute time limit. Due to the fact that significant reforms had occurred during the previous decade in only two areas, education and divorce, the concerns expressed at the 1889 congress largely reiterated those of the earlier event.

In contrast to the similarity in format, the positions taken at the second congress differed markedly from those taken at the first. Consistent with the purpose of Richer's *Le Code des femmes* (1883) and the orientation of his League, the 1889 congress strove to limit resolutions to immediately realizable reforms. Rather than duplicate the dozens of sweeping demands made in 1878, the centennial congress passed only nine resolutions. These called for:

1. a wife's right to control her own income and woman's right to defend her financial interests through participation on regulatory boards;

2. equal pay for women teachers;

3. access of women to all liberal careers and to the practice of law;

4. admission of women to bureaus of public assistance as employees, investigators, and visitors;

5. establishment of work shelters for women and the transfer of apprenticeship programs from workshops to schools;

6. suppression of the morals police;

7. demolition of the prison of Saint-Lazare and the erection of women's refuges in all *arrondissements*;

8. revision of the Napoleonic Code to conform to the principle of justice and absolute equality; and

9. abrogation of Code Article 340 forbidding women to file paternity suits.

The congress concluded its work by attempting to formulate a response to the international woman's rights movement. Under pressure to cooperate with foreign activists but wary of slipping into an even more subordinate position, Richer announced the creation of a new ten-nation International Federation for the Demand of Woman's Rights (Fédération internationale pour la revendication des droits de la femme). Paris would serve as the Federation's headquarters, with *Le Droit des femmes* as its official organ. The League would represent France, but other feminist groups could participate by cooperating with the League. As president of the Federation, Richer acknowledged a similarity between his coalition and the recently formed International Council of Women (1888), but he did not expect the new organization to succumb to its tacit rival. Inasmuch as the goal was to succeed, he pointed out, the more combatants the better.[50]

CONCLUSION

As the last grand act in a career devoted to moderate feminism, Richer viewed the second Congress for Women's Rights as a moment of personal triumph. Aside from the procedural setback, he achieved nearly all that he had desired. The *assautistes* had little opportunity to raise the suffrage issue, and when Jules Allix attempted to do so Deraismes censured him and struck part of his statement from the official record for expressing "an injurious qualification against the Chamber."[51] The congress then proceeded to pass resolutions whose limited number and specific scope reflected the cautious program that had become Richer's hallmark. Finally, in laying the basis for the International Federation, Richer emerged from the congress with a vehicle through which he expected to rejuvenate the fortunes of the League, maintain the dominance of *la brèche* within the French movement, and assert that movement's claim for greater international recognition.

But Richer's triumph proved illusory. Although the Chamber sustained Richer's belief in limited reform for about a week by debating and finally passing the *commerçante* vote, the Senate blocked the measure for another five years. None of the congress's other resolutions fared even that well. The Federation also floundered. Hardly anything could be done about it during the summer, although in April 1890 Richer added a new subtitle to *Le Droit des femmes*: "International Review of the Feminine Movement: Official Organ of the International Federation" ("Revue internationale du mouvement féminin: organe officiel de la fédération internationale). But more words on the masthead could not reverse the attrition that had already halved the League's strength, and, like Auclert's similar effort six years before, Richer's Federation expired in silence.

Illusion also characterized the momentary dominance of *la brèche* over *l'assaut*. No sooner had the congress ended than Léon Giraud, a cofounder of Auclert's *La Citoyenne*, accused Richer of deleting a woman suffrage motion from *Le Droit des femmes's* coverage of the congress. Giraud claimed to have personally inserted a demand for "the civil and political emancipation of woman" into a text of the resolution on wives' financial rights. Richer had also confused civil and penal rights, Giraud charged, thereby acquiescing in relegating women to the status of convicted criminals.

Richer denied the accusations and mocked Giraud for writing under the feminine pseudonym "Camille." If taken literally, Richer wrote, Giraud's motion would imply that only working women should vote, "that is, if salaries were sufficient and work days not so excessively [long] or if all women lived off their *rentes*, there would be no reason to claim political emancipation for them." Furthermore, whatever the motion meant, it had come up when hardly anyone remained in the hall and even *La Citoyenne* had neglected to note it at the time. Then, shifting to the attack, Richer charged Giraud with criminal culpability for supporting the Napoleonic Code in opposition to equal rights for illegitimate children. He challenged Giraud to a formal debate on the issue, which never took place, and, after a double set of press forays, the dispute got lost in another controversy, the 1889 shadow campaign.[52]

The 1889 shadow campaign barely materialized. None of the 1885 activists participated, and no woman presented herself as a candidate. Its sponsoring organization was the Women's Socialist League (Ligue socialiste des femmes), created in the fall of 1889 to bridge the gap between bourgeois indifference to the working class and socialist indifference to women. Hardly had the Women's Socialist League come into existence, however, than it dissolved amid innumerable quarrels. Indeed, the entire demonstration could easily have escaped Richer's attention had not one of the Socialist League's founders also been one of *Le Droit des femmes*'s principal editors, Eugénie Potonié-Pierre. She had rejected a candidacy in 1885 because too many women had run. On the occasion of the revolutionary centennial, however, she felt the need to make at least a minimal protest against woman's political subordination. Even the threat of General Boulanger could not dissuade her:

Various journals have accused [me]...of playing into the hands of *boulangisme* by diverting a certain number of republican votes...I have only wished...to make an act of propaganda in favor...of the equity of the demand for woman's civil and political rights....I was and remain convinced that the few isolated votes that might go to women would exercise no influence on the struggle between the Republic and reaction.

Richer naturally objected, warning that "ten votes taken from a republican candidate could assure victory to a reactionary." He acknowledged Potonié-Pierre's sincerity, "but I say that, given the gravity of the circumstances the moment was badly chosen for a feminine demonstration." The campaign collapsed in any case when Potonié-Pierre learned from the press that the prefect of the Seine, who refused to communicate with her directly, had ruled against her candidacy.[53]

The conduct of Giraud, Potonié-Pierre, and de Gasté in the immediate aftermath of the 1889 congress, coupled with the attrition in the French League for Women's Rights and the collapse of the International Federation, reflected Richer's inability to impose his personal direction on the French feminist movement. He had managed for an instant to reassert the preeminence of *la brèche*, but he could neither annihilate the *assautistes* through direct attack nor undercut their campaign through successes of his own. He hung on for two more years until December 1891, when age, poor health, and disappointment combined to effect the suspension of *Le Droit des femmes* and his retirement from the movement. Thereafter, his service to the cause evoked an occasional article in the feminist press, and the League honored him with a four-franc banquet in 1902. Otherwise, his retirement separated him almost completely from the movement that he had done so much to create. Richer died on 25 June 1911, at the age of eighty-seven. He had written what might pass for his epitaph in January 1889, at the beginning of the year that brought him so much joy and so much sorrow: "Always, I have been wrong in being right too soon."[54]

CONCLUSION

It [feminism] appears less as a political, philosophical or social doctrine than as a state of mind.

Léon Abensour, 1927

The Women's Rights Congress of 1889 coincided with a dynamic mutation in the evolution of the French feminist movement. At roughly that moment in the struggle against *masculinisme*, due in part to the death or retirement of many of the movement's founders, second-generation feminists not only began to assume control of the campaign for women's rights but also came to view the 1889 congress as more a time of beginning than a triumph of unfolding. Beneath the second generation's reassessment of the 1889 congress lay a repudiation of the founders' liberal-political feminism and the priority that they had accorded to the political question over the woman question. Once the second generation rejected the founders' priority, however, the tension that had formerly held the mother-teacher "woman ideal" in balance with the liberal republican "political ideal" also relaxed. The effect of this relaxation profoundly altered liberal feminism in France. For, without the countervailing political question, the answer to which upheld woman as man's equal in liberalism, the post-1889 generation could only raise the woman question, the response to which increasingly identified woman as man's equivalent in special naturism. Hence, although the founders of the movement succeeded in imparting to liberal feminism an impulse to ongoing struggle, their successors partly repudiated the strategical, organizational, and theoretical bases on which the movement originally developed.

TRANSFORMATION AND REPUDIATION

The ranks of the movement's founders suffered a striking depletion in the late 1880s and early 1890s. Each of the three principal founders left the movement between 1888 and 1894, with Auclert's withdrawal to Algeria at the earlier date, Richer's retirement in 1891, and Deraismes's death in the latter year. The much younger Auclert eventually returned to the movement, but her four-year absence undercut her authority at about the same moment that Richer and Deraismes relinquished theirs. Among the other individuals who inspired the movement, death took Eugénie Niboyet in 1883, Caroline de Barrau in 1888, Olympe Audouard and Jenny d'Héricourt in 1890, and Jeanne Deroin in 1894. Amélie Bosquit, who had submitted a woman suffrage request to the National Assembly in 1871, lived until 1904, but reached her eightieth year in 1895. Of the small number of politicians who supported women's rights during the movement's first generation, Victor Hugo died at eighty-three in 1885, Alfred Talandier at seventy-seven in 1890, Joseph de Gasté at eighty-one in 1893, Jean Macé at seventy-nine in 1894, and Charles Boudeville at seventy-one in 1895.

Among the movement's rank and file, at least three indicators also suggest a large turnover during the immediate era of the 1889 congress. One indicator is the Amelioration Society's roster for 1894, which reveals that half of Deraismes's sixteen original colleagues had died by the time of her death, and two of the remaining seven had reached advanced age, Deputy Émile Corneau (1826–1906), who retired from the Chamber in 1893 at the age of sixty-seven, and Virginie Griess-Traut (1814–1898), who passed her eightieth birthday in 1894. Nearly as old as Griess-Traut was Jules Allix, who served for years as the Society's secretary and died in 1897 at the age of seventy-nine. Another indicator is the roster of the 1889 Women's Rights Congress, which reveals that only twenty-five of the individuals who participated in the first congress of 1878 attended the second eleven years later, although the combined official attendance at the two congresses totaled nearly four hundred. A third indicator is the 1892 roster of Richer's French League for Women's Rights, which reveals that, of the ninety-six women and men who founded the group in 1882–1883, no more than forty retained their membership throughout the League's first decade.[1]

This transformation in the movement's cadres found a complement in the assessment and reassessment of the 1889 congress itself. The congress initially elicited plaudits from the ranks of the founders themselves. The authorized report of the congress stressed, for example, that in comparison to "all the [other] congresses held during the Universal Centennial Exposition, that of women's rights attracted the most attention and obtained the most publicity; the total of foreign as well as French articles devoted to the subject surpassed six-hundred!"[2] Similarly, Jules Allix later reflected, "One can very well say that, from these two congresses of 1889 [the official congress and the women's rights congress], truly date, in principle, all the numerous groups that have since emerged one after the other, and still exist [in 1897]."[3] The year before, even the otherwise hostile Marie Dronsart paid grudging homage to the importance of the two gatherings: "These two congresses drew no more than a thousand people. Party divisions somewhat confused the foreigners, and the nation ignored [the events]. However, they were the point of departure for a kind of organization."[4]

By the late 1890s, however, the shift from assessment to reassessment, already implicit in the statements of Allix and Dronsart, began to take full hold. Second-generation feminist Avril de Saint-Croix typified the tendency to subordinate antecedents to aftermath by citing the 1889 event as important to women but especially to Jeanne Schmahl and Marya Chéliga, two second-generation leaders of immigrant background. "It is from that date," wrote Avril de Saint-Croix in 1907, "and thanks as well to the contribution brought to it by two talented foreigners, that feminism definitely came of age."[5] Chéliga herself maintained that the 1889 congresses represented "incontestably the beginning of a prosperous epoch for the French feminist movement," an opinion shared by feminist historian Li Dzeh-Djen, who in 1934 wrote that 1889 constituted a decisive date for the French feminist movement by "posing the first bases of a national and international tactic."[6] Perhaps Li Dzeh-Djen was influenced by Léon Abensour, the most industrious of the movement's historians and a prolific propagandist for the second generation's moderation, who, although he knew better, wrote in 1921 that "the congresses began to appear, and that of 1889, the first, opened in an atmosphere of sympathetic attention."[7]

In focusing on what followed the 1889 congress rather than on what preceded it, the movement's second generation sought in historical subtlety to divorce itself from the founders' liberal-political feminism.

Not so subtle, however, were the two main grounds for divorce. Tactically, according to Abensour, the founders in general and the *assautistes* in particular had acted in a singularly inappropriate manner. "Perhaps France would have little by little accustomed itself to feminism," he noted, "if some militants had not too hastily wanted to pick still unripe fruit and to pass on to direct action." The shadow campaigns had been especially disastrous: "From such demonstrations, which reinforce the facile jests whose influence is so strong on the public, undoubtedly flowed more bad than good for the cause."[8] Jane Misme, who founded *La Française (The French Woman)* in 1906 and played a dominant role in French feminism for the next thirty years, also sought to draw a sharp line between moderates like herself and the "impulsive" *assautistes* in Auclert's "radical party." Urging "discreet envelopment" of apathetic women, she railed against Auclert's "gaudy demonstrations" and "puerile gestures." Misme acknowledged Auclert's devotion to the cause when the latter died in 1914, but the strategy of *l'assaut* struck her at best as appropriate only to times past.[9] Jeanne Schmahl, whom Misme described as "remarkably intelligent and distinguished," refused to concede even that. Shortly after forming the Advance Messenger in 1893, Schmahl blasted Auclert for engaging in "uproarious proceedings" reminiscent of the French Revolution's women militants.

Schmahl also gave voice to the second generation's other main ground for divorce: the founders' strategy. Aside from Deraismes's despotism and inability "to recognize and utilize [her followers'] talent and merit," the demand for lay girls' schools "was undoubtedly a mistake," Schmahl charged in an English-language article: "This mixing up of politics and religion with the women's question has been one of the great reasons of the unsuccess of the movement in France." The founders had also acted prematurely in declaring their liberal republican sympathies: "Until women have got the franchise they can neither be Republicans nor Monarchists; it is thereore foolish to stamp them beforehand as belonging to this or that political camp." The net effect of the pioneers' foolishness was predictable, Schmahl concluded: women remain the greatest obstacles to feminism "not only because they are profoundly ignorant of its signification, but because they disapprove of the socialistic and irreligious attitudes of most of the leaders." So well in fact did Schmahl make her point that Abbé Lecoeur, director of the Join-Lambert day school, described her as a "woman distinguished by talent, mind, and character" who "has resolutely separated herself from Maria Deraismes, especially from Louise Michel, and has oriented feminism in a practical way where moderation will lead to victories in the near future."[10]

In resolving to effect a break from their predecessors, second-generation feminists like Misme and Schmahl and sympathizers like Abbé Lecoeur in effect shattered the revolutionary mold into which the founders had poured the movement. Consequently, after a long decade of organizational and strategical confusion stretching from the 1889 congress to the founding of the National Council of French Women in 1901, the substance of French feminism reset in a shape that Abensour characterized in one of his last works on the subject, the aptly named *Le Problème féministe* (*The Feminist Problem*):

In fact, feminism is at the same time a reaction of the individual conscience and the collective conscience of women against the injustice and the illogicality of the condition that certain societies have imposed on them....It appears less as a political, philosophical or social doctrine than as a state of mind.[11]

Although enigmatic on its face, this "state of mind" reflected the absence of a clear-cut notion about what constituted women's emancipation. By stripping away the first generation's overt political orientation, the movement's beneficiaries, although no less liberal than their benefactors, also stripped from liberal feminism the one rationale that had provided the movement with a referent for determining its progress, namely the consolidation of the Third Republic itself.

LIBERAL-POLITICAL FEMINISM: AN ASSESSMENT

In contrast to both their Anglo-Saxon counterparts and their successors, whose efforts on behalf of women's emancipation took place within solidly liberal political contexts, the founders of the liberal feminist movement in France saw themselves not only as social revolutionaries but as political revolutionaries as well. Against the ever-present danger of monarcho-clerical reaction, they fought first to achieve and then to preserve a liberal republican redistribution of power, which for them constituted the essential political precondition for any improvement in woman's status. In pursuit of this precondition, Deraismes maintained a republican salon, directed *Le Républicain de Seine-et-Oise*, and assumed leadership of the republican forces in her home department. Richer wrote for *L'Opinion nationale* and other liberal republican journals, served as editor-in-chief of the *République radicale*, and twice ran for a seat in the Chamber of Deputies. Auclert also subscribed to the precondition, despite frequent criticism of the Third Republic for perpetuating *masculinisme*. During the crisis of 16 May 1877, for example, she temporarily set aside the woman question, and throughout her long campaign for woman suffrage she held steadfastly to "my country and my republic," even if these, her twin idols, meant a slave's life in France rather than freedom elsewhere. In addition, danger from the Right drew Deraismes into promoting anticlericalism, Richer into penning journalistic assaults on clerical abuses, and Auclert into mocking anyone who fostered religious escapism in women by denying them the vote. All of the movement's founders sought a system of free, universal, and lay education to offset Church influence, and all also considered the reenactment of divorce in 1884 as much as a defeat of the Church as a victory for women.

Despite Schmahl's accusation of "socialistic" attitudes, the principles that underlay the founders' political activism came straight out of the liberal tradition. In contrast to the emergent Marxist feminist movement on their left, which saw classes as the basic units of society and the resolution of class conflict as the precondition for women's emancipation, or the emergent Catholic feminist movement on their right, which sought to ameliorate woman's condition by restoring the "natural" social hierarchy and by compelling all levels of it to fulfill their responsibilities to family and society, the founders of the liberal feminist movement saw society as a conglomeration of individuals and the elimination of prescriptive barriers to equal opportunity and individual advancement as the precondition for solving the woman question. "If it is too early [for woman suffrage], let us wait," Richer wrote in 1877; "but let us not create special privileges, let us not establish classes."[12] "When at the proper time, I shall call for political equality, as I call today for civil equality," Richer repeated during the convoluted debate with Giraud in 1889:

I shall not speak in the name of particular class interests, but in the name of lofty principle, in the name of right, in the name of justice; I shall rest my case, without distinguishing between categories, on the quality of the [individual] human being which encompasses woman as much as man.[13]

Liberalism likewise informed Deraismes's 1872 assessment of *France et progrès* (*France and Progress*):

Thank God, we can rest assured, because that faction [the communists] is composed of only the most ignorant and least honorable individuals. . . . Certainly, it is not impossible to seize riches violently, but what remains inalienable, indivisible, immovable are the sources which produce them: [individual] talent, genius, knowledge, character, beauty, health, etc. These are riches that cannot be expropriated and cannot be held in common.[14]

Finally, in the name of liberalism, Auclert too railed against the collectivists, whose vision of economic transformation would "only operate to the profit of men."[15]

As a group, then, the founders of the French feminist movement brought to their task a dynamic attachment to liberalism that placed them politically in an historic seam between the new Left and the old Right. Of the two alternatives, however, the threat from the Right far outweighed the danger from the Left in the outlook of the founders. As a fairly homogeneous generational cadre born within a few decades of 1789, weaned around 1830, in full youth in 1848, and middle-aged during the troubled transition from the Second Empire to the Third Republic, the founders projected into their militancy (and into their younger colleagues like Auclert) life-long experiences that simultaneously reinvigorated their liberal faith while heightening their concern about its successful realization. Having witnessed reaction, they never forgot it. Even after the Third Republic achieved relative stability they brought to its defense the cumulative fears and frustrations that had once gone into its creation. Without a liberal republic, they believed, no one could enjoy liberty. Or, more specifically, without a permanent liberal answer to the "first stage" political question, there could be no answer to the "second stage" woman question.

Nor so long as this two-stage vision of societal transformation remained pitched at so general a level could there by any disagreement among the founders of the liberal feminist movement. Once brought down to specifics, however, the vision provoked differences over strategy and organization and confusion about how to interpret and alleviate women's subordination. In the bitter controversy over woman suffrage, for example, the demand itself as well as the tactics employed by the *assautistes* provoked angry objections from the *brèchistes*, not because the vote conflicted with feminist ideals but because it seemed to threaten the republic. Auclert and the other pioneer suffragists, who sought at one and the same time to strengthen the republic and to emancipate women politically, thus found themselves cut off from the psychological sustenance felt by the *brèchistes* when they looked at republican France. Furthermore, by so persistently denouncing the *assautistes* on political grounds, Richer not only reinforced popular impressions of women's reactionary tendencies but also provided subsequent opponents of woman suffrage with a "feminist authority."[16]

Richer interjected yet another strategic ambiguity by relying so heavily on men in positions of power, a reliance that introduced a contradiction of "types" into the movement. On the one hand, the founders of the French feminist movement sought to construct the type of collective endeavor called a social movement, the general characteristics of which are a strong goal orientation, a high degree of idealism, and a deep commitment to fundamental change. On the other hand, by attempting to curry favor with the male power structure, the movement also displayed characteristics typical of political parties, which are generally power oriented, realistic, and concerned with the capture of offices. Rarely can a movement remain pure, but when the two types become too intermingled the effect is usually a loss of direction. In the case of the French feminist movement, the intermingling and resultant loss of direction stemmed largely from the magnitude of the undertaking. On behalf of a female population numbering from seventeen to twenty million, the movement managed to attract less than a thousand activists in its first two decades. In Richer's view, this immense discrepancy required a shift of tactical locus from the movement's apathetic mass constituency to parliament, where sympathetic legislators might give to all women what only a few forthrightly demanded.

Such "realism," however, had at least three serious drawbacks. First, as long as the political question retained primacy, the movement refused to open its ranks to nonrepublicans, and, conversely, most nonrepublicans refused to join an effort dominated by pacifists, utopian socialists, Freemasons, and free thinkers. Soon, in fact, liberal feminism became so well integrated into bourgeois republicanism that "feminists were not so much outsiders, challenging the republic, as they were insiders, seeking readjustment of it." And what of liberal feminism's limited appeal among rural and small-town people in the provinces; what accounts for "why a middle-class, republican, urban, anticlerical movement did not attract conservative, Catholic peasants; why an integral part of the bourgeois governing regime did not attract workers?" "The question," Steven Hause has observed, "answers itself." Eventually by focusing on the larger towns, "feminists reached the provincial audience they sought," but the majority remained beyond reach. So determined to break the shackles of *masculinisme*, liberal feminists nonetheless remained the "prisoners of their social class and their national history."[17]

Second, although the movement existed to emancipate women, the priority accorded to republicanism helped to produce a governing elite that cared only secondarily, if at all, about women's rights. Indeed, the pivotally important and politically powerful liberal republican Radical Socialist party waited until the eve of World War I to create a women's rights group, and even then the Federation of Radical and Radical-Socialist Women (Fédération des femmes radicales et radicales-socialistes) excluded woman suffrage from its program. Moreover, when at last, three years after passage in the Chamber of Deputies by a count of 334 to 97, the issue of woman suffrage finally came to a vote in the Senate in 1922, the opposition of 70-plus percent of liberal republicans generally and the younger senators particularly loomed large in the bill's close 156 to 134 defeat.[18]

Finally, despite declaring a year before the 1878 congress that woman "would be mistaken to wait for our good will to obtain the freedom that she aspires to" and that "woman's emancipation will come from woman,"[19] Richer and his followers strove with considerable effectiveness to prevent liberal feminism from straying outside the political boundaries delimited for women by France's male-dominated institutions and male-defined procedures. Due in part no doubt to a pragmatic calculation that men had more power and could therefore act with greater speed than women as well as perhaps to a normative bias that the enlightened had to lead the ignorant and that more men than women had seen the light, Richer in effect relegated women to auxiliary status within his branch of the movement. In doing so, however, not only did he perpetuate within the movement a mode of discrimination similar to that which characterized the whole of French society, but he also added to the contradiction between women's emancipation and republican security an even deeper contradiction between those he claimed to serve and those he chose for service.

Organizational disunity compounded the founders' strategical dilemma. After the 1889 congress, Auclert reconstructed her Suffrage Society upon returning to Paris in 1892, and the Amelioration Society passed into the hands of Féresse-Deraismes upon her sister's death in 1894, with both groups surviving at least until World War I. The French League for Women's Rights also survived, with Maria Pognon as the first of Richer's several successors, and it exists to this day. But by then a revolt against the old groupings had already begun. One of the first to rebel was Madame Vincent, who in 1888 created the Feminist Society "Equality" (Société féministe "Égalité"), the first French group to use the word *feminist* in its title.[20] Next came Marya Chéliga's Universal Union of Women (Union universelle des femmes), which grew out of the 1889 congress and succeeded on a smaller scale in founding the international organization that Richer had hoped to lead.[21] Then in short order appeared Astié de Valsayre's short-lived Women's Emancipation League (Ligue de l'affranchissement des femmes) in 1890, which numbered de Gasté among its members and imposed higher dues on men to symbolize women's inferior wages; the Women's Solidarity Group in 1891, which represented an effort by Maria Martin and Potonié-Pierre to bridge the gulf between socialist and bourgeois women; and Jeanne Schmahl's Advance Messenger of 1893, whose conservative cadre included the Duchess d'Uzès and Madame Adam, the former Juliette Lamber.[22]

Such organizational disunity reflected the second generation's penchant for imitating the founders' practice rather than implementing the founders' ideal. The practice itself had begun when, after a few years in the ranks of André Léo's Society for the Demand of Women's Rights, Deraismes joined Richer in founding the Society for the Amelioration of Woman's Condition. Six years later Auclert created the Women's Rights Society, and, after another six years, Richer fashioned the French League for Women's Rights. Auclert then launched her abortive National Society for Women's Suffrage, and at the time of the 1889 congress Richer announced his equally unsuccessful International Federation for the Demand of Women's Rights. Indeed, the only instance of consolidation during the movement's formative years was the Amelioration Society's cooptation of André Léo's Society in the early 1880s, an act that amounted to little more than a transfer of funds. A near success came two years after the 1889 congress when eleven groups tried to contain the "polyfederal epidemic" by forming under Potonié-Pierre and Martin the French Federation of Feminist Societies (Fédération française des sociétés féministes) and by hosting, with Chéliga's Universal Union, the Feminist Congress of 1892—the first congress in France to use the word *feminist* in its title.[23] But soon thereafter the Federation also collapsed.

While the liberal feminist movement slipped into disarray during the 1890s, despite yet another congress in 1896, the prospect of expanding the movement's base leftward or rightward became increasingly remote. To their left, liberal feminists found themselves cut off from socialist women, who identified liberal feminism with class oppression. Following the lead of Elisabeth Renaud and especially Louise Saumoneau, who together in 1899 founded the Feminist Socialist Group (Groupe féministe socialiste), socialist women singled out liberal feminists as their "natural adversaries," arguing that, since the "general interest of the feminine bourgeoisie lay with the interests of their parasitic class," a "profound antagonism" separated them from the "feminine proletariat, equally attached to the interests of their exploited class."[24] To their right, liberal feminists found themselves at odds with a small group of Catholic feminists, led by Marie Maugeret who in 1896 founded *Le Féminisme chrétien* (*The Christian Feminism*) and the Catholic Circle of Ladies (Cercle catholique de dames), and with a great many nonfeminist Catholic women, who at the turn of the century organized by the tens of thousands in opposition to the government's anticlerical policies.[25]

In 1900 the problem of liberal feminist coordination both came to a head and began to move toward resolution. Three women's congresses took place that year. Catholic women, provoked in particular by the recent exoneration of the falsely convicted Captain Alfred Dreyfus, held their first such event, while bourgeois women once again, as in 1889, split their forces between a second philanthropically oriented International Congress of Feminine Works and Institutions (Congrès international des oeuvres et institutions féminines) and another International Congress on the Condition and the Rights of Women (Congrès international de la condition et des droits des femmes). The latter in turn signaled the definitive rupture between socialist and liberal feminists, with the liberals accusing the socialists of trying to divide bourgeois women from working women by erecting a "wall of hate."[26] Boxed in this time by the balance of political forces rather than the founders' political commitment, however, and under pressure from representatives of the International Council of Women, liberal feminists moved quickly toward coalescing with their sisters in the other bourgeois congress. The result manifested itself the following year in the National Council of French Women.

Planned by a committee composed of three representatives from each of the two bourgeois congresses, the National Council of French Women enabled liberal feminists to break out of their isolation but also reaccentuated the movement's moderation.[27] Affiliated with the 1888 International Council of Women, the National Council leaped from 30- odd federated groups with 20,000 members in 1901 to well over 100 groups with 100,000 members in 1914, and by 1929 it represented nearly a quarter of a million women. It also reached out into the provinces by establishing eight departmental branches between 1908 and the end of World War I.[28] Yet most of the National Council's member groups were not explicitly feminist. By its own count, for instance, the National Council in 1911 employed the designation "feminist" for only nine of its 102 member groups.[29] Furthermore, not until 1907–1908 did the Council establish a special section to press for woman suffrage, and even then most suffragists agreed that the quest for political rights required a separate organization. This came in 1909 when Jeanne Schmahl founded the French Union for Women's Suffrage (Union française pour le suffrage des femmes), which grew between 1911 and 1914 from 3,000 members to 14,000 and from six provincial chapters to eighty-one.

The majority with whom the liberal feminists coalesced in joining the National Council of French Women came primarily from the ranks of Protestant moral reformers. Through the journal *La Femme*, founded in the late 1870s, and annual Versailles conferences, the first of which took place in 1890, these reformers eschewed the kind of direct political involvement that marked the liberal feminist movement's early years in favor of a concentration on various women-related social problems. Many of the reformers worked hard on Josephine Butler's abolitionist campaign, and "in the 1870s the issue of state-regulated prostitution provided a point of convergence for radical republicans and women reformers."[30] Other reformers, focusing less on abolitionism and more on such evils as white slavery and pornography, rallied to groups like Senator René Bérenger's League for Public Morality (Ligue de la moralité publique) and his French section of the Association for the Repression of the White Slave Trade and for the Protection of Young Women, founded at London in 1899. In general, as Elisabeth Weston has pointed out, such reform efforts and especially abolitionism reflected a "nascently feminist" consciousness, and, although these women reformers did not initially join the small but growing women's rights movement, "they did develop a systematic critique of woman's oppression, particularly in the realm of sexuality."[31]

In addition to this critique and their own isolation, liberal feminists saw in their coalition partners women of similar social standing and, even if downplayed in the name of decorum, similar political outlook. All of the leaders of the National Council—as well as of the French Union for Women's Suffrage—possessed wealth, exercised a profession, or belonged by either birth or marriage to prominent liberal republican families. Some displayed all three characteristics, and, according to one feminist in 1910, the Council's officer corps alone included forty to fifty millionaires.[32] Not surprisingly, the National Council of French Women established its central office at the Musée Social, founded in 1894 as "a kind of corporate headquarters within which captains of industry periodically gathered to discuss the progress made toward social peace" and to undertake "a common effort to promote enlightened capitalism and class harmony."[33] Although financed by the Comte de Chambrun, an unreconstructed monarchist and reforming entrepreneur, the Musée Social remained under the direction of Jules Siegfried until his death in 1922. A Protestant, a good republican, a millionaire, and an intimate of "the brightest stars in the French liberal firmament," such as the laissez-faire conservative Léon Say and Deraismes's "clerical" opponent Jules Simon, Siegfried "acted as a personal focus for the diverse tendencies of social reform" and, according to Sanford Elwitt, "comes the closest in French political life to the consummate professional philanthropist and social conscience of the *haute bourgeoisie*."[34] His wife Julie, moreover, served from the outset as one of the vice-presidents of the National Council of French Women and then, upon the death of Sarah Monod in 1912, succeeded to the presidency, which she held until her own death in 1922.

Thus, although subscribing rhetorically to an apoliticism, the National Council nonetheless accentuated the liberal feminism of the founders, the two orientations differing only in respect to how much feminists should engage in direct political action. Once the second generation of liberal feminists abandoned such direct action and made common cause with the

Protestant reformers, however, the expanded movement as a whole raised moderation, or what might be called *neo-brèchisme*, to the level of unquestioned principle. Aside from two incidents in 1908—Auclert smashing a ballot box and socialist-feminist Madeleine Pelletier stoning a polling station—liberal feminism adamantly opposed any behavior resembling that of the English suffragettes, and both Auclert and Pelletier garnered the movement's severest condemnation. In part such moderation was due to the power and willingness of the state to suppress illegality with violence, as evidenced by the not infrequent repression of workers' demonstrations in blood. In part, too, it was due to a fear that the Left and the Right continued to pose a danger to the Third Republic as well as to a sense that the legal options available under the republic offered in any case sufficient avenues for protest and occasional successes. "Might" was also viewed as the man's way in contrast to "right" as the woman's. Yet, the principal effect of coalition was to reaccentuate the sociopolitical character of liberal feminism. With the right to vote as the movement's main objective and moderation as the movement's means in the years just prior to World War I, Steven Hause and Anne Kenney have suggested, "the generalized personality of French suffragism as liberal, middle class, and republican, as dreading ridicule and esteeming dignity, does not alone explain the limits suffragists imposed on their behavior." "But," Hause and Kenney added, "it is certainly the predominant factor."[35]

Predominant as well was the ambiguity that from the outset had characterized liberal feminism's theoretical approach to women's emancipation. In part this ambiguity stemmed from the founders' interest in effecting rapid change, which in the circumstances seemed to require action rather than study—a possible defect that Jeanne Oddo-Deflou apparently tried to correct by founding in 1898 the Group for Feminist Studies and the Civil Rights of Women (Groupe d'études féministes et des droits civils des femmes).[36] The journalistic talents of the founders also contributed to this ambiguity. Reams of reportage and polemics flowed from the pens of the movement's founders, but, pressed from all sides by feminist commitments and masculinist constraints, none managed to produce a synthetic analysis of *masculinisme*. Finally, consistent with the moral paradigm that informed the movement's sense of history, the movement's founders seemingly considered *masculinisme* so self-evidently unjust that they saw little need for theoretical disquisitions. The optimistic titles of the founders' journals and groups, which emphasized women's "future" and women's "rights," impart this impression, and Richer, for example, took pride in reversing Bismarck's "Might makes right" as the motto for his *Le Droit des femmes*. Not until the end of the second generation in fact did journals, usually with a left-wing slant, appear bearing titles more in keeping with the magnitude of the task: *Le Combat féministe (Feminist Combat)* of 1913–1914, *Le Cri des femmes (Women's Cry)* of 1914, and *La Lutte féministe (Feminist Struggle)* of 1919–1921. Whatever the reasons, though, the founders of the liberal feminist movement bequeathed ambiguous theoretical guidelines in the three key areas of constituency, goal, and rationale.

The movement's constituency seemed obvious enough. It was women; however, inasmuch as many women accepted and even defended woman's subordination while at least a few men fought against it, the movement could count women among its opponents and men among its friends. First-generation feminists exhibited an appreciation of how woman's socialization had helped to produce this situation. Auclert, for instance, claimed a contrast between most women and Jewish women, who as "modern Judiths" had translated their awareness of anti-Semitic persecution into a concern for sex equality, although she herself eventually wrote woman suffrage pieces for Édouard Drumont's virulently anti-Semitic *La Libre Parole*. Yet, because the founders attached as much importance to republicanism as feminism, the result was a movement whose internal composition, if defined by social-sex criteria, sometimes included both "friends" and "enemies." The second generation rejected overt political "right thinking" as the essential criterion for membership in the feminist movement and increased the ratio of women to men within its ranks, but it nonetheless preserved a subtle form of right thought—as evidenced in 1909 by Oddo-Deflou's expulsion from the National Council of French Women for questioning liberal feminism's pacifist tendencies—while drifting into defining the cause by numbers rather than a well-wrought critique of *masculinisme*. In the absence of clear-cut theoretical guidelines, in short, the movement tended to subordinate basic insight to body count in determining its strength. Indeed, if a specific moment could signify the beginning of this drift on the part of liberal feminism, it would be 2 May 1886, the date on which Richer announced that his dwindling League had entered into an informal alliance with the moral reformers of Pastor Tommy Fallot's French League for the Improvement of Public Morality.

The movement's goal also seemed obvious enough. *Masculinisme* imposed countless constraints on women. Those had to go, along with anything else that prevented women from realizing their full individual potential. In practice, however, the movement focused almost exclusively on securing women's legal rights, a focus which reflected a deep-rooted tradition, if the analysis of working-class aspirations by the Belgian theorist Henry de Man can be expanded to include France's liberal feminists:

In Britain and the United States, the workers are led by their longing for equality to demand *freedoms* from the State; in continental European countries, the workers clamor for *rights*. In the English-speaking lands, the demand is that the State shall not hinder the process of change. In Latin countries, the demand is that changes shall be regulated by law.[37]

This focus also reflected the limited aspirations of the liberal bourgeoisie, from whose ranks most of the founders of the French feminist movement came and in the name of which they sought to emancipate women. Yet, by focusing so exclusively on rights, the liberal feminist movement in France, like the liberal feminist movements elsewhere in the nineteenth century, drifted into a legalism which, in the absence of a general concept of women's emancipation, confused legislation with liberation.

Not so obvious was the movement's rationale. Even in the limited area of liberal rights, the founders displayed a marked ambivalence about why women should enjoy an improved legal status. Were women the equals of men, as some feminists sometimes maintained, or equivalent, as others asserted? Perhaps they were both, equal in some respects, equivalent in others? "Feminism," wrote Nelly Roussel, "is the doctrine of natural equivalence and of social equality of the two factors of the human genre."[38] Kaethe Schirmacher expressed a similar notion: "Woman, in her sphere, is entirely the equal of man in his."[39] Richer suggested that "man and woman are equivalent. In this sense one can say EQUAL: that is, equality in dissimilarity."[40]

In immediate impact, this ambivalence led the movement to employ contradictory emancipation themes. At times the founders portrayed women as integral parts of a larger unit—the nation, the West, all humanity—and demanded their emancipation in the name of universal justice and right. At other times the founders emphasized woman's special relationship to smaller units, particularly the family, and claimed her freedom in the name of unique "feminine" qualities. Often the two themes merged, especially in the assertion that woman's unique characteristics would contribute to a more peaceful and harmonious social order. Deraismes typified the movement's tendency in this respect by stressing the potential benefit of woman's domestic virtues to the whole of society: "She will bring to public life her beautiful qualities: sagacity, perseverance, abnegation." Without full utilization of these qualities, she exclaimed, society must necessarily suffer because "any law, any institution that does not bear the imprint of the human duality will be neither viable, nor durable."[41]

The long-range impact of this ambivalence inclined the movement to expediency. Aware that for nearly a century the trend in favor of the rights of man had bypassed women, liberal feminists tried but failed and then partially abandoned even the attempt to effect a transfer of universal "people" principles from the one sex to the other. Coincidentally, popular belief and the "patriarchal feminism" of men like Richer enclosed women in a prison of sexist metaphysics, the bars of which stood firmly implanted in the widespread assumption that women possessed innate aptitudes. By thus drawing attention to women's "beautiful qualities," which liberal feminists tended more and more to do as appeals to principal failed, they simply reinforced the already well-established belief that sex represented a legitimate criterion for discrimination. Furthermore, to the extent that women occasionally secured new legal rights in the name of their "equivalent" natures, the net effect was to strengthen the metaphysical notion of separate spheres on which *masculinisme* rested in the first place.

The principal metaphysical notion to which the founders of the liberal feminist movement lent the weight of their collective ambivalence was that of the mother-teacher. According to this image of *woman*, all women possessed an innate aptitude for playing two social-sex roles, motherhood and wifehood. To fulfill these two roles, women had to confine themselves to the social sphere that revolved around the home, where they had in turn to devote themselves to maintaining domestic order and to guiding the next generation through childhood. Combined with the structural constraints made possible by emerging capitalism, this "myth" placed women, and especially bourgeois women, in a position where they found themselves isolated from one another and in daily "loving" contact with their "superiors." In their child-rearing capacity, they also found themselves charged with the noble responsibility, especially for "inferiors," of molding the society's young. Together the concrete constraints and the "myth" insidiously interacted in subtly depriving women of any meaningful options for their lives. Moreover, as Linda Gordon has observed of the women's movements in the late nineteenth century generally, "the cult of motherhood was thus argued as passionately by feminists as by antifeminists: conservatives argued that motherhood was the basic reason women should stay at home; feminists argued that motherhood was the main reason women needed more power, independence, and respect."[42] Thus, too, the founders of the liberal feminist movement not only perpetuated the ambiguity from which the ideal of the mother-teacher drew life, but, if anything, they also strengthened the myth by relying increasingly on special nature arguments to obtain the rights that increasingly became ends in themselves.

At the outset of the movement, Jenny d'Héricourt had protested against the tendency of utopian socialists and others to envelop the woman question in "theology," whereas Juliette Lamber had asserted that "I, like Proudhon, believe that woman's first duty is to be wife and mother." Somewhat paradoxically the founders of the liberal feminist movement, siding in effect with Lamber, likewise attached great value not only to Proudhon's priority but also to the notion of separate spheres on which it rested. Consequently, although the movement contributed to a gradual improvement in women's legal status, the gains in law were partially offset by the simultaneous reinforcement of the special nature premise that constituted the ideological basis of women's subordination.

APPENDIX A
1876 Program of Léon Richer's
L'Avenir des Femmes

THE LAW SAYS:

The girl, from fifteen years of age, is alone responsible for her virtue.

WE DEMAND:

That the young girl, even older than fifteen years, should be protected against the designs of pleasure seekers (*surprises des coureurs d'aventures*).

Seduction is not a crime (*délit*).[1]

That seduction should be punished.

Corruption, even of a female minor, is not a crime.[2]

That corruption should be punished.

The search for paternity is forbidden.

That the search for paternity should be permitted, as is the search for maternity.

SOURCE: *L'Avenir des femmes*, January 1876.

[1]*Simple* seduction does not fall under the arm of the law, for which *violence* is required. VIOLATION and RAPE are crimes, *seduction* is not.

[2]Here is the text of the law: — "Anyone who has violated morality in exciting, favoring, or facilitating *habitually* the debauchery or the corruption of an individual *below the age of twenty-one*, will be punished by imprisonment from six months to two years and fined from fifty to five-hundred francs." (C.P., 424) — It follows that the law does not punish *accidental, isolated* corruption; to be treated as a crime corruption must be a regular practice, a profession, what is called, in a word, procuring (*proxénétisme*). A judgment of the correctional tribunal of Niort, of 7 December 1861, ruled as follows: *It is in principle and in jurisprudence that the individual who has excited to debauchery in order to satisfy his own passions, is not at all regarded as culpable by our legislation.*—We could multiply the examples.

Children born outside of wedlock (*les enfants naturals*) are the sole responsibility of the mother.

That the natural father should be held *responsible* [and] that the child should be cared for by both of its parents.

Every promise of marriage is null, even if it leads to the abandonment of the child.

That a promise of marriage should not be considered less serious than a promise of sale, and that it gives a right, in case of rupture, to moral or other reparations, proportionate to the damages caused.

The man, in marriage, alone exercises paternal authority.

That authority over children should be shared by the father and the mother.

For children to marry, the father's consent suffices; if the mother refuses hers, it does not matter.

That the consent of the mother should be as necessary, for marriage, as that of the father.

The husband administers the personal wealth of his wife.

That the administration of the personal wealth of the wife should not belong by right and exclusively to the husband.

The husband may sell, whenever it pleases him, the furnishings of the household (*le mobilier conjugal*).

That the husband may not sell, without the consent of his wife, the goods outfitting the home.

He can dispose of all movable effects, securities, furniture, jewels, etc., without consulting his wife, and this [he can do] *free of charge*, and even to the profit of a *third person* (read: to a *concubine*).

That he cannot dispose freely and alone, either *free* of charge or as a debt (*à titre onéreux*), of securities or movable effects forming part of the joint estate or belonging to one of the spouses.

The wife can neither make nor receive a donation, even from a member of her family, without her husband's consent.

That the wife can make and receive donations without the consent of her husband, in conformity with the prescriptions of law.

Ineligible to be tutors or members of family councils, *minors, convicts, men of notorious misconduct, individuals condemned to loss of civil rights*...and WOMEN!

That she ceases, in what concerns family councils, to be grouped with *minors, imbeciles, and habitual criminals*.

The husband's adultery, perpetrated outside the conjugal domicile, is not punishable. The wife's adultery, in whatever place it has been consummated, is punishable. The murder committed by the husband on the wife as well as on the accomplice, in the instant when he surprises them *en flagrant délit* in the conjugal home, is excusable. The murder committed by the wife, in the same circumstances, *is not excusable*.

That the husband's adultery should be put in the same category as the wife's adultery; that is to say that adultery perpetrated by the husband, outside the home, should be as criminal as adultery in the common residence.

The woman cannot serve as a witness to acts of birth, marriage, or death, wills, leases, sales, family property divisions or public acts; HER SIGNATURE CARRIES NO VALUE (*ne fait pas foi*).

That the witness of the woman should count (*fasse foi*) in civil acts and public acts, as it counts before criminal tribunals.

WE DEMAND IN ADDITION:

There is what the law says—and a host of other offensive things that women ignore or that they learn only too late, when misfortune itself has compelled them to open their eyes.

In the name of the sanctity of marriage itself.
In the name of moral purity.
In the name of morality.
That the hypocritical law of separation—which breaks marriage without dissolving it, separates spouses without disuniting them and opens the door to shameful compromises—should be replaced by divorce qualified in accordance with all the legal guarantees judged necessary.

The problem thus posed, there is not an honest woman, a mother anxious about her dignity and her interests, of the dignity and the interest of her children, who refuses to join us.

This is why we appeal to all, without distinction of opinion, of rank and of fortune, begging them to help us, by all the means in their power, in the accomplishment of the great task that we have undertaken.

Our goal is to revise the law.

If it is said that the hour is inopportune, it is in epochs of social and political reorganization like that through which we pass, that it is good to think of reforms.

No moment would be more propitious.

APPENDIX B
1877 Program of the Society for the Amelioration of Woman's Condition

1. Complete identification of man and woman in respect to the possession and exercise of civil rights.
2. Preservation by woman of the plentitude of her rights in marriage: no more subordination of the wife to the husband; right of the mother equal to the right of the father.
3. Reestablishment of divorce.
4. Progressive initiation of woman into civic life.
5. A single morality for the two sexes; what is excusable for the one cannot be blamable, sometimes even criminal, for the other.
6. Absolute right for woman to develop her intelligence through study, to cultivate her reason, to extend the circle of her knowledge, without other limits than those resulting from her aptitude and her will.
7. Free access of women to all professions and to all careers for which they will prove, in the same degree as men, and after similar examinations, the necessary capacities and aptitudes.
8. Rigorous application, without distinction of sex, of the economic formula: "Equal pay for equal work."

SOURCE: *L'Avenir des femmes*, 1 April 1877.

APPENDIX C
Program of Hubertine Auclert's Women's Rights Society (1876-1880)

The Society, considering the political emancipation of woman as the sole means of obtaining the economic and civil emancipation of woman, writes into its program the exercise of the right to vote [and] the right to eligibility for women in the [local] Community, as in the State.

The Society writes into its program integral education for woman. No need to burden the budget to obtain this goal; it suffices that *lycées* [and] existing schools be mixed [coeducational] schools open to girls as well as boys.

The Society demands for woman access to all careers, to all professions, and equality of salary with man for equality of production.

The Society demands the search for paternity.

The Society believes that marriage should be an association freely contracted and based on equality between spouses. At the present time, it [the Society] advocates the regime of separation of goods.

Like every association, marriage should be dissolvable, the human being can much less alienate his person and his freedom than his interest.

The right of spouses to separate does not reduce the duty imposed on them to raise their children.

The Society, desiring impartial justice, wants women to be named consular judges, civil judges, and jurors.

Finally, the Society wants for woman, of whom is demanded the fulfillment of all duties, the recognition and exercise of all rights: the equality of the two sexes before the law.

SOURCE: Hubertine Auclert, *Historique de la société le droit des femmes 1876-1880* (Paris: Robert et Buhl, 1881), 6-7.

APPENDIX D
Principles and Program of Léon Richer's French League for Women's Rights (1892)

OUR PRINCIPLES

The question of civil and civic equality for women is posed everywhere.

It makes in England, in Switzerland, in Italy, in America, rapid and considerable progress.

France cannot remain behind.

Our most eminent thinkers, our best known writers, our most influential political men, pronounce themselves in favor of a prompt revision of the restrictive laws that place so heavy a burden on an entire half of the human species, particularly on wives and mothers.

It is incontestable that woman occupies, neither in society, nor in the family, the place that is her legitimate due.

Everywhere she is *inferiorized*, everywhere she is *sacrificed*.

The code makes her a minor and an unfit [person]; customs make her almost a slave.

Even in work, this duty for all, this supreme necessity for the poor, she confronts, in suffering, the inferiority of her sex.

Such a state of things cannot be maintained for long.

Man and woman have a right to the same rights.

There must be [only] one law, permitting to woman what is permitted to man.

SOURCE: *Circulaire* of the Ligue française pour le droit des femmes of 1892, at BMD, Dossier Ligue française pour le droit des femmes.

There must be [only] one morality, and what is reputed as a crime or an infraction for woman must not be a licit thing for man.

Every woman must be able to live honestly on the product of her labor, without being forced to turn to the filthy resources of public or clandestine prostitution.

It is in order to defend these principles and to seek their application that the review *Le Droit des femmes* was founded in 1869.

The goal to achieve is clearly determined. In these conditions, with the problem thus posed, there is not an honest woman who can repudiate it, not a mother concerned for her dignity and her interests, for the dignity and the interest of her children, who can legitimately refuse us her support.

So what if some might say that the time is not right. It is precisely in epochs of social and political reorganization, like those that affect France at present, that it is good to think of reforms.

No moment would be more propitious.

Already we have obtained the reestablishment of divorce.

Already we have obtained the creation of *écoles supérieures*, the creation of *collèges* and of *lycées* for girls.

We have obtained the admission of women to faculty examinations. Thanks to our long and persevering efforts, women can today be *bachelières ès-lettres, bachelières ès-sciences, licenciées, docteurs*. They can practice medicine.

There is yet to resolve the question of civil equality, to ameliorate the situation of women in marriage.

In order to bring about this second part of our work, we appeal to the devoted support of women themselves.

Let them help us to expand our action; let them join our ranks, as members of the French League. The next step is up to them, the future of their daughters is the question at hand.

OUR PROGRAM

1. Complete identification of man and woman, in respect to the legal possession and exercise of civil rights, while waiting for the legal possession and exercise of political rights.

2. Retention by woman of her full rights in marriage. No more subordination of the wife to the husband. Rights of the mother equal to the rights of the father.

3. Revision of the divorce law.

4. Search for paternity.

5. Progressive initiation of woman into civic life.

6. One and the same morality for the two sexes: what is excusable for the one being no longer inexcusable—sometimes even criminal—for the other.

7. Abolition of regulated prostitution; immediate closing of all whore houses; suppression of the police improperly designated by the name morals police (*police des moeurs*).

8. Absolute right for woman to develop her intelligence through study, to cultivate her reason, to extend the circle of her knowledge, without other limits than those resulting from her aptitudes and her will.

9. Open access of women to all professions and to all careers for which they prove, in the same degree as men and after identical examinations, the necessary capacities and aptitudes.

10. Rigorous application, without distinction of sex, of the economic formula: "Equal pay for equal work."

NOTES

INTRODUCTION

1. Kaethe Schirmacher, *The Modern Woman's Rights Movement*, trans. Conrad Eckhardt, 2nd ed. (New York, 1912), 175.

2. Hubertine Auclert, *Historique de la société le droit des femmes 1876-1880* (Paris, 1881), 19.

3. The suffragist Hubertine Auclert used the word *masculinisme* in an article published in *La Citoyenne* of 9-15 January 1882. Its use throughout the text is intended to evoke a sense of something French as well as to suggest the symmetrical opposite of *feminisme*, a word which Auclert introduced to the French in a letter to the prefect of the Seine in 1882, according to her sister Marie Chaumont, "Hubertine Auclert," *Les Femmes au gouvernail* (Paris, 1923), 5. Somewhat like the word *patriarchy*, rejected here because of its misleading symmetrical opposite, and the word *sexism*, dropped here because of its ambiguous popularity, the word *masculinisme* is supposed to denote the systematic combination of ideology and power that in a thousand ways has perpetuated the subordination of women as a group to men as a group.

4. Jeanne E. Schmahl, "Progress of the Women's Rights Movement in France," *Forum* 22 (September 1896), 82.

5. *Le Droit des femmes* (18 August 1889).

6. Maria Deraismes, *Oeuvres complètes de Maria Deraismes*, ed. Anna Féresse-Deraismes (Paris, 1895), 273.

7. Jenny d'Héricourt, *La Femme affranchie*, 2 vols. (Brussels, 1860).

8. Zillah R. Eisenstein, *The Radical Future of Liberal Feminism* (New York, 1981), 19. Eisenstein analyzes the contradictions within as well as the potential of the liberal feminist tradition as expressed in the writings of John Locke, Jean-Jacques Rousseau, Mary Wollstonecraft, John Stuart Mill and Harriet Taylor, Elizabeth Cady Stanton, and Betty Friedan.

9. Suzanne Blaise, *Des Femmes de nulle part ou le préféminisme politique* (Paris, 1980). For insights into the contemporary movement, see Elaine Marks and Isabelle de Courtivron, *New French Feminisms: An Anthology* (Amherst, Mass., 1980).

CHAPTER 1. CONDITIONS AND CONSTRAINTS: WOMEN AND FEMINISTS UNDER *MASCULINISME*

1. Olympe Audouard, *Guerre aux hommes* (Paris, 1866), 57.
2. *La Citoyenne* (2 July-6 August 1882).
3. Winifred Stephens, *Women of the French Revolution* (New York, 1922), 166.
4. Francis I. Clark, *The Position of Women in Contemporary France* (London, 1937), iii. Gordon Wright, *France in Modern Times* (Chicago, 1960), 90.
5. Françoise Guelaud-Leridon, *Recherches sur la condition féminine dans la société d'aujourd'hui* (Paris, 1967), 93.
6. For information on the Napoleonic Code and feminist reaction to it, see H. M. J. Wattel, ed., *Code Napoléon* (Amsterdam, ca. 1888); *Women's Position in the Laws of Nations*, prepared by the International Council of Women (Karlsruhe, 1912), 97-126; Léon Richer, *Le Code des femmes* (Paris, 1883); Maria Vérone, *La Femme et la loi* (Paris, 1920); Ph. Sagnac, *La Législation civile de la Révolution française (1789-1804)* (Paris, 1898). The Napoleonic Code, referred to above in the singular, included not only the Civil Code of 1804, but four other codes (penal, commercial, civil procedure, and criminal procedure). Due to the influence of the Roman legal tradition, "French law was, accordingly, more apt to intervene in relations *within* the family than English law." Ross Evans Paulson, *Women's Suffrage and Prohibition: A Comparative Study of Equality and Social Control* (Glenview, Ill., 1973), 43. For a survey of the current legal status of French women, see Isabelle Journet-Durca and Paulette Aulibé-Istin, *La Femme et ses nouveaux droits* (Paris, 1975). Although the extent to which the Code's legal strictures actually impinged on women's daily lives is unclear, the principles that it embodied at the very least powerfully reinforced the ideology of *masculinisme*.
7. Fathers could imprison offspring for one month if under sixteen, six months if between sixteen and twenty-one. Illegitimate children had no inheritance rights whatsoever. "Society has no interest in having these bastards recognized," Napoleon exclaimed. Robert B. Holtman, *The Napoleonic Revolution* (New York, 1967), 90-91.
8. Sanche de Gramont, *The French: Portrait of a People* (New York, 1969), 400.
9. *La Citoyenne* (7 January-4 February 1883), (5 March-1 April 1883).
10. On l'Avant courrière, see Schmahl, "Progress of the Women's Rights Movement in France."
11. Ephesians 5:23.
12. Le Vicomte Louis de Bonald, *Législation primitive, considérée dans le dernier temps par les seules lumières de la raison, suivie de divers traités et discours politiques*, 4th ed. (Paris, 1847), 414-17.
13. Ibid.
14. Le Vicomte Louis de Bonald, *Démonstration philosophique du principe constitutif de la société, suivie de méditations politiques tirées de l'Évangile* (Paris, 1830), 102.
15. Ibid., 190-93.
16. Anne Delalande, "Les Femmes et la franc-maçonnerie," *Le Devoir des femmes françaises* (October 1902), 209.
17. G[abrielle] de Villepin (Mme. Le Roy Liberge or Leroy-Liberge), "Pour et contre le féminisme français," *Le Devoir des femmes françaises* (November 1903), 357-58.

18. Octave Chambon, *Le Devoir social de la femme française*, Address delivered at Ploermel on 21 December 1902 (Auxerre, 1902), 22.

19. Jean Lagardère, "Causerie du mois: Le Libéralisme féminin," *La Femme contemporaine* (April 1913), 241.

20. AN F⁷ 13215. Report No. 6852 to Interior Ministry dated 5 September 1917.

21. *Le Devoir des femmes françaises* (August 1903), 250.

22. In his *Syllabus of Errors* (1864), Pius IX specifically condemned divorce as one "of the principal errors of our time." It was wrong to believe, Pius maintained in error number 67, that "by the law of nature, the marriage tie is not indissoluble, and in many cases divorce properly so called may be decreed by the civil authority." Anne Fremantle, ed., *The Papal Encyclicals in Their Historical Context* (New York, 1955), 143-50. The 1850 education reform bore especially hard on women. "It provided that nuns could teach without obtaining the certificate of capacity which was obligatory for lay teachers. The congregations' schools were thereby given an enormous competitive advantage over the secular schools and quickly outnumbered them," according to Persis Hunt, "Feminism and Anti-Clericalism Under the Commune," *Massachusetts Review* 12 (Summer 1971), 419-20.

23. On the family economy, see Olwen Hufton, "Women and the Family Economy in Eighteenth-Century France," *French Historical Studies* 9, no. 1 (Spring 1975), 1-22, as well as Louise A. Tilly and Joan W. Scott, *Women, Work, and Family* (New York, 1978).

24. Unless otherwise noted, the data in this section are drawn from: Évelyne Sullerot, *Histoire et sociologie du travail féminin* (Paris, 1968); Jean Daric, *L'Activité professionelle des femmes en France* (Paris, 1947); and Madeleine Guilbert, *Les Femmes et l'organisation syndicale avant 1914* (Paris, 1966). See also Kaethe Schirmacher, *Le Travail des femmes en France* (Paris, 1902); Alva Myrdal and Viola Klein, *Women's Two Roles: Home and Work* (London, 1956); Michel de Juglart, "L'Émancipation juridique de la femme en France et dans le monde," in *Histoire mondiale de la femme: Sociétés modernes et contemporaines*, under the direction of Pierre Grimal (Paris, 1965), 293-346; and Clark, *The Position of Women in Contemporary France*. For an analysis of the women's movement and unionization, see Marie-Hélène Zylberberg-Hocquard, *Féminisme et syndicalisme en France* (Paris, 1978). For sources on the subject, see Marie-Hélène Zylberberg-Hocquard, Madeleine Guilbert, and Nicole Lowit, *Travail et condition féminine (bibliographie commentée)* (Paris, 1977).

25. Sullerot, *Histoire et sociologie*, 19.

26. Roger L. Williams, *The World of Napoleon III 1851-1870* (New York, 1957), 29.

27. Guilbert, *Les Femmes et l'organisation syndicale avant 1914*, 18.

28. Jules Simon, *L'Ouvrière* (Paris, 1861), cited in Edith Thomas, *The Woman Incendiaries*, trans. James and Starr Atkinson (New York, 1966), 6.

29. Julie Daubié, *La Femme pauvre au XIXe siècle* (Paris, 1866), cited in Thomas, *The Woman Incendiaries*, 8.

30. Elisabeth Anne Weston, "Prostitution in Paris in the Later Nineteenth Century: A Study of Political and Social Ideology" (Ph.D. diss., State University of New York at Buffalo, 1979), 6.

31. The Factory Law of 22 March 1841 covered only children without distinction as to sex. The law of 2 March 1848, which also made no sex distinctions, limited the work day to twelve hours in mines and factories, but it died with the provisional government that enacted

it. The law of 19 May 1878 forbade night work to women under twenty-one and to men under sixteen; it also forbade all underground work to women. The law of 2 November 1892 prohibited women, irrespective of age, to work at night and limited their work day to eleven hours. It also required a weekly day of rest for women workers and provided for better supervision. However, as inspection reports indicate, enforcement proved extremely difficult, and, moreover, the law itself permitted a great many exceptions to its provisions. Guilbert, *Les Femmes et l'organisation syndicale avant 1914*, 232-24. For an opinion pro and con on the law of November 1892 see *Rapport du Comité de résistance pour la défense de la loi du 2 Novembre 1892* (Lyon, 1896), and Yves Guyot, *La Réglementation officielle du travail* (Paris, 1894). Feminists opposed the 1892 law from the moment debate began; see the article by Marya Chéliga in the *Bulletin de l'Union universelle des femmes* (15 April 1890). The only piece of protective legislation that won feminist endorsement was the "seat law" of 29 December 1900, which required shop owners to provide chairs for female clerks. "Feminists, adversaries of all special legislation in matters of work, have not, as far as we know, protested against this concession, however humiliating in their eyes for commercial employees." Schirmacher, *Travail des femmes,* 351.

32. For Comte's views on women, see Louise-Marie Ferré, *Féminisme et positivisme* (Saint-Léger-en-Yvelines, 1938).

33. Fremantle, ed., *The Papal Encyclicals in Their Historical Context,* 186. The difficulty of establishing the relationship between the ideal of woman and the actual conditions under which women live and work is suggested by Sullerot, who points out that "prevailing ideology is insufficient to explain differences in the rates of employment that often run counter to the dominant social norms and reflect economic or demographic pressures." Évelyne Sullerot, *Woman, Society and Change,* trans. Margaret Scotford Archer (New York, 1971), 111.

34. Richard J. Evans, *The Feminists: Women's Emancipation Movements in Europe, America and Australasia 1840-1920* (New York, 1977), 28-35.

35. Antoine Prost, *Histoire de l'enseignement en France 1800-1967* (Paris, 1968), 191.

36. Carlo M. Cipolla, *Literacy and Development in the West* (Baltimore, 1969), 113-30.

37. Williams, *The World of Napoleon III,* 173-208.

38. Cipolla, *Literacy and Development in the West,* 36.

39. Evelyn Martha Acomb, *The French Laic Laws* (1879-1889) (New York, 1967), 153-82.

40. Prost, *Histoire de l'enseignement en France,* 263.

41. Françoise d'Eaubonne, *Histoire et actualité du féminisme* (Paris, 1971), 108.

42. Clark, *The Position of Women in Contemporary France,* 54-55.

43. Hunt, "Feminism and Anti-Clericalism under the Commune," 419.

44. Ibid., 420.

45. Prost, *Histoire de l'enseignement en France,* 268-69.

46. Observance of the law excluding women from political rallies seemed to depend on the prevailing political climate. In 1875, with fear of reaction in the air, Louis Blanc spoke at Saint-Mandé to a gathering of six hundred men. The women who accompanied them waited in a nearby garden while the rally took place behind closed doors and windows. A year later, women attended political gatherings throughout France, including a 14 July

celebration at the Saint-Mandé hall from which they had been excluded the year before. *L'Avenir des femmes* (6 August 1876), (6 January 1877).

47. In 1880 the Union internationale des amies de la jeune fille, founded earlier by the Fédération britannique et continentale, became the Union des amies de la jeune fille. The importance of the name change stemmed from a new service, providing intranational, as well as international, assistance to young female travelers. In France the Union had its headquarters at Lyon, with an 150-member branch at Paris. Paris hosted the Union's international congress in 1888. Under the direction of Mlle. Venet and M. and Mme. Siegfried, the Union secured permission to post its address in French train stations. *Bulletin de l'Union universelle des femmes* (April 1891).

48. The law forbidding women to wear pants was enacted on 9 Brumaire IX, and it remains on the books. Évelyne Sullerot, *La Presse féminine*, 102. For an interesting article on the corset controversy, see David Kunzle, "The Corset as Erotic Alchemy: From Rococo Galanterie to Montaut's Physiologies," in *Woman as Sex Object: Studies in Erotic Art, 1730-1970*, ed. Thomas B. Hess and Linda Nochlin (New York, 1972), 90-165.

49. D'Eaubonne, *Histoire et actualité du féminisme*, 102. In general in the nineteenth century, wrote John Demos, "the whole subject of sex was enveloped in a pervasive hush, which remained virtually unbroken until our own [twentieth] century.... Masturbation became *the* phobia of the times; to practice this secret sin was to risk intemperance, insanity and death.... For many women, of every status, the situation was more tortured still [than for men]. Recent research on the history of gynecology has uncovered a demand, in an astonishing number of cases, for the surgical procedure of clitoridectomy. Evidently this was the last resort of women who, contrary to expectation, found themselves afflicted with 'sensual' wishes." John Demos, "The American Family in Past Time," *American Scholar* 43 (Summer 1974), 437. A principal cause of female masturbation lay in youthful drinking, according to an 1886 report to the Société française de tempérance. If young girls drank, explained Dr. A.-J. Devoisins, two consequences would "almost inevitably" result: premature menstruation and *l'onanisme*. Marital drunkenness would also cause women to bear idiotic, epileptic, and hysterical infants. Women possessed a "marvelous" ability to adapt to their "natural destination," but the traumatic passage through puberty had to come at the proper moment without external stimuli: "It is perhaps at that epoch of life when the sensitivity of woman is the most strangely tormented in a contrary sense. It is also without doubt one of the stormiest periods of her existence. Her nervous system assumes attributes of the most accentuated susceptibility. Woman effects due to menstrual hemorrhage an excessive irritability; her imagination takes on an unusual activity, sometimes even disordered; her senses splinter; and, among subjects so predisposed, attacks of hysteria or epilepsy appear or recur. One also ascertains peculiar caprices, bizarre tastes, and changes in character, which grow into a disposition to melancholia, irascibility, hypochondria, etc." A[lbert] -J[oseph] Devoisins, *La Femme et l'alcoolisme* (Paris, 1885), 33-34.

50. From a review of Dr. Lion's *Hygiène des écoles* (1863) in the *Annales d'hygiène publique et de médecine légale* 33 (January 1865), cited in Karen M. Offen et al., eds., "The Female Experience: Victorian Heritage," 3 vols., MSS, Center for Research on Women at Stanford University (1978), part 3, document 42. Other documents from this collection have appeared under the title *Victorian Women: A Documentary Account of Women's Lives in Nineteenth-Century England, France, and the United States* (Stanford, California, 1981).

51. Edward Lewis, ed., *The French on Life and Love* (Kansas City, 1967), 39. The tendency of women to create distance between each other and to demean each other is characteristic of minority groups, according to Helen Hacker. As with racial and ethnic minorities, women tend to accept the dominant group's stereotyped conceptions, which result in "mea culpa" breastbeating, applying severe moral standards to other women, preferring to work under men, and finding the company of women repugnant. In short, "like those minority groups whose self-castigation outdoes dominant group derision of them, women frequently exceed men in the violence of their vituperations of their sex" Helen Meyer Hacker, "Women as a Minority Group," condensed in Nona Glazer-Malbin and Helen Youngelson Waehrer, eds., *Woman in a Man-Made World* (Chicago, 1972), 39-40.

52. Simone de Beauvoir, *The Second Sex*, trans. H. M. Parshley (New York, 1952), 122.

53. Marie Dronsart, "Le Mouvement féministe," *Le Correspondant* (10 October 1896), 116.

54. Jean Larnac, *Histoire de la littérature féminine en France* (Paris, 1929), 248.

55. Aldous Huxley, *Grey Eminence: A Study in Religion and Politics* (New York, 1941), 26. Bonald, *Législation primitive*.

56. Flaubert, *Dictionary of Accepted Ideas*, trans. Jacques Barzun (New York, 1954), 91. Évelyne Sullerot, *Histoire de la presse féminine en France, des origines à 1848* (Paris, 1966), 136.

57. George C. S. Adams, *Words and Descriptive Terms for "Woman" and "Girl" in French and Provençal and Border Dialects*. University of North Carolina Studies in the Romance Languages and Literatures, no. 11 (Chapel Hill, 1949). See also Pierre Guiraud, *Sémiologie de la sexualité* (Paris, 1978); and Marina Yaguello, *Les Mots et les femmes* (Paris, 1979).

58. S. C. Burchell, *Imperial Masquerade: The Paris of Napoleon III* (New York, 1971), 67-69. See also Theresa M. McBride, "A Woman's World: Department Stores and the Evolution of Women's Employment, 1870-1920," *French Historical Studies* 10, no. 4 (Fall 1978), 664-83; and Michael B. Miller, *The Bon Marché: Bourgeois Culture and the Department Store, 1869-1920* (Princeton, N.J., 1980).

59. Maurice Bardèche, *Histoire des femmes*, 2 vols. (Paris, 1968), 2: 314-29.

60. For the feminine/feminist press, see Évelyne Sullerot, *La Presse Féminine*, and *Histoire de la presse féminine en France, des origines à 1848* as well as Pamela Langlois, "The Feminine Press in England and France" (Ph.D. diss., University of Massachusetts, 1979). *La Fronde*'s initial run of 200,000 copies probably reflected an attempt to advertise the new venture rather than an indication of the number of subscribers.

61. Twenty-eight of the seventy-one feminine journals that appeared between 1800 and 1845 employed one or more of the following words in their titles: *mode, vogue, fashion, toilette, bon ton, miroir, boudoir, élégant, nouveauté, galant*. Sullerot, *Histoire de la presse féminine en France, des origines à 1848*, 217-18.

62. Sullerot, *La Presse féminine*, 22.

63. Sullerot, *Histoire de la presse féminine en France, des origines à 1848*, 189.

64. Ibid., 81-83, 117, 171-74.

65. For an insightful inquiry into the relationship of myth to sex-roles, see Elizabeth Janeway, *Man's World, Woman's Place* (New York, 1971).

66. Théodore Joran, *Le Suffrage des femmes* (Paris, 1914). In addition to *Le Suffrage des femmes*, Joran's works on feminism included *Le Mensonge du féminisme* (Paris, 1905); *Autour du féminisme* (Paris, 1906); *Le Féminisme à l'heure actuelle* (Paris, 1907); *Au coeur du feminisme* (Paris, 1908); *La Trouée féministe* (Paris, 1909); and *Les Féministes avant le féminisme*, 2 vols. (Paris, 1910, 1935). He also wrote the preface to Naera's [Anna Radius Zuccari] *Les Idées d'une femme sur le féminisme* (Paris, 1908). His nonfeminist works reflected an interest in language and education and included *Le Péril de la syntaxe et la crise de l'orthographe, recueil de locutions vicieuses, dressé par ordre alphabétique*, 6th ed. (Paris, 1916), and *Université et enseignement libre, deux systèmes d'éducation*, 2nd ed. (Paris, 1905). In a review of Joran's *Suffrage*, the Earl of Cromer agreed that even moderate feminists showed defects of character that would "render it undesirable that direct political power should be conferred on women." Like Joran, Cromer identified feminists with a trinity of "anarchism, collectivism, and anti-militarism," seeing in them a threat to family, religion, and morality. E. B. Cromer, "Feminism in France," *Living Age* 279 (6 December 1913), 589-93. Some of Joran's letters on feminism can be found in BMD, Dossier Misme. For feminist reaction to his opinions, see *L'Entente* (June 1906) and (February 1908); Léon Abensour, *Le Problème féministe: Un cas d'aspiration collective vers l'égalité* (Paris, 1927), 167-68; and *La Française* (29 November 1908).

67. Léon Abensour, *La Femme et le féminisme avant la révolution* (Paris, 1923), 374.

68. Charles Laurent, *Les Droits de la femme: Droits politiques* (Paris, 1888), 4.

69. Joran, *Les Féministes avant le féminisme*, 2:309.

70. Josephine E. Butler, *Personal Reminiscences of a Great Crusade* (London, 1896), 129.

71. Joran, *Les Féministes avant le féminisme*, 2:138.

72. For an analysis of the *pétroleuses*, see Thomas, *The Woman Incendiaries*.

73. Bishop Dupanloup (of Orleans), *Les Alarmes de l'épiscopat justifiées par les faits. Lettre à un cardinal par Mgr. l'évêque d'Orléans* (Paris, 1868).

74. Larnac, *Histoire de la littérature féminine en France*, 34-35.

75. Jules Barbey d'Aurevilly, *Les Bas-Blues* (Paris, 1878), xxiii.

76. Sullerot, *Histoire de la presse féminine en France, des origines à 1848*, 152.

77. Jane Misme, "La Vie et la mort du féminisme," BMD, 26.

78. Jean Jacques Rousseau, *Émile* (1762), cited in Sullerot, *Histoire de la presse féminine en France, des origines à 1848*, 16.

79. Abensour, *La Femme et le féminisme avant la révolution*, 426-28.

80. Jeanne Bouvier, *Les Femmes pendant la révolution* (Paris, 1931), 283-89.

81. Sullerot, *Histoire de la presse féminine en France, des origines à 1848*, 63-64.

82. Ibid., 64.

83. Ibid., 65.

84. Ibid., 50.

85. Ibid., 66.

86. *La Citoyenne* (2 July-6 August 1882).

87. France, Chambre des Députés, *Journal officiel* (2 February 1891), 185.

88. Philippe Ariès, *Centuries of Childhood: A Social History of Family Life*, trans. Robert Baldick (New York, 1960), 364.

89. Ibid.

90. Ibid., 406.

91. Ibid.

92. Ibid., 407.

93. For an interesting interpretation of Ariès's thesis, see Shulamith Firestone, *The Dialectic of Sex: The Case for Feminist Revolution* (New York, 1970), 72-104. For a comparison of Ariès to Eric Erikson, see David Hunt, *Parents and Children in History: The Psychology of Family Life in Early Modern France* (New York, 1970).

94. Ariès, *Centuries of Childhood*, 414-15.

95. Frédéric Le Play, *L'Organisation de la famille selon le vrai modèle signalé par l'histoire de toutes les races et de tous les temps* (Paris, 1874), xvi.

96. Philippe Ariès, "L'Évolution des rôles parentaux," in *Familles d'aujourd'hui* (Brussels, 1968), 45.

97. Ariès, *Centuries of Childhood*, 365, 403-4, 412-13.

98. Ariès stopped short of making this connection. "What Ariès fails to grasp, then, is that the phenomenon he is witnessing comes more from a changing conception of manhood than from a developing view of childhood," according to the thoughtful criticism of Hilda Smith, "Feminism and the Methodology of Women's History," in *Liberating Women's History*, ed. Berenice A. Carroll (Chicago, 1976), 381.

99. Margaret H. Darrow, "French Noblewomen and the New Domesticity, 1750-1850" *Feminist Studies* 5, no. 1 (Spring 1979), 53.

100. Ariès, "L'Évolution des rôles parentaux," 53. Sullerot, *Histoire et sociologie*, 78-83.

101. Barbara Corrado Pope, "Maternal Education in France, 1815-1848," *Proceedings of the Third Annual Meeting of the Western Society for French History* 3 (4-6 December 1975), 368-77.

102. Sullerot, *Woman, Society and Change*, 63.

103. Sullerot, *Histoire de la presse féminine en France, des origines à 1848*, 66.

104. *Women's Position in the Laws of Nations*, 98.

105. D'Eaubonne, *Histoire et actualité du féminisme*. Libussa Slavenko first used the word *phallocrate* in an article for Auclert's *La Citoyenne* of 25 December 1881, according to Jean Rabaut, *Histoire des féminismes français* (Paris, 1978), 176.

CHAPTER 2. CONSCIOUSNESS AND CONTRADICTIONS: ROOTS AND ROUTES OF FEMINIST AWARENESS

1. Sheila Rowbotham, *Women, Resistance and Revolution* (New York, 1972), 39.

2. Joan Cassell, *A Group Called Women: Sisterhood and Symbolism in the Feminist Movement* (New York, 1977), 18-19.

3. Évelyne Sullerot, *Woman, Society and Change*, trans. Margaret Scotford Archer (New York, 1971), 19.

4. Rowbotham, *Women, Resistance and Revolution*, 39.

5. *La Citoyenne* (December 1887).

6. Ibid. (5 June-2 July 1882).

7. Camille Belilon, *La Fronde* (March 1898).

8. F. W. J. Hemmings, *Culture and Society in France 1848-1898: Dissidents and Philistines* (New York, 1971), 51-67. Évelyne Sullerot, *Histoire de la presse féminine en France, des origines à 1848* (Paris, 1966), 124-26.

9. Claire Goldberg Moses, "The Evolution of Feminist Thought in France, 1829-1889" (Ph.D. diss., George Washington University, 1978), 228.

10. *La Citoyenne* (May 1890).

11. See the section in this chapter on "The Revival of Literary Feminism: Lamber and d'Héricourt."

12. Elisabeth Anne Weston, "Prostitution in Paris in the Later Nineteenth Century" (Ph.D. diss., State University of New York at Buffalo, 1979).

13. Steven C. Hause, "The Failure of Feminism in Provincial France, 1890-1920" (Unpublished paper presented to the Western Society for French History, Eugene, Oregon, October, 1980), 1.

14. Weston, "Prostitution in Paris," 134. Weston estimated that in the 1880s 2 percent of the population of Paris annually underwent treatment for venereal disease.

15. Hause, "The Failure of Feminism in Provincial France," 2.

16. For instances of maimings and murders, see Madame Anne Levinck, *Les Femmes qui ne tuent ni ne votent*, 3rd ed. (Paris, 1881), 13-15. Although estimates vary, the abortion rate in nineteenth- and twentieth-century France was certainly high. Doctor André Cauchois calculated that there was one abortion for every live birth. *Démographie de la Seine Inférieure* (Rouen, 1929), 248, cited in Wesley D. Camp, *Marriage and the Family in France Since the Revolution: An Essay in the History of Population* (New York, 1961), 113. Simone de Beauvoir estimated: "In France abortions number each year from 800,000 to 1,000,000—about as many as there are births—two-thirds of those aborted being married women, many already having one or two children." Simone de Beauvoir, *The Second Sex*, trans. H. M. Parshley (New York, 1952), 135.

17. *La Citoyenne* (September 1885).

18. Ibid. (February 1884).

19. *La Fronde* (30 December 1899), (10-12 January 1900).

20. *Le Droit des femmes* (7 September 1890). *Journal des femmes* (December 1897). *La Fronde* (28 November 1898). When the French parliament opened the École Nationale des Beaux-Arts to women in 1897, the school's administration attempted to circumvent the reform by setting up auxiliary courses for women. Males protested nonetheless, causing a month-long closing of the school. With the school's reopening, women secured full student status, but of the 180 who applied for the year 1897-1898, only two were admitted. Three women attended in 1898-1899. *Almanach féministe 1899* (Paris, 1899), 52-53.

21. *Journal des femmes* (December 1899). Perhaps the delegation should have been forewarned. The month before, in November 1899, Millerand had instituted a new pay scale at the Ministry of Posts and Telegraphs, starting women at 1,000 francs per year with a top salary of 2,300—less than men at both ends of the scale. *La Fronde* (3 November 1899).

22. George Guéroult, *Du rôle de la femme dans notre rénovation sociale* (Caen, 1891), 7-8. Guéroult's reliance on Bishop Fénelon (1651-1715) as a guide for women's education under the Third Republic reflected the belief that the family constituted the basis of society and that women represented the basis of the family. With that belief in mind, Fénelon inspired Madame de Maintenon (1635-1719) to establish the first lay school for girls in France at Saint-Cyr. Through the instruction provided there, Fénelon hoped to steer

women away from frivolity, which he identified with the French court and which led de Maintenon to reduce reading materials to an absolute minimum, and to revive the middle ranks of the nobility by training women to become "professional" wives, mothers, and estate managers. Fénelon distrusted women, but he recognized their potential as a collective force for social transformation. Leaders of the Third Republic also recognized that potential, and, as a result, despite the shift from aristocratic to bourgeois values, they ascribed to women a similarly limited but exalted role. Thus, although the Third Republic's education reforms affected many more women than Fénelon's, the effect was roughly the same: to control women and to employ them as a force for social change rather than to permit women to develop their individual talents. See Carolyn C. Lougee, *Le Paradis des Femmes: Women, Salons, and Social Stratification in Seventeenth-Century France* (Princeton, N.J., 1976), 173–214, as well as Lougee, "The Impact of Fénelon and Madame de Maintenon: Education of Women for Domestic Fulfillment in the Late Seventeenth Century," and Karen M. Offen, "French Feminists Challenge the Third Republic's Public Education for Girls: The Campaign for Equal Access to the Baccalaureate, 1880–1924" (Papers read at the annual American Historical Association Convention in December 1973); Madame Pauline Rebour "L'Éducation civique des femmes," *Bulletin 1914–1916* (Union française pour le suffrage des femmes), 72–77; François de Salignac de La Mothe-Fénelon, *Éducation des filles* (Paris, 1687); and Jean Larnac, *Histoire de la littérature féminine en France* (Paris, 1929), 95–100.

23. *La Citoyenne* (April 1881).

24. "Woman creates luxury, luxury creates industry, industry transforms man....The proscription of luxury! but that is suicide for France, and not only for economic France, but also for artistic France. Our workers would have to emigrate, and our artists throw themselves into the Seine with heavy stones round their necks." Olympe Audouard, *Le Luxe des femmes; réponse d'une femme à M. la procureur général Dupin* (Paris, 1865), 26–27.

25. Olympe Audouard, *Le Luxe effréné des hommes, discours tenu dans un comité de femmes,* (Paris, 1865), 5–7.

26. Olympe Audouard, *À travers mes souvenirs,* cited in Jean Rabaut, *Histoire des féminismes français* (Paris, 1978), 148.

27. Olympe Audouard, *Guerre aux hommes* (Paris, 1866), 57.

28. Olympe Audouard, *Lettre aux députés* (Paris, 1867). See also Baron Marc de Villiers, *Histoire des clubs de femmes et des légions d'Amazons 1793–1848–1871* (Paris, 1910), 381–82. Léon Abensour, *Histoire génerale du féminisme* (Paris, 1921), 267.

29. On Michelet and Proudhon, see in particular Moses, "The Evolution of Feminist Thought in France," 176–93; for all three, see Rabaut, *Histoire des féminismes français,* 142–45.

30. Pierre-Joseph Proudhon, *De la justice dans la révolution et dans l'église,* 3 vols. (Paris, 1858), 3: 375, cited in Charles Thiébaux, *Le Féminisme et les socialistes depuis Saint-Simon jusqu'à nos jours* (Paris, 1906), 88, 91–93.

31. Proudhon, *De la justice,* 3: 380, cited in Thiébaux, *Le Féminisme et les socialistes,* 95.

32. Stewart Edwards, ed., *Selected Writings of Pierre-Joseph Proudhon,* trans. Elizabeth Fraser (New York, 1969), 256.

33. Proudhon, *Qu'est-ce que la propriété?* (Paris, 1966), 274–75, originally published in 1840. Cited in Moses, "The Evolution of Feminist Thought in France," 185.

34. Pierre-Joseph Proudhon, *La Pornocratie ou les femmes dans les temps modernes* (Paris, n.d.), 463. Cited in Rabaut, *Histoire des féminismes français*, 143.

35. Article by Proudhon in *Le Représentant du peuple* (31 May 1848), reprinted in Edouard Dolléans, *Proudhon* (Paris, 1948), 167. Cited in Moses, "The Evolution of Feminist Thought in France," 184.

36. Reported in Juliette Lamber, *Idées anti-proudhoniennes sur l'amour, la femme, et le mariage*, 2nd ed. (Paris, 1861), 12.

37. Cited in Rabaut, *Histoire des féminismes français*, 145–46.

38. For two years Lamber had been working on a similar study, according to Saad Morcos, *Juliette Adam* (Dar Al-Maaref, Lebanon, 1962), cited in Moses, "The Evolution of Feminist Thought in France," 209. Family pressure drove Lamber into an early and unsatisfactory marriage with Alexis La Messine. With divorce unavailable, she attempted to disguise the second edition of *Idées anti-proudhoniennes* under the name of "J. Lambert" to protect its royalties from seizure and to arrange a legal separation. After lengthy negotiations, her husband, who exercised control over her property and royalties, agreed to settle for 15,000 francs. His death in 1867, on the eve of the formal agreement, ended the dispute and led Lamber to record that day as one of the happiest of her life. A year later she married Edmond Adam. Juliette Lamber, *Mes sentiments et mes idées avant 1870*, 6th ed. (Paris, 1895), 131–34.

39. Lamber, *Idées anti-proudhoniennes*, 13.

40. Ibid., 41–42.

41. *Le Droit des femmes* (6 September 1885).

42. Cited in Winifred Stephens, *Madame Adam (Juliette Lamber). La Grande Française: From Louis Philippe until 1917* (New York, 1917), 60–61.

43. Lamber, *Idées anti-proudhoniennes*, 132, cited in Moses, "The Evolution of Feminist Thought in France," 214. For Moses' interpretation of Lamber's views, with a different emphasis than the above, see pages 207–15.

44. Cited in Stephens, *Madame Adam*, 59.

45. Jenny d'Héricourt, *La Femme affranchie*, 2 vols. (Brussels, 1860). The Second Empire's censors initially banned *La Femme affranchie*, but the emperor lifted the ban after he received a personal appeal from d'Héricourt. The quotations are taken from the English edition: Madame d'Héricourt, *A Woman's Philosophy of Woman: or Woman Affranchised. An Answer to Michelet, Proudhon, Girardin, Legouvé, and Other Modern Innovators* (New York, 1864), 33.

46. D'Héricourt, *A Woman's Philosophy of Woman*, ix–x.

47. Ibid., 17, 20. "Woman, *according to Michelet*, is a being of a nature opposite to that of man," wrote d'Héricourt, "a creature weak, *always wounded, exceedingly barometrical*, and consequently, unfit for labor. . . . *Created for man*, she is the altar of his heart, his refreshment, his consolation" (p. 17). D'Héricourt's references were to Jules Michelet's *La Femme* (Paris, 1860) and *L'Amour* (Paris, 1858).

48. D'Héricourt, *A Woman's Philosophy of Woman*, 202–3.

49. Ibid., 203.

50. D'Héricourt, *La Femme affranchie*, 1: 89–90, 2: 209. Cited in Moses, "The Evolution of Feminist Thought in France," 220–22. For Moses' account of d'Héricourt, see pp. 215–25.

51. D'Héricourt, *A Woman's Philosophy of Woman*, vii. The unidentified author of the

introduction to the English translation wrote: "This remarkable book of Madame d'Héricourt on woman is conceded to be the best reply to these philosophers extant." This tribute may have stemmed solely from prior awareness. Without mention of Lamber, contemporary American feminists had earlier recorded: "A very curious controversy, on paper, is going on at present in the *Revue Philosophique et Religieuse*, between M. Proudhon and Mme. Jenny d'Héricourt. The latter defends, with great warmth, the moral, civil, and political emancipation of woman. Proudhon, in reply, declares that all the theories of Mme. d'Héricourt are inapplicable, in consequence of the inherent weakness of her sex. The periodical in which the contest is going on was founded and is conducted by the old St. Simoniens." Elizabeth Cady Stanton et al., *History of Woman Suffrage*, 6 vols. (New York, 1969), 1: 870.

52. Abensour, *Histoire générale du féminisme*, 266.

53. Jane Misme, "Les Grandes Figures du féminisme: Madame Adam," *Minerva* (1 February 1931). See also Stephens, *Madam Adam*; Joseph O. Baylen, "Mme. Juliette Adam, Gambetta, and the Idea of a Franco–Prussian Alliance," *Social Studies No. 4* (Stillwater, Okla.) 57, no. 15 (20 May 1960); and Helene Brion, ed., "Encyclopédie féministe," BMD, vol. 1. For Adam's attitude toward feminism (in English), see the reprint of her *Humanitarian* article of February 1897 that appeared as "Position of Women in France," *Review of Reviews* 15 (April 1897), 480.

54. Stephens, *Madame Adam*, 22, 48.

55. Jeanne E. Schmahl, "Progress of the Women's Rights Movement in France," *Forum* 22 (September 1896), 79–92.

56. Cited in Edith Thomas, *The Woman Incendiaries*, trans. James and Starr Atkinson (New York, 1966), 24–25.

57. *Le Droit des femmes* (5 January 1889).

58. Sullerot, *Histoire de la presse féminine en France, des origines à 1848*, 144. On the relationship of utopian socialism to feminism and women, see C. Bouglé, *Chez les prophètes socialistes* (Paris, 1918), 51–110; Edith Thomas, *Pauline Roland. Socialisme et féminisme aux XIXe siècle* (Paris, 1956); Marguerite Thibert, *Le Féminisme dans le socialisme français de 1830 à 1850* (Paris, 1926); É. Dessignolle, *Le Féminisme d'après la doctrine socialiste de Charles Fourier* (Lyon, 1903); Frank E. Manuel, *The Prophets of Paris* (New York, 1962), 53–248; Thiébaux, *Le Féminisme et les socialistes*; Abensour, *Histoire générale du féminisme*, 205–14. See also *Le Devoir*, journal of the Familistère de Guise, and *La Rénovation*, journal of the École sociétaire phalanstérienne. The most recent and fullest treatment is by Claire Goldberg Moses, "The Evolution of Feminist Thought in France, 1829–1899," a Ph.D. dissertation currently being revised for publication by the State University of New York Press, forthcoming 1982.

59. Sullerot, *Histoire de la presse féminine en France*, 153–63.

60. Étienne Cabet, *Réalisation d'Icarie* (Paris, 1846), 122, cited in Thiébaux, *Le Féminisme et les socialistes*, 73. See also Christopher H. Johnson, *Utopian Communism in France: Cabet and the Icarians, 1839–1851* (Ithaca, N.Y., 1974).

61. C. Bouglé and Élie Halévy, eds., *Doctrine de Saint-Simon. Exposition, première année, 1829* (Paris, 1924), 164. Cited in Manuel, *The Prophets of Paris*, 172.

62. *Procès en la cour d'assises de la Seine, les 27 et 28 août, 1832* (Paris, 1832), 210–17, 221. Cited in Manuel, *The Prophets of Paris*, 187–88.

63. "The word upheaval is always associated with a blind and brutal force having as its goal destruction. . . . This doctrine [of Saint-Simon] does not itself possess or recognize for the direction of men any other power but that of persuasion and conviction." *Doctrine de Saint-Simon*, 278–79. Cited in Manuel, *The Prophets of Paris*, 181.

64. *Oeuvres complètes de Saint-Simon et d'Enfantin publiées par les membres du Conseil institué par Enfantin, pour l'exécution de ses dernières volontés*, 42 vols. (Paris, 1865–1876), 14: 39. Cited in Thiébaux, *Le Féminisme et les socialistes*, 18.

65. François Marie Charles Fourier, *Théorie des quatre mouvements et des destinées générales*, 2nd ed. (Paris, 1841), 225. Cited in Thiébaux, *Le Féminisme et les socialistes*, 49.

66. Pierre Leroux, *De l'égalité, suivi d'aphorisme sur la doctrine de l'humanité* (Boussac, 1848), 46. Cited in Thiébaux, *Le Féminisme et les socialistes*, 39–40.

67. Cited in Thiébaux, *Le Féminisme et les socialistes*, 42.

68. Fourier, *Théorie des quatre mouvements*, cited in Thiébaux, *Le Féminisme et les socialistes*, 58.

69. Sullerot, *Histoire de la presse féminine en France, des origines à 1848*, 160.

70. *Oeuvres complètes de Saint-Simon et d'Enfantin*, 27: 191, cited in Thiébaux, *Le Féminisme et les socialistes*, 25.

71. Abel Transon, *Religion Saint-simonienne. Affranchissement des femmes, prédication du 1er janvier 1832* (Paris, 1832). Cited in Frank E. Manuel and Fritzie P. Manuel, eds., *French Utopias* (New York, 1966), 294. Christian patience collapsed sooner than Christian principles. The imprisonment of Enfantin in 1832 for outrages against public morality decapitated Saint-Simonianism and brought about the dispersal of its disciples, some of whom embarked for Egypt in search of a "female messiah."

72. Misme, "La Vie et la mort du féminisme," 26.

73. Rowbotham, *Women, Resistance and Revolution*, 52.

74. Utopian influence declined during the movement's second generation, but many of the older, first-generation feminists remained heavily indebted to it. Consequently, they tended to share opinions like Adolphe Alhaiza's, whose *De phalanstérien à socialiste* (Paris, 1900) branded class-struggle socialists as money-hungry, traitorous politicians. With Dr. E. Verrier, who wrote *Le Meilleur des socialismes pratiques: le socialisme phalanstérien* (Toulouse, 1905), they subscribed to the *methode sociétaire*, the principles of Fourier, and the practice of the Familistère de Guise. To first-generation feminists, as to Verrier, the socialism of Guesde and Jaurès represented a "return to primitive barbarism" and "the annihilation of all social life."

75. Sullerot, *Histoire de la presse féminine et France, des origines à 1848*, 186–87.

76. Ibid., 151–52, 186. Deroin's "utopian" perspective on the woman question can be seen in a statement she made in 1848: "Woman, still slave, remains veiled and in silence. She has lost the memory of her divine origin, she is unable to understand her noble social mission, she has neither name nor country, she is banished from the sanctuary, she seems to have accepted shameful servitude. Held down by man's yoke, she has not even the aspirations toward liberty, man must liberate her." Jeanne Deroin, *Cours de droit social pour les femmes* (Paris, 1848), 6. Cited in Rowbotham, *Woman, Resistance and Revolution*, 53.

77. Thomas, *The Woman Incendiaries*, 9–11. Bernard Noël, *Dictionnaire de la Commune* (Paris, 1971), 103, 234–35, 347–48.

78. As with Deroin, Tristan too eventually shifted to the position that men should liberate women. On Tristan, see in particular Moses, "The Evolution of Feminist Thought in France," 136–49.

79. Manuel, *The Prophets of Paris*, 191.

80. *Le Journal des femmes* (January 1899). *La Fronde*, (11 December 1894). BMD, Dossier Griess-Traut.

81. Jean-Baptiste-André Godin (1817–1888) made a fortune through developing new smelting processes. Influenced by the ideas of Saint-Simon, Robert Owen, Cabet, Fourier, and Considérant (whose abortive utopian experiment in Texas cost Godin a third of his wealth), and despite the opposition of the Second Empire (which stripped him of his patents for espousing radical notions), Godin created the Familistère de Guise between 1859 and 1865. The Société du familistère de guise secured legal recognition on 13 August 1880, as a cooperative association capitalized at 4.6 million francs. Its journal, *Le Devoir*, first appeared in 1878. Between the period 1879–1880 and 1898–1899, the Familistère de Guise and its branch at Schaerbeek served approximately 1,500 to 2,000 people each year. Louis Lestelle, *Étude sur le Familistère de Guise* (Paris, 1904). See also Fernand Duval, *J.-B.-A. Godin et le Familistère de Guise* (Law thesis, University of Lille, 1905); Verrier, *Le Meilleur des socialismes pratiques*, 9; *Bulletin de l'Union universelle des femmes* (15 April 1890); and Godin's works listed in the *Catalogue général des livres imprimés de la bibliothèque nationale*, vol. 61 (Paris, 1924), 662–64.

82. Maria Deraismes, *France et progrès* (Paris, 1873), cited in *Oeuvres complètes de Maria Deraismes*, ed. Anna Féresse-Deraismes (Paris, 1895), 183, 185–86.

83. Paul Gide and Adhémar Esmein, *Étude sur la condition privée de la femme dans le droit ancien et moderne* (Paris, 1867), 7, cited in Thiébaux, *Le Féminisme et les socialistes*, 47.

84. Fourier, *Théorie des quatres mouvements*, 43, cited in Rowbotham, *Women, Resistance and Revolution*, 52.

85. Fourier, *Théorie des quatres mouvements*, 195, cited in Thiébaux, *Le Féminisme et les socialistes*, 47.

86. Cited in an article by Elisabeth Renaud that originally appeared in the *Rappel*: "Glimpse of the Feminist Movement in France," *Review of Reviews* 44 (September 1911), 355.

87. Roger Henry Soltau, *French Political Thought in the 19th Century* (New York, 1959), 95.

88. Ibid., 95–96.

89. In the course of transforming the Second Republic into the Second Empire, Louis Napoleon initiated a reign of repression that resulted in 27,000 arrests, 1,500 expulsions, and 9,800 deportations (9,500 to Algeria and 300 to Guiana). Paul A. Gagnon, *France Since 1789* (New York, 1964), 163.

90. Michelet, *La Femme*, 34.

91. Paul Granotier, *L'Autorité du mari sur la personne de la femme et la doctrine féministe* (Law thesis, University of Grenoble, 1909), 37. See also Misme, "La Vie et la mort du féminisme," 32; and Hubertine Auclert, *Le Vote des femmes* (Paris, 1908), 100–1.

92. For information on Deraismes and Richer, see Chapter 3.

93. For selected bibliographical information on corsets, vivisection, temperance, vegetarianism, positivism, and spiritualism, see the author's "The Feminist Movement in France:

The Formative Years, 1858–1889'' (Ph.D. diss., Michigan State University, 1975), 96–99.

94. Léon Richer, *Le Divorce, projet de loi précédé d'un exposé des motifs et suivi des principaux documents officiels se rattachant à la question, avec une lettre-préface par Louis Blanc* (Paris, 1873).

95. Hubertine Auclert, *Le Nom de la femme* (Paris, 1905).

96. *La Citoyenne*, 1881.

97. The prevalence of Biblical imagery in feminist writings can be seen in the titles of Maria Deraismes's two principal works: *Ève contre Monsieur Dumas fils* (Paris, 1872), and *Ève dans humanité* (Paris, 1891). Audouard mockingly reversed the standard "rib" interpretation by arguing that what came last was best. As humans were superior to mollusks, so women were superior to men, because "the divine creator wanted to finish the act of creation with the most perfect, most complete creature." *Guerre aux Hommes*, 19.

98. Léon Richer, *Lettres d'un libre-penseur à un curé de village, précédé d'une introduction par M. Ad. Guéroult*, 2 vols. (Paris, 1868–1869). For an example of Richer's continuing interest in "priest baiting," once feminism became his primary pursuit, see the report he published on Abbé Baque, a young priest who seduced a parishioner. The girl in question received five years' imprisonment at hard labor for infanticide; Baque received a transfer. *Le Droit des femmes* (4 September 1887).

99. Gagnon, *France Since 1789*, 235.

100. Charles Lemonnier, *Élisa Lemonnier, fondatrice de la Société pour l'enseignement professionel des femmes* (Saint-Germain, 1866). For a later assessment of professional education for girls in France, see Clémence Royer, "L'Enseignement professionel en France," *La Société Nouvelle* 10 (1889), 306–29.

101. Michel Tricot, *De l'instruction publique à l'éducation permanente* (Paris, 1973), 29. A Comité des dames de la Ligue de l'enseignement included Madame Jules Ferry, Paul Bert, and Ferdinand Buisson. Louli Sanua, *Figures féminines 1909–1939* (Paris, 1949), 69.

102. Tricot, *De l'instruction publique*, 28.

103. Edmond Potonié-Pierre, *Historique du mouvement pacifique* (Berne, 1899), 83–89.

104. Jules Tixerant, "Le Mouvement féministe sous le Second Empire," *Ligue française pour le droit des femmes. Bulletin trimestriel* (April 1911), 3.

105. On Émile de Girardin as a feminist, see Moses, "The Evolution of Feminist Thought in France," 199–206.

106. Potonié-Pierre, *Historique du mouvement pacifique*, 88.

107. France, Ministry of the Interior, AN F[7] 13266, "La Campagne féministe en faveur de la paix" (1915).

108. See in particular Weston, "Prostitution in Paris." Weston characterized the system as follows: "The state regulation of prostitution entails the seeking out, registration and regular medical inspection of prostitutes by police or medical authorities. It implies legal toleration of prostitution, in that prostitutes are not prosecuted for the act of prostitution but rather for infractions of the rules to which they are subjected by the police or medical authorities. It is ultimately a matter of administrative rather than criminal law" (p. 20).

109. Potonié-Pierre, *Historique du mouvement pacifique*, 88. See also Arthur C. F. Beales, who cites 1867 as the year in which Santallier founded his Peace Union, *The History of Peace: A Short Account of the Organised Movements for International Peace* (New York, 1931), 120.

110. Tricot, *De l'instruction publique*, 25.

111. Marianne Monestier, *Les Sociétés secrètes féminines* (Paris, 1963), 129. See also Éliane Brault, *La Franc-Maçonnerie et l'émancipation des femmes* (Paris, 1953); Gaston Martin, *Manuel d'histoire de la franc-maçonnerie française* (Paris, 1929); Jacques Mitterand, *La Politique des Francs-Maçons* (Paris, 1973); Charles Laurent, *Les Droits de la femme: Droits politiques* (Paris, 1888); Docteur Henri Fischer, *Le Rôle de la femme, conférence faite à la loge "le Lien des peuples"* (Brussels, 1904); Robert Freke Gould et al., eds., *A Library of Freemasonry*, vol. 3 (London, 1906), 391–449; Gérard Serbanesco, *Histoire de la franc-maçonnerie universelle*, vol. 4 (Paris, 1969), 523–56. For a hostile opinion, see J. Tourmentin, *La Femme chez les francs-maçons d'après les derniers convents du G. ˙ . O. ˙ .* (Paris, 1902).

112. Mildred J. Headings, *French Freemasonry Under the Third Republic*, John Hopkins University Studies in Historical and Political Science, vol. 66 (Baltimore, 1949), 79–80.

113. In the cabinet of 2 February 1879, for example, six out of ten ministers were Protestants. Prominent Protestant politicians included Waddington, Freycinet, Léon Say, Le Royer, Eugène Pelletan, Nefftzer, Réville, Jauréguiberry, and Paul Bert. Jules Ferry married a Protestant in a civil ceremony. A prominent Protestant feminist and educator, Ferdinand Buisson felt that free thinking and Protestantism had much in common inasmuch as both beliefs emphasized a positivist approach to free examination and opposed reliance on dogmas, miracles, and priests. Evelyn Martha Acomb, *The French Laic Laws (1879–1889)* (New York, 1967), 54–58.

114. Tixerant, "Le Mouvement féministe sous le Second Empire," 2.

115. Barbara Corrado Pope, "Maternal Education in France, 1815–1848," *Proceedings of the Third Annual Meeting of the Western Society for French History* 3 (4–6 December 1975), 368–69.

116. Karen M. Offen, "The Male Feminist Phenomenon in Mid-Nineteenth Century France: The Case of Ernest Legouvé (1807–1903)" (Paper prepared for the Third Berkshire Conference on the History of Women, 9–11 June 1976), 1–5.

117. Ernest Legouvé, *La Femme en France au dix-neuvième siècle* (Paris, 1864). Paul Thouzery, *La Femme au XIXe siècle: Ce qu'elle est. Ce qu'elle doit être* (Paris, 1866). Eugène Pelletan, *La Femme au XIXe siècle* (Paris, 1869). *Catalogue des thèses et écrits académiques: Année scolaire 1884–85, 1894–95, 1904–05* (Paris, 1885, 1895, 1905).

118. BMD, Dossier Durand. See also Sue Helder Goliber, "The Life and Times of Marguerite Durand (Ph.D. diss., Kent State University, 1975).

119. BMD, Dossier Bogelot.

120. Lula McDowell Richardson, *The Forerunners of Feminism in French Literature of the Renaissance from Christine de Pisan to Marie de Gournay*, Johns Hopkins Studies in Romance Literatures and Languages, vol. 12 (Baltimore, 1929). Larnac, *Histoire de la littérature féminine en France*.

121. Beauvoir, *The Second Sex*, 120.

122. Abensour, *La Femme et le féminisme avant la révolution*.

123. For the complete text of Olympe de Gouges's *Déclaration des droits de la femme et de citoyenne*, see Bouvier, *Les Femmes pendant la révolution*, 283–89. Lydie Martial cited an advocate of woman's emancipation who expressed the typical feminist impression

of Joan of Arc: "A woman, Joan of Arc, has certainly saved France, feminism can certainly save society." Lydie Martial, *La Femme intégrale* (Paris, 1901), 40.

124. Mary Wollstonecraft, *A Vindication of the Rights of Woman with Strictures on Political and Moral Subjects* (London, 1792). John Stuart Mill, *"The Subjection of Women"* (London, 1869), in *Essays on Sex Equality, John Stuart Mill and Harriet Taylor Mill*, ed. Alice S. Rossi (Chicago, 1970), 125–242. August Bebel, *Woman Under Socialism*, trans. Daniel de Leon from original German of 33rd ed. (New York, 1971). For a feminist reaction to Bebel's work, see Eugénie Potonié-Pierre's three-part review in *La Citoyenne* (5 July 1891), (19 July 1891), and (2 August 1891). Although Wollstonecraft's *Vindication* is perhaps the best known of the late eighteenth-century works on women, Mélanie Lipinska considered Theodor Gottlieb Hippel's *Uber die bürgerliche Verbesserung der Weiber* (1792) to be the best contemporary examination of the subject. Mélanie Lipinska, *Histoire des femmes médecines depuis antiquité jusqu'à nos jours* (Paris, 1900), 291.

125. Miriam Schneir, ed., *Feminism: The Essential Historical Writings* (New York, 1972). For the complete text of this communication, see Stanton et al., *History of Woman Suffrage*, 1: 234–37.

126. Olympe Audouard, *À travers l'Amérique, le Far-West* (Paris, 1869), and *À travers l'Amérique. North America. États-Unis. Constitution, moeurs, usages, lois, institutions, sectes religieuses* (Paris, 1871). Élie Reclus, "Études sociologiques: Visite aux perfectionnistes d'Oneida," and "Études sociologiques: Visite aux Shakers du Mount Libanon," *La Société nouvelle* 3 (1885–1886), 5–29, 45–71. Americans acquired an impression of the French situation through the works of French feminists, like André Léo's *The American Colony in Paris in 1867* (Boston, 1868), and the works of Americans in France, like Theodore Stanton's chapter on "France" in his edited collection *The Woman Question in Europe* (New York, 1884). Stanton conveyed this picture of feminism in France: "For the moment, the woman question in Europe is pushed into the background by the all-absorbing struggle still going on in various forms between the republican and the monarchical principle, between the vital present and the moribund past.... During the second empire, in spite of the oppressive nature of the government, the movement took on a more definite form; its advocates became more numerous; and men and women who held high places in literature, politics and journalism, spoke out plainly in favor of ameliorating the condition of French women. Then came the third republic, with more freedom than France had enjoyed since the beginning of the century. The woman movement felt the change, and, during the past ten years, its friends have been more active than ever before." Stanton, et al., *History of Woman Suffrage* 3: 895–96. Considerably less accurate was the selection of Alexandre Dumas *fils* and Victor Hugo as the only two French "Eminent Advocates of Woman Suffrage." Stanton et al., *History of Woman Suffrage*, 4: 1084.

127. Elizabeth Cady Stanton, *Eighty Years and More: Reminiscences 1815–1897* (1898; reprint ed., New York, 1971), 177.

128. Ibid., 400. In a letter dated 26 March 1889, Maria Deraismes personally invited her "eminent *Conseour*," Elizabeth Cady Stanton, to attend the second French Congress for Women's Rights. Library of Congress. Manuscript Division. Papers of Elizabeth Cady Stanton: General Correspondence 1885–1889.

129. BMD, Dossier Griess-Traut. *Le Journal des femmes* (January 1889). *La Fronde* (11 December 1898). *Le Droit des femmes* (3 February 1889). *Le Devoir* (Familistère de Guise) (28 September 1879), (15 August 1880), (29 August 1880), (8 May 1881), (29 May 1881), (26 November 1882), (12 April 1885), (26 April 1885).

130. *Le Devoir* (Familistère de Guise) (26 November 1882).

131. Ibid. (28 September 1879).

132. *La Fronde* (11 December 1898).

133. Beauvoir, *The Second Sex*, 114.

134. Margaret H. Darrow, "French Noblewomen and the New Domesticity, 1750-1850," *Feminist Studies* 5, no. 1 (Spring 1979), 48.

135. Hilda Smith, "Feminism and the Methodology of Women's History," in *Liberating Women's History*, ed. Berenice A. Carroll (Chicago, 1976), 382.

136. William L. O'Neill, *The Woman Question: Feminism in the United States and England* (Chicago, 1969), 17.

CHAPTER 3. CRISIS AND COOPERATION: MARIA DERAISMES, LÉON RICHER, THE STRATEGY OF *LA BRÈCHE*, AND THE CONGRESS OF 1878

1. For information on and references to the life of Maria Deraismes, see Dossier Deraismes at the Bibliothèque Marguerite Durand; Léon Abensour, *Histoire générale du féminisme: Des origines à nos jours* (Paris, 1921), 269-71; Éliane Brault, *La Franc-Maçonnerie et l'émancipation des femmes* (Paris, 1953), 62-126; Louli Sanua, *Figures féminines 1909-1939* (Paris, 1949), 127-28; Suzanne Grinberg, *Historique du mouvement suffragiste depuis 1848* (Paris, 1926), 59-73; Zhenia Avril de Sainte-Croix, *Le Féminisme* (Paris, 1907), 85-86; Li Dzeh-Djen, *La Presse féministe en France de 1869 à 1914* (Paris, 1934), 23-27; Theodore Zeldin, ed., *Conflicts in French Society: Anticlericalism, Education and Morals in the Nineteenth Century* (London, 1970), 44-45; Marianne Monestier, *Les Sociétés secrètes féminines* (Paris, 1963), 124-54; Evelyne Sullerot, *La Press féminine* (Paris, 1966), 30-31; Simone de Beauvoir, *The Second Sex*, trans. H. M. Parshley (New York, 1952), 137; Edith Thomas, *Louis Michel ou la Velléda de l'anarchie* (Paris, 1971), 60-61; Evelyn Martha Acomb, *The French Laic Laws (1879-1889): The First Anti-Clerical Campaign of the Third French Republic* (New York, 1967), 117; Geneviève Gennari, *Le Dossier de la femme* (Paris, 1965), 12-13; J. Tourmentin, *La Femme chez les francs-maçons d'après les derniers convents du G.˙.O.˙.* (Paris, 1902); Eugen Lennhoff and Oskar Posner, eds., *Internationales Freimaurerlexikon* (Austria, 1932), 355; *Dictionnaire de biographie française*, vol. 10 (Paris, 1962), 1118; *Almanach féministe 1899* (Paris, 1899), 36-37; *Bulletin de l' Union universelle des femmes* (15 March 1891); *Journal des femmes* (February-March 1894), (August 1898); *La Française* (28 June 1919); Hélène Brion, ed., "Encyclopédie féministe," vol. 1, BMD; Jane Misme, "La Vie et la mort du féminisme," BMD, 35; Marie Dronsart, "Le Mouvement féministe," *Le Correspondant* (10 October 1896), 110-37; Jeanne E. Schmahl, "Progress of the Women's Rights Movement in France," *Forum* 22 (September 1896), 81-86; Jean-Bernard [Passerieu], "Notice" on Maria Deraismes, *Oeuvres complètes de Maria Deraismes* (Paris, 1895), v-lv; Claire Goldberg Moses, "The Evolution of Feminist

Thought in France" (Ph.D. diss., George Washington University, 1978), 229–37; Jean Rabaut, *Histoire des féminismes français* (Paris, 1978); Charles Sowerwine, *Les femmes et le socialisme* (Paris, 1978).

2. Amélie Hammer in *La Française* (28 June 1919).

3. Jean-Bernard [Passerieu], "Notice," liv. The quotation is from Amélie Hammer in *La Française* (28 June 1919). Both Ernest Hamel and Maria Pognon mentioned in their eulogies that Deraismes refused to marry because of woman's subordination in marriage. *Obsèques de Maria Deraismes: Discours prononcés sur sa tombe le 9 février 1894*, by Annie Jackson-Daynes, Virginie Griess-Traut, Ernest Hamel, Mme. Vincent, Eugénie Potonié-Pierre, M. Dide, Mme. Béquet de Vienne, Gustave Hubbard, Mme. Pognon, M. Raqueni, Mme. Valette, Paule Mink, Mme. Rouzade, M. Schacre, M. Frinquet (Paris, 1895), 8, 29, cited in Moses, "The Evolution of Feminist Thought in France," 229–30.

4. Maria Deraismes published the following plays: *A bon chat bon rat, comédie-proverbe en un acte, en prose* (Paris, 1861); *Un Neveu, s'il-vous plaît, comédie en 3 actes et en prose* (Paris, 1862); *Le Père coupable, comédie en 4 actes et en prose* (Paris, 1862); *Retour à ma femme, comédie en 1 acte et en prose* (Paris, 1862).

5. Maria Deraismes, *Aux femme riches* (Paris, 1865); *Thérésa et son époque* (Paris, 1865).

6. Jeanne Barrelet-Bernier, *La Française* (28 June 1919).

7. Jules Barbey d'Aurevilly, *Les Bas-Bleus* (Paris, 1878), xxiii.

8. Amélie Hammer, *La Française* (28 June 1919).

9. Opinion of M. Siebacker, cited in Jean-Bernard [Passerieu], "Notice," xvii. See also Moses, "The Evolution of Feminist Thought in France," 232.

10. Jules Tixerant, "Le Mouvement féministe sous le Second Empire," Ligue française pour le droit des femmes. *Bulletin trimestriel* (April 1911), 3.

11. Amélie Hammer, *La Française* (28 June 1919).

12. For comment on Revendication and its members, see Bernard Noël, *Dictionnaire de la Commune* (Paris, 1971), 258; Hélène Miropolsky's obituary of Madame Vincent in *L'Excelsior* (12 March 1914); Li Dzeh-Djen, *La Presse féministe*, 29; Baron Marc de Villiers, *Histoire des clubs de femmes et des légions d'Amazons 1793–1848–1871* (Paris, 1910), 382; Edith Thomas, *Louise Michel ou la Velléda de l'anarchie* (Paris, 1971), 60 and *The Woman Incendiaries*, trans. James and Starr Atkinson (New York, 1966), 33; Dronsart, "Le Mouvement féministe," 112; Supplement to *Bulletin de l'Union française pour le suffrage des femmes* (1914), 15–16.

13. Li Dzeh-Djen wrote of the 1870 Association pour le droit des femmes: "Ce fut l'origine de l'organisation actuelle du féminisme." *La Presse féministe*, 28. See also Évelyne Sullerot, *La Presse féminine* (Paris, 1966), 31; Hubertine Auclert, *Le Vote des femmes* (Paris, 1908), 102; Monestier, *Sociétés secrètes féminines*, 130; Brault, *Franc-Maçonnerie et l'émancipation des femmes*, 92.

14. Jean-Bernard [Passerieu], "Notice," xix.

15. Maria Deraismes, *Ève contre Monsieur Dumas fils* (Paris, 1872) and *France et progrès* (Paris, 1873).

16. *L'Avenir des femmes* (24 September 1871).

17. Villiers, *Histoire des clubs de femmes*, 412. Alexandre Dumas *fils*, *L'Homme-femme. Réponse à M. Henri d'Ideville* (Paris, 1872). Forty editions of *L'Homme-femme* appeared during its first year, forty-five by 1889.

18. Maria Deraismes, *Ève dans l'humanité* (Paris, 1891).

19. *Oeuvres complètes de Maria Deraismes*, 222.

20. Monestier, *Sociétés secrètes féminines*, 130.

21. *Oeuvres complètes de Maria Deraismes*, 4, 259.

22. *Revue internationale* (1 June 1899), 303.

23. *Oeuvres complètes de Maria Deraismes*, 263.

24. Ibid., 260, 266.

25. Ibid., iv.

26. From Deraismes's printed report to the 1893 Congress of Women in Chicago. BMD, Dossier Deraismes.

27. *Oeuvres complètes de Maria Deraismes*, 240, 287.

28. Ibid., 261.

29. BMD, Dossier Deraismes.

30. This and the following two quotations are from *Oeuvres complètes de Maria Deraismes*, 245, 276, 278.

31. Ibid., 273, 279.

32. Jean-Bernard [Passerieu], "Notice," xxiii.

33. Ibid., xxv.

34. Maria Deraismes, *Lettre au clergé français* (Paris, 1879).

35. Jean-Bernard [Passerieu], "Notice," xxvii–xxviii.

36. Ibid., xxvii.

37. Fernand Tourret, *La Franc-Maçonnerie* (Paris, 1975), 74–75. In addition to Maria Deraismes, the founders of the Droit humain included her sister Anna Féresse-Deraismes, Clémence Royer, Béquet de Vienne, Louise David, Docteur Marie Pierre, Marie-Georges Martin, Julie Pasquier, Eliska Vincent, Florestine Mauriceau, Myrtille Rengnet, Lévy-Maurice, Charlotte Duval, Marie Martin, Maria Pognon, Louisa Wiggishoff, and Senator Georges Martin. Gérard Serbanesco, *Histoire de la franc maçonnerie universelle*, 4 vols. (Paris, 1969), 4: 542–43.

38. Maria Deraismes, *Nos principes et nos moeurs* (Paris, 1868), 208–50, cited in Zeldin, ed., *Conflicts in French Society*, 44–45.

39. *Le Devoir: Journal des reformes sociales* (Familistère de Guise) (14 March 1880), 168–70.

40. Maria Deraismes, *Discours sur la vivisection* (Paris, 1884), 26–29.

41. Quotations in this paragraph are from Maria Deraismes, *France et progrès*, cited in *Oeuvres complètes de Maria Deraismes*, 183–87.

42. See official report of *Congrès français et international du droit des femmes* (Paris, 1889).

43. Madame Vincent, "Le Vote des femmes dans les élections consulaires," *La Revue féministe* (5 November 1895). Maria Deraismes, *Ève dans l'humanité*, 356–77.

44. Schmahl, "Progress of the Women's Rights Movement in France," 85.

45. Abensour, *Histoire générale du féminisme*, 271.

46. Monestier, *Sociétés secrètes féminines*, 128.

47. Gennari, *Le Dossier de la femme*, 12–13.

48. Jane Misme, *La Française* (28 June 1919).

49. Jane Misme, from an undated, unidentified press clipping, BMD, Dossier Deraismes.

50. Schmahl, "Progress of the Women's Rights Movement in France," 81–86.

51. Dronsart, "Le Mouvement féministe," 113–15.

52. Unidentified press clipping of March 1894 from Dossier Ligue française pour le droit des femmes, BMD. An obituary notice of Anna Féresse-Deraismes, who died on 19 January 1910, accused Maria of using Anna as a stand-in for photographs. The notice described Maria as a supreme coquette who wished to employ Anna's beauty in order to enhance her own image in posterity's eyes. *La Française* (30 January 1910).

53. *Bulletin* (Société pour l'amélioration du sort de la femme et la revendication de ses droits; hereafter cited as Amelioration Society) (October-December 1896).

54. Jane Misme, *La Française* (28 June 1919).

55. Jean-Bernard [Passerieu], "Notice," x.

56. Abensour, *Histoire générale du féminisme*, 271.

57. For information on and references to the life of Léon Richer, see Beauvoir, *The Second Sex*, 137; Misme, "La Vie et la mort du féminisme," 33-37; Sullerot, *La Presse féminine*, 30; Monestier, *Société secrètes féminines*, 128; Brault, *La Franc-Maçonnerie et l'émancipation des femmes*, 49-126; Thomas, *Louise Michel*, 63; Li Dzeh-Djen, *La Presse féministe*, 11-22, 51-71; Françoise d'Eaubonne, *Histoire et actualité du féminisme* (Paris, 1971), 138; Trevor Lloyd, *Suffragettes International: The World-Wide Campaign for Woman's Rights* (London, 1971), 14; Abensour, *Histoire générale du féminisme*, 274 and *Le Problème féministe: Un cas d'aspiration collective vers l'égalité* (Paris, 1927); *La Française, (30 December 1906), (25 June 1911), (28 June 1919); Le Droit des femmes* (24 June 1919) (letter from Richer's son Paul); introduction by Victor Poupin to Richer's *Le Livre des femmes* (Paris, 1872); Moses, "The Evolution of Feminist Thought in France," 241-55; Rabaut, *Histoire des féminismes français*; Sowerwine, *Les femmes et le socialisme*.

58. *La Française* (25 June 1911).

59. Li Dzeh-Djen, *La Presse féministe*, 21.

60. *Le Droit des femmes* (20 May 1888).

61. *L'Avenir des femmes* (January 1876). For complete text, see Appendix A.

62. Léon Richer, *Le Livre des femmes*; *Le Divorce* (Paris, 1873); *La Femme libre* (Paris, 1877); *Le Code des femmes* (Paris, 1883).

63. *Le Droit des femmes* (February 1883), (6 July 1884). *Oeuvres complètes de Maria Deraismes*, 355. *La Citoyenne* (June 1884).

64. *L'Avenir des femmes* (January 1876).

65. Richer, *La Femme libre*, 142-43. Cited in Moses, "The Evolution of Feminist Thought in France," 244.

66. Richer, *La Femme libre*, 197. Cited in Moses, "The Evolution of Feminist Thought in France," 245.

67. Richer, *Le Livre des femmes*, ix.

68. Richer, *La Femme libre*, 147.

69. Ibid., 36. Cited in Moses, "The Evolution of Feminist Thought in France," 245.

70. Brault, *Franc-Maçonnerie et l'émancipation des femmes*, 74, 92. *Le Droit des femmes* (24 June 1919). Li Dzeh-Djen, *La Presse féministe*, 202. *Bulletin* (Amelioration Society) (July-September 1894).

71. *L'Avenir des femmes* (1 April 1877). For complete text, see Appendix B.

72. *Le Droit des femmes* (24 April 1870). Cited in Moses, "The Evolution of Feminist Thought in France," 259-60.

73. *Le Droit des femmes* (January 1876), (6 January 1877), (6 February 1877).

74. Ibid., (3 March 1878), (1 September 1878), (3 November 1878).

75. Ibid., (January 1876).

76. *Bulletin* (Amelioration Society) (April-June 1894). For a roster of The Amelioration Society's members in 1894, see the author's "The Feminist Movement in France: The Formative Years, 1858-1889" (Ph.D. diss., Michigan State University, 1975), 359-61.

77. *L'Avenir des femmes* (6 January 1877). Brault, *Franc-Maçonnerie et l'émancipation de femmes*, 76. Monestier, *Sociétés secrètes féminines*, 128. Richer may have confused Laboulaye with Ernest Legouvé, who wrote a work of the same title, *Histoire morale des femmes* (Paris, 1849).

78. *L'Avenir des femmes* (4 August 1872), (1 September 1872). Cited in Moses, "The Evolution of Feminist Thought in France," 258.

79. *L'Avenir des femmes* (6 January 1877), (4 March 1877). Li Dzeh-Djen, *La Presse féministe*, 61.

80. *Le Droit des femmes* (5 January 1899). Li Dzeh-Djen, *La Presse féministe*, 53-54.

81. Li Dzeh-Djen, *La Presse féministe*, 64. *L'Avenir des femmes* (1 July 1877), (5 August 1877), (4 November 1877).

82. *L'Avenir des femmes* (5 March 1876), (3 December 1876), (6 May 1877).

83. Ibid., (24 March 1873). Cited in Moses, "The Evolution of Feminist Thought in France," 264.

84. *L'Avenir des femmes* (6 July 1873). Cited in Moses, "The Evolution of Feminist Thought in France," 264.

85. There are at least four contemporary accounts of the 1878 congress: *Congrès international du droit des femmes. Ouvert à Paris, le 25 juillet, clos le 9 août suivant. Actes. Compte rendu des séances plenières* (Paris, n.d.); Léon Giraud, *Souvenirs du congrès pour le droit des femmes, tenu à Paris en août 1878* (Paris, 1879); Léon Richer's articles for *L'Avenir des femmes* (7 July 1878), (4 August 1878), (1 September 1878), (1 December 1878); Eugénie Pierre's articles for *Le Devoir* (Familistère de Guise), (28 July 1878), (25 August 1878), (8 September 1878), (22 September 1878). The following account is drawn from these sources unless otherwise noted. For a roster of the members of the 1878 congress, see the author's "The Feminist Movement in France," 362-67.

86. *L'Avenir des femmes* (1 September 1878). Rabut, *Histoire des féminismes français*, 173.

87. Li Dzeh-Djen, *La Presse féministe*, 15.

88. *L'Avenir des Femmes* (1 September 1878).

89. Ibid. (4 August 1878).

90. Ibid. (1 September 1878).

91. *Le Devoir* (Familistère de Guise), (25 August 1878), 397.

92. Schmahl, "Progress of the Women's Rights Movement in France," 85.

CHAPTER 4. CONFLICT: HUBERTINE AUCLERT AND THE STRATEGY OF *L'ASSAUT*

1. *La Citoyenne* (13 February 1881).

2. Ibid.

3. Recalling their youth together in the family home, Auclert's sister wrote: "Already at that moment, the *petite fille* manifested precious gifts, she was admired for the manner in which she dressed her dolls, the ease with which she knew how to pull apart the tiniest piece of moire or taffeta to fashion beautiful robes for them imitating those of ladies. She embroidered just as marvelously and took an interest in all the details of domestic [life], she thus acquired all the qualities of an accomplished woman of the house," Marie Chaumont [Hubertine Auclert's sister], "Hubertine Auclert," pp. 1-91, in Hubertine Auclert, *Les Femmes au gouvernail* (Paris, 1923), 1-2. For additional information on Hubertine Auclert (10 April 1848-8 April 1914), see Jane Misme, "La Vie et la mort du féminisme," BMD, 36-38; *La Française* (18 April 1914); Edith Thomas, *Louise Michel ou la Velléda de l'anarchie* (Paris, 1971), 186; Hélène Brion, ed., "Encyclopédie féministe," BMD, vol. 1; Marie-Hélène Lefaucheux, ed., *Women in a Changing World: the Dynamic Story of the International Council of Women since 1888* (London, 1966), 9-11; Li Dzeh-Djen, *La Presse féministe en France de 1869 à 1914* (Paris, 1934), 38-50; Vital Gougeon, *Du vote des femmes* (Rennes, 1907), 40-75; Francis I. Clark, *The Position of Women in Contemporary France* (London, 1937), 217-18; Léon Abensour, *Histoire générale du féminisme* (Paris, 1921) 275; *Dictionnaire de biographie française*, vol. 4 (Paris, 1947), 327; Alcyone, "Les Femmes voteront-elles? Hubertine Auclert, la première des suffragistes françaises," *La Lumière* (16 February 1935); Elizabeth Cady Stanton et al., *History of Woman Suffrage*, 6 vols. (New York, 1969), 3: 899, 4: 23, 27, 44-49; BMD, Dossier Auclert and Dossiers VOT 396 for the period 1880-1914; *Le Droit des femmes* (15 April 1914); Jean Maitron, ed., *Dictionnaire biographique du mouvement ouvrier français*, vol. 10 (Paris, 1973), 165-66; Henri Avenel, *Histoire de la presse française depuis 1789 jusqu'à nos jours* (Paris, 1900), 818; Claire Goldberg Moses, "The Evolution of Feminist Thought in France" (Ph.D. diss., George Washington University, 1978), 268-77; Jean Rabaut, *Histoire des féminismes français* (Paris, 1978), 173-83. Charles Sowerwine, "Women and Socialism in France 1871-1921" (Ph.D. diss., University of Wisconsin, 1973), 14-17, 245-47, now revised and available in French as *Les Femmes et le socialisme* (Paris, 1978).

4. Li Dzeh-Djen, *La Presse féministe*, 38.

5. Chaumont, "Hubertine Auclert," 3-4.

6. Ibid., 4.

7. It was Auclert herself who described the group she joined in the early 1870s as a "*comité féministe*," but, in addition to the problem of identifying the particular group, the word *feminist* had not yet come into popular usage. Auclert first used the word in a letter to the prefect of the Seine in 1882. Ibid., 5.

8. Misme, "La Vie et la mort du féminisme," 34. Auclert later recalled, "In citing our great poet, the Press awakened among the exploited the idea of rights and, within a year, I was not the only recruit, who came from a hundred places to enroll in the feminist army." Hubertine Auclert, *Le Vote des femmes* (Paris, 1908), 102-3.

9. Hubertine Auclert, *Historique de la société le droit des femmes 1876-1880* (Paris, 1881), 11.

10. Hubertine Auclert, *Le Droit politique des femmes, question qui n'est pas traitée au congrès international des femmes* (Paris, 1878).

11. Auclert, *Historique*, 18-19.

12. Ibid., 6.

13. *L'Avenir des femmes* (6 May 1877). Misme, "La Vie et la mort du féminisme," 37.

14. Auclert, *Historique*, 7-11. *L'Avenir des femmes* (6 May 1877). For the text of the program of Auclert's Society in the late 1870s, see Appendix C.

15. Taken from statutes of the Société le suffrage des femmes in a two-page handout distributed sometime after 1903. BMD, Dossier Auclert.

16. Auclert, *Historique*, 8-10.

17. *L'Avenir des femmes* (6 January 1877), (4 May 1877). Auclert, *Historique*, 10. Buisson assumed leadership of the woman suffrage faction in the Chamber of Deputies upon the death of Paul Dussaussoy (Pas-de-Calais), who introduced a measure for granting women the vote in municipal, *arrondissement*, and general council elections in 1906. Dussausoy died in 1909. Buisson served as president of the Chamber's Committee on Universal Suffrage. His views on the issue can be found in Ferdinand Buisson, *Le Vote des femmes* (Paris, 1911). For a roster of Auclert's followers, see the author's "The Feminist Movement in France," 369-71.

18. Giraud's works on women include *Le roman de la femme chrétienne, étude historique avec une lettre-préface par Mlle. Hubertine Auclert* (Paris, 1880); *Les Femmes et les libres-penseurs. Réponse à M. Benjamin Gastineau pour sa brochure "Les Femmes et les prêtres"* (Paris, 1880); *La Femme et la nouvelle loi sur le divorce* (Paris, 1885); *La Vérité sur la recherche de la paternité* (Paris, 1888); and *Contradictions du Code Napoléon et nécessité de le réviser* (Paris, 1889). He also wrote an account of the first feminist congress: *Souvenirs du congrès pour le droit des femmes, tenu à Paris en août 1878* (Paris, 1879).

19. *La Citoyenne* (29 May 1881), (11-18 September 1881), (19-25 December 1881); Li Dzeh-Djen, *La Presse féministe*, 42.

20. *La Citoyenne* (1889-1890).

21. Ibid. (February 1884), (April 1884), (January 1885), (December 1885).

22. Ibid. (2-8 January 1882).

23. Ibid. (5-11 February 1881), (13 February 1881), (7 January-4 February 1883).

24. Ibid. (5 February-4 March 1883).

25. Ibid. (19-25 March 1882), (5 June -2 July 1882), (5 February-4 March 1883), (6 August-2 September 1883), (September 1884), (January 1885).

26. Ibid. (March 1888).

27. Stanton et al., *History of Woman Suffrage*, 3: 899, 4: 27.

28. *La Citoyenne* (4 December 1882-7 January 1883), (5 February-4 March 1883), (February 1884), (March 1884), (April 1884), (November 1884).

29. Ibid. (20 February 1881), (6 May-4 June 1881), (2 July-6 August 1882), (6 August-3 September 1882), (6 November-5 December 1882), (January 1885).

30. Ibid. (4 September 1881), (11-18 September 1881), (February 1889).

31. Ibid. (22 May 1881), (April 1885), (November 1885).

32. Ibid. (7-13 November 1881), (2 April-6 May 1883), (October 1884), (December 1885), (June 1886), (December 1887). For a synopsis of these and other arguments advanced by Auclert in support of woman suffrage, see her *Le vote des femmes* and *Les Femmes au gouvernail*.

33. *La Citoyenne* (8 May 1881), (19-25 February 1882), (April 1884).

34. Ibid. (17 April 1881), (September 1884), (May 1887), (20 March 1881), (8 May 1881).

35. Ibid. (April 1881), (May 1885).

36. Ibid. (10 April 1881), (8 May 1881).

37. Ibid. (21 August 1881), (July 1887). Chaumont, "Hubertine Auclert," 18-19.

38. *La Citoyenne* (9-15 January 1882), (16-22 January 1882), (December 1887), (1 December 1891).

39. Ibid. (3 April 1881), (24-30 October 1881), (12-18 March 1882), (7 May-3 June 1883), (July 1888), (March 1889).

40. Stanton et al., *History of Woman Suffrage*, vols. 1-4. Seven hundred women out of a total population of 42,000 received the full franchise on the Isle of Man in 1881. After the assassination of Alexander II in 1881, Auclert reported, the mayor of St. Petersburg, Baranoff, permitted women to drop their own ballots into the urn. *La Citoyenne* (31 October-6 November 1881).

41. *La Citoyenne* (6 March 1881), (4 December 1882-7 January 1883), (4 June-1 July 1883), (6 August-2 September 1883).

42. Auclert, *Historique*, 15-20. For these and other written protests, see *La Citoyenne* (7 August 1881), (10-16 October 1881), (6 May-4 June 1882), (2 July-6 August 1882), (6 August-3 September 1882), (March 1884), (March 1885), (1 June 1891).

43. Auclert, *Historique*, 22.

44. *La Citoyenne* (5 June-2 July 1882), (6 August-3 September 1882).

45. Ibid. (8 May 1881), (April 1885), (November 1885), (December 1885), (November 1886).

46. Ibid. (June 1885). For Auclert's attitude toward Bastille Day and Joan of Arc, see *La Citoyenne* (10 July 1881), (17 July 1881), (23 July 1881), (2 July-5 August 1883), (2 July-6 August 1882), (July 1884), (June 1885), (October 1889). *Le Libérateur* (23 July 1881). Chaumont, "Hubertine Auclert," 60-63.

47. Auclert, *Historique*, 26.

48. Ibid., 27. Suzanne Grinberg, *Historique du mouvement suffragiste depuis 1848* (Paris, 1926), 76. Auclert named eight of her fellow tax-strikers on 8 April 1880 in a press release: J. Coulassez, Marie Chevassus (of Lyon), and six widows (Leprou, Blondit, Marc, Rioux, Dupénet, and Jamier). Unidentified press clipping of 11 April 1880, BMD, Dossier Auclert. Auclert's sister recalled that Auclert paid her back taxes. Chaumont, "Hubertine Auclert," 11. Others disagreed. According to an official history of the International Council of Women, "Hubertine Auclert, future founder of the French Women's Suffrage Movement allowed her household goods to be seized by bailiffs rather than pay taxes in obedience to laws she had not voted." Lefaucheux, ed., *Woman in a Changing World*, 9-10. Clark maintained that Auclert went to prison rather than pay. Clark, *The Position of Women in Contemporary France*, 217. Auclert's tax bill came to 30 francs and 85 centimes based on her rent of 550 francs. The applicable law of 1852 exempted rents under 400 francs. *Le Soleil* (12 August 1880). Widow Leprou had her furniture seized, according to *La Citoyenne* (2-8 January 1882).

49. Alexandre Dumas *fils*, *Les Femmes qui tuent et les femmes qui votent* (Paris, 1880). Auclert, *Historique*, 25. Auclert, *Le vote des femmes*, 107. Grinberg, *Historique du mouvement suffragiste depuis 1848*, 65. Misme, "La Vie et la mort du féminisme," 39-41. Henri Fouquier, unidentified newspaper clipping of 30 July 1880, BMD.

50. Auclert, *Le Vote des femmes*, 60-61.

51. *Le Droit des femmes* (5 April 1885). *La Citoyenne* (29 May 1881), (17 July 1881), (12-18 December 1881), (January 1884), (November 1886).

52. *La Citoyenne* (10-16 October 1881), (31 October-6 November 1881). *Le Libérateur* (23 July 1881), (20 August 1881). The expulsion vote was twenty-nine to two, although neither Épailly nor Drouin attended the dismissal meeting.

53. *La Citoyenne* (26 December 1881-1 January 1882).

54. Thomas, *Louise Michel*, 219-20, 280-81. *Le Droit des femmes* (6 September 1885).

55. *La Citoyenne* (5 February-4 March 1883), (2 April-6 March 1883), (2 July-5 August 1883).

56. Ibid. (5 February-4 March 1883), (1 October-5 November 1882).

57. Ibid. (5 February-4 March 1883), (June 1888).

58. Ibid. (12 June 1881), (19 June 1881), (1 October-5 November 1882), (October 1885), (May 1885), (8 October-4 November 1883). *Le Droit des femmes* (15 March 1885), (17 May 1885).

59. *La Citoyenne* (April 1885), (September 1889).

60. Ibid. (28 November-4 December 1881), (19-25 December 1881).

61. Ibid. (26 December 1881-1 January 1882), (January 1886), (June 1887).

62. Ibid. (April 1885), (December 1888).

63. Ibid. (26 June 1881), (3 July 1881). Despite Pelletan's refusal to promote women's rights, *La Citoyenne*'s obituary praised him for his republicanism and for his interest in revising the Napoleonic Code. *La Citoyenne* (January 1885). Perhaps the worst of the political opponents of woman suffrage was Henri Brisson, a vice president of the Chamber, who wielded his influence on behalf of antidivorce clericals. He apparently led an unblemished personal life, however, because Senator Camparan's opposition to divorce earned him *La Citoyenne*'s exposure as an adulterer. *La Citoyenne* (April 1884). Nonetheless, Brisson's delay of Naquet's divorce bill led Lévrier to charge him with complicity in every marital murder and to urge the voters of Saint-Denis and Saint-Martin to defeat him. *La Citoyenne* (7 August 1881). In a similar political intervention, Auclert embarrassed a socialist's bid for the Chamber in 1881 by pointing out that, in addition to being ''an enemy of women's rights,'' he had served as Mac-Mahon's doctor during the crisis of 16 May 1877. *La Citoyenne* (19-25 December 1881).

64. Cited in Chaumont, "Hubertine Auclert," 35-40.

65. *La Citoyenne* (7 January-4 February 1883), (22 May 1881), (7 August 1881), (21 August 1881), (21-27 November 1881), (5-11 February 1882), (5 February-4 March 1883).

66. Sowerwine, "Women and Socialism in France 1871-1921," 7-12.

67. Ibid. See also Sowerwine, *Les femmes et le socialisme*.

68. *Le Droit des femmes* (December 1879).

69. *La Citoyenne* (May 1885).

70. Louise Saumoneau, *Le Mouvement féministe socialiste* (Paris, 1903), 3.

71. Auclert, *Les Femmes au gouvernail*, 359-64.

72. *La Citoyenne* (13 February 1881), (20 February 1881), (10 April 1881), (19-25 December 1881), (June 1884), (July 1884).

73. *Le Droit des femmes* (6 September 1885).

74. *La Citoyenne* (October 1885). Auclert, *Le vote des femmes*, 111.

75. *La Citoyenne* (October 1885). *Bulletin* (Amelioration Society) (January-April 1900). Sowerwine, "Women and Socialism in France 1871-1921," 46. According to Sowerwine, Auclert's distaste for Barberousse became public knowledge when *Le Figaro* published a private letter by Auclert denouncing Barberousse for her handling of the campaign.

76. Sowerwine, "Women and Socialism in France 1871-1921," 45. Maitron, ed., *Dictionnaire biographique*, 4: 108-9. The snail proposal, which Allix repeatedly advanced, involved raising two snails together from birth. The two snails would then develop a bond of empathy that would permit them to communicate with each other as adults. At that point they could be separated and employed as transmitters and receivers. The sender of a message had only to move his snail to a spot on a lettered board, which would cause the "paired" snail to do likewise some distance away.

77. *Le Droit des femmes* (1 March 1885).

78. Ibid.

79. *La Bataille* (13 September 1885), cited in Sowerwine, "Women and Socialism in France 1871-1921," 45, 66.

80. *Le Droit des femmes* (6 September 1885).

81. *La Citoyenne* (September 1885).

82. Thomas, *Louise Michel*, 322.

83. *Le Droit des femmes* (6 September 1885).

84. Ibid. Thomas incorrectly identifies Madame Adam as one of the organizers of the 1885 shadow campaign. See Thomas, *Louise Michel*, 280. *La Citoyenne* (September 1885).

85. Alexandre Zévaès, *Ombres et silhouettes* (Paris, 1928), 234-43. *Le Droit des femmes* (1 December 1884), (1 February 1885), (6 September 1885), (20 September 1885). Richer asked what honest woman would have the courage to cast the first stone at Mme. Hugues and concluded by saying that she "has avenged her outraged honor, her sullied daughter, and her tarnished home." *Le Droit des femmes* (1 December 1884).

86. *Le Droit des femmes* (20 September 1885).

87. *La Citoyenne* (September 1885), (October 1885). *Le Droit des femmes* (20 September 1885). For a sketch of Rousade, see Sowerwine, "Women and Socialism in France, 1871-1921," 12-18, 30-44.

88. *Bulletin* (Union française pour le suffrage des femmes) (January-March 1914). *Bulletin* (Amelioration Society) (September-October 1903). In 1911, Mme. Vincent became the president of the Union française pour le suffrage des femmes, founded in 1909.

89. *La Citoyenne* (October 1885).

90. Maitron, ed., *Dictionnaire biographique*, 9: 77. *Le Droit des femmes* (6 September 1885). *La Citoyenne* (September 1885).

91. *Le Voltaire* (24 August 1885).

92. Ibid.

93. Sowerwine, *Les femmes et le socialisme*, 245-47.

94. *La Citoyenne* (October 1885), (January 1886). For the totals for the Federation's male candidates, of whom Allix received 171 votes, see Sowerwine, "Women and Socialism in France, 1871-1921," 50-51.

95. Auclert, *Le Vote des femmes*, 111.

96. *La Citoyenne* (October 1885).

97. Ibid.

98. *Le Droit des femmes* (1 November 1885).

99. Gougeon, *Du vote des femmes*; Antoine Martin, *De la situation politique des femmes* (Paris, 1902); Jean le Couteulx du Molay, *Les Droits politiques de la femme* (Paris, 1913); Paul de Poulpiquet, *Le Suffrage de la femme en France* (Paris, 1912).

100. *Bulletin bimestriel* (Amelioration Society) (June-July 1897).

101. Unless otherwise indicated, all quotations are from Auclert's diary. Hubertine Auclert, "Diary," (Provisional Code 4248), at the Bibliothèque historique de la ville de Paris.

102. Dr. Eugène Verrier, *La Femme devant la science, considerée au point de vue du système cérébral* (Paris, 1883).

103. BMD, Dossier Auclert. Auclert, *Le vote des femmes*, 111.

104. Hubertine Auclert, *Les Femmes arabes en Algérie* (Paris, 1900); *L'Égalité sociale et politique de l'homme et de la femme* (Marseille, 1879); *L'Argent de la femme* (Paris, 1904); *Le Nom de la femme* (Paris, 1905).

105. Auclert, *Le vote des femmes*, 41, 120, 178. Gougeon, *Du vote des femmes*, 41. *Le Journal des femmes* (December 1904). Molay, *Les Droits politiques de la femme*, 261.

106. Auclert, *Le Vote des femmes*, 121

107. *Le Matin* (23 March 1910).

108. Abensour, *Histoire générale du féminisme*, 275.

109. Schmahl, "Progress of the Women's Rights Movement in France," 83-84.

110. *Le Journal des femmes* (June 1906). Grinberg, *Historique du mouvement suffragiste depuis 1848*, 91. See also Steven C. Hause, "Hubertine Auclert's Second Suffragist Career, 1893-1914: To an Unchanging Goal with Constantly Changing Tactics" (Paper read to the Fourth Berkshire Conference on the History of Women, 24 August 1978). On the subject of feminism and violence, see Hause and Anne R. Kenney, "The Limits of Suffragist Behavior: Legalism and Militancy in France, 1876-1922," *American Historical Review* 86, no. 4 (October 1981), 781-806.

CHAPTER 5. COUNTERATTACK: THE FRENCH LEAGUE FOR WOMEN'S RIGHTS AND THE CONGRESS OF 1889

1. *La Citoyenne* (1 October-November 1882).

2. Richer's emphasis. *Le Droit des femmes* (December 1882). Léon Richer, *Le code des femmes* (Paris, 1883), 374-400.

3. *Le Droit des femmes* (December 1882), (November 1882).

4. Ibid. Mildred J. Headings, *French Freemasonry Under the Third Republic* (Baltimore, 1949), 99.

5. *Le Droit des femmes* (December 1882).

6. *Le Droit des femmes* (December 1882-December 1883).

7. Ibid. (April 1883).

8. Ibid. (February 1883).

9. For a roster of the League's membership in the 1880s and early 1890s, see the author's "The Feminist Movement in France: The Formative Years, 1858-1889" (Ph.D. diss., Michigan State University, 1975), 374-78.

10. *Le Droit des femmes* (January 1883), (February 1883).

11. Headings, *French Freemasonry under the Third Republic*, 95-98. A comparison of the roster of the League for 1892 with the Masons mentioned by Headings indicates that eleven of the League's thirty-three men had been Masons.

12. *Le Droit des femmes* (15 May 1887).

13. Ibid. (June 1883). Bonnetain's book was entitled *Charlot s'amuse*, 2nd ed. (Brussels, 1883). According to the entry by P. Leguay in the *Dictionnaire de biographie française*, vol. 6 (Paris, 1954), 1028-29, Paul Bonnetain published his first work at Brussels in 1882, *Le Tour du monde d'un troupier:* "He truly made his debut the following year, and by a work of scandal, *Charlot s'amuse*, a case study in pathology, filled with all the extreme naturalistic details in vogue at the time. *Charlot* brought its author, in December 1884, before the *cour d'assises* of Paris." Bonnetain was acquitted, "but the author seemed drawn to rowdy literature." Vergoin accused Richer of obtaining his information from the conservative press, a charge that Richer denied. *Le Droit des femmes* (April 1886), (May 1886), (August 1886), (November 1886).

14. *Le Droit des femmes* (6 September 1885), (1 November 1885), (2 May 1886).

15. For information on *Le Droit des femmes*'s financial problems, see the following issues: February 1882, 4 January 1885, 1 February 1885, 15 February 1885, 3 May 1885, 6 September 1885, 15 November 1885, 3 May 1888, 21 December 1890, 2 August 1891.

16. Ibid. (1 March 1885). The Gironde group had twenty-nine members.

17. Ibid. (15 May 1887). See also the issues of 1 March 1885 and 2 May 1886.

18. Léon Richer, *Le Femme libre* (Paris, 1877), 77-78. Cited in Claire Goldberg Moses, "The Evolution of Feminist Thought in France 1829-1889," (Ph. D. diss., George Washington University, 1978), 253.

19. *Le Droit des femmes* (7 June 1891), (22 May 1892).

20. Ibid. (15 March 1885).

21. Ibid. (2 May 1886).

22. Ibid. In a thirteen-month period spanning 1885 and 1886 the League spent 1,283.55 francs: 195.80 on stationary and other operating expenses, 400 on the subsidy for *Le Droit des femmes*, 150 on flowers for Hugo's funeral, 345 on circulars explaining the League's program, and 192.75 on the banquet.

23. Ibid.

24. Ibid. (April 1883), (2 May 1886). At the end of 1886, Richer announced with evident pride that Senators Schoelcher (who replaced Hugo as the League's honorary president), Naquet, Couturier, and Georges Martin had joined with Deputies Passy, Lefèvre, Laisant, Guyot, and Victor Poupin to form a parliamentary caucus on women's rights. Ibid. (19 December 1886).

25. Ibid. (5 April 1885).

26. Ibid. (15 March 1885).

27. Ibid. (15 March 1885), (5 April 1885), (3 May 1885).

28. Ibid. (20 May 1888).

29. Ibid. (7 September 1884).

30. Ibid. (17 May 1885).

31. Ibid. (20 May 1888).

32. Ibid. (20 May 1888), (20 October 1889).

33. Ibid. (7 September 1884), (5 April 1885).

34. Ibid. (20 September 1885).

35. Ibid. (19 April 1885). *La Citoyenne* (April 1885).

36. *Le Droit des femmes* (15 June 1890), (6 July 1890).

37. Ibid. (17 May 1885), (1 November 1885), (1 February 1888).

38. Ibid. (3 January 1886), (17 January 1886), (7 February 1886), (21 February 1886).

39. *La Citoyenne* (November 1886).

40. The idea for an official congress originated with de Morsier, who convinced Guyot in June 1888 to raise the matter within the commission. The commission delayed its approval until February 1889. *Exposition universelle internationale de 1889: Actes du Congrès international des oeuvres et institutions féminines* (Paris, 1890), i. (Hereafter cited as *Actes*.) For the whole of the celebration, see Brenda Flo Nelms, "The Third Republic and the Centennial of 1789" (Ph.D. diss., University of Virginia, 1976).

41. *Le Journal des femmes* (February 1896). See also Elisabeth Anne Weston, "Prostitution in Paris in the Later Nineteenth Century" (Ph.D. diss., State University of New York at Buffalo, 1979).

42. *Actes*, iv, x.

43. Jeanne E. Schmahl, "Progress of the Women's Rights Movement in France," *Forum* 22 (September 1896), 86; Dossier Deraismes, BMD; *Bulletin bimestriel* (Amelioration Society) (June-July 1897).

44. *Le Droit des femmes* (3 February 1889).

45. Ibid. (17 March 1889).

46. Ibid. (March-June 1889). The official report of the 1889 congress presents a slightly different picture of the participants and donations than the above account, which was taken from *Le Droit des femmes*. The official report lists 206 individuals and groups and total receipts of 5,034 francs. *Congrès français et international du droit des femmes* (Paris, 1889). For a roster of the people who registered for the 1889 Women's Rights Congress, see the author's "The Feminist Movement in France," 382-86.

47. *Bulletin* (Ligue d'électeurs pour le suffrage des femmes) (1911-1914).

48. *Le Droit des femmes* (4 November 1888).

49. *La Citoyenne* (May 1889), (July 1889).

50. *Le Droit des femmes* (21 July 1889), (18 August 1889).

51. *Congrès français et international du droit des femmes*, 146.

52. *La Citoyenne* (August 1889), (September 1889). *Le Droit des femmes* (18 August 1889), (15 September 1889). The controversial resolution read: "The Congress, considering that the question of women's work, their insufficient salaries, their excessive days, cannot be resolved except by legal and constitutional reforms, demands the civil and political emancipation of women, which will give notably to the wife the [free] dispensation of her salary, and to woman in general a representation for her economic interests, consequently for the salaries of women workers."

53. *Le Droit des femmes* (15 September 1889), (6 October 1889).

54. Ibid. (5 January 1889). *Le Journal des femmes* (May 1902). *La Française* (30 December 1906), (25 June 1911). *La Fronde* (25 May 1902).

CHAPTER 6. CONCLUSION

1. For these rosters, see the author's "The Feminist Movement in France; The Formative Years, 1858-1899" (Ph.D. diss., Michigan State University, 1975), 359-67, 374-86.

2. *Congrès français et international du droit des femmes* (Paris, 1889), i.

3. *Bulletin* (Amelioration Society) (June-July 1897).

4. Marie Dronsart, "Le Mouvement féministe," *Le Correspondant* (10 October 1896), 115.

5. Ghenia Avril de Saint-Croix, *Le Féminisme* (Paris, 1907), 133-34.

6. Li Dzeh-Djen, *La Presse féministe en France de 1869 à 1914* (Paris, 1934), 35.

7. Léon Abensour, *Histoire générale du féminisme* (Paris, 1921), 274.

8. Ibid., 274-75.

9. Jane Misme, "La Vie et la mort du féminisme," BMD, 36. *La Française* (30 December 1906), (29 November 1908), (18 April 1914).

10. Jeanne E. Schmahl, "Progress of the Women's Rights Movement in France," *Forum* 22 (September 1896), 81-84. Abbé Lecoeur, "Le Mouvement féministe," *Quatre conférences blanches* (Rouen, 1897), 123, 131.

11. Léon Abensour, *Le Problème féministe* (Paris, 1927), 159.

12. Léon Richer. *La Femme libre* (Paris, 1877), 240. Cited in Claire Goldberg Moses,"The Evolution of Feminist Thought in France, 1829-1889," (Ph.D. diss., George Washington University, 1978), 255.

13. *Le Droit des femmes* (18 August 1889).

14. Maria Deraismes, *Oeuvres complètes de Maria Deraismes*, ed. Anna Féresse-Deraismes (Paris, 1895), 186-87.

15. *La Citoyenne* (May 1885).

16. In the interwar years, for example, Richer received praise for establishing the only "true" brand of feminism and for opposing woman suffrage from Fernand Goland, *Les Féministes françaises* (Paris, 1925), 157-64.

17. Steven C. Hause, "The Failure of Feminism in Provincial France, 1890-1920" (Unpublished paper presented to the Western Society for French History, Eugene, Oregon, October, 1980), 11-12.

18. Among liberal republican senators grouped in the Gauche démocratique, the vote went 112 to 28 against woman suffrage. Among senators between the minimal constitutional age of 40 and the age of 49, the vote went 20 to 8 against. Steven C. Hause, "The Rejection of Women's Suffrage by the French Senate in November 1922: A Statistical Analysis," *Third Republic/Troisième République*, nos. 3-4 (1977), 209, 225.

19. Richer, *La Femme libre*, 230. Cited in Moses,"The Evolution of Feminist Thought in France," 255.

20. BMD, Dossier Madame Vincent.

21. *Bulletin de l'Union universelle des femmes* (May 1891).

22. *La Citoyenne* (November 1890), (1 July 1891). Charles Sowerwine, "Women and Socialism in France 1871-1921" (Ph.D. diss., University of Wisconsin, 1973), 99-110. Schmahl, "Progress of the Women's Rights Movement in France," 79-92.

23. *Le Droit des femmes* (20 December 1891). The eleven groups were: l'Allaitement maternel et le refuge pour les femmes enceintes; la Société pour l'amélioration du sort de la femme et la revendication de ses droits; le Groupe Étienne Dolet; la Fédération de la libre-pensée; la Ligue française pour le droit des femmes; la Ligue du bien public; la Ligue pour la réform du costume féminin et la liberté du costume; le Patronat du 6e arrondissement; le Patronat de la rue de Buci; l'Union universelle des femmes; and la Solidarité des femmes. Several more groups joined before the Federation finally collapsed.

24. Louise Saumoneau, *Études et critiques* (Paris, 1903), 3. See also Sowerwine, *Les*

Femmes et le socialisme (Paris, 1978), and Marilyn J. Boxer, "Socialism Faces Feminism: The Failure of Synthesis in France, 1879-1914," in *Socialist Women*, ed. Marilyn J. Boxer and Jean H. Quatacrt (New York, 1978), 75-111.

25. Marie Maugeret, "Notre programme," *Le Féminisme chrétien* (1896), 1-7. The largest of the Catholic women's groups was the Ligue patriotique des françaises, which grew to over a half million members between its founding in 1902 and the eve of World War I. See also Steven C. Hause and Anne R. Kenney, "The Development of the Catholic Women's Suffrage Movement in France, 1896-1922," *Catholic Historical Review* 67, no. 1 (January 1981), 11-30 and the author's "Right-Wing Feminism in France: The Theory and Practice of the *Association patriotique du devoir des femmes françaises* 1901-1913" (Paper delivered at the annual meeting of the Society for French Historical Studies, March 1981).

26. Boxer, "Socialism Faces Feminism," 96.

27. The three representatives from the Congress of Feminine Works and Institutions were Mlle. Sarah Monod, Mme. Avril de Saint-Croix, and Mme. Jules Siegfried. The representatives from the Congress on the Condition and Rights of Women were Mmes. Maria Pognon, Marie Bonnevial, and Wiggishoff.

28. The eight branches of the National Council of French Women were in the departments of Gironde, Indre-et-Loire, Rhône, Bouches-du-Rhône, Tarn-et-Garonne, Finistère, and two in Seine-Inférieure.

29. In addition to the nine feminist groups, the National Council of French Women included the following types of groups in 1911: work assistance (7), charity (20), circles and study groups (9), cooperatives (3), education (17), emigration (1), pacifism (1), provident societies (6), professional (7), women's syndicates (8), temperance (2), and preservation (12). *L'Action fèminine. Bulletin officiel du Conseil national des femmes françaises* (December 1911), 319.

30. Weston, "Prostitution in Paris in the Later Nineteenth Century," 73.

31. Ibid., 72.

32. Héra Mirtel, "Féminisme mondial," *Les Documents du progrès* (May 1910), 436. Cited in Hause, "The Failure of Feminism in Provincial France," 9.

33. Sanford Elwitt, "Social Reform and Social Order in Late Nineteenth-Century France: The Musée Social and its Friends," *French Historical Studies* 11, no. 3 (Spring 1980), 431.

34. Ibid., 437. Overall, indeed, the outlook of the liberal feminists closely approximated the "solidarist ideology" that Elwitt has identified as "an essential component of a social ideology integral to perpetuation of bourgeois class rule." Sanford Elwitt, *The Making of the Third Republic: Class and Politics in France, 1868-1884* (Baton Rouge, La., 1975), 313.

35. Cited from a preliminary draft, subsequently revised, of Stephen C. Hause and Anne R. Kenney, "The Limits of Suffragist Behavior: Legalism and Militancy in France, 1876-1922," *American Historical Review* 86, no. 4 (October 1981), 781-806. See also Charles Sowerwine, "Socialism, Feminism, and Violence: The Analysis of Madeleine Pelletier." Paper presented to Western Society for French History. Eugene, Oregon (October 1980).

36. *La Française* (5 July 1915).

37. Henry de Man, *The Psychology of Socialism*, trans. Eden and Cedar Paul from the 2nd German edition (London, 1928), 121. Cited in Donald N. Baker, "Seven Perspectives

on the Socialist Movement of the Third Republic,'' *Historical Reflections/Réflexions historiques* 1 (Winter 1974), 179.

38. *Le Petit Almanach Féministe pour 1907* (Paris, 1907), 4.

39. Kaethe Schirmacher, *The Modern Woman's Rights Movement*, trans. Conrad Eckhardt, 2nd ed. (New York, 1912), xiv.

40. Léon Richer, *Le Livre des femmes* (Paris, 1872), viii.

41. *Oeuvres complètes de Maria Deraismes*, 273.

42. Linda Gordon, ''The Struggle for Reproductive Freedom: Three Stages of Feminism,'' in *Capitalist Patriarchy and the Case for Socialist Feminism*, ed. Zillah R. Eisenstein (New York, 1979), 112.

SELECTED BIBLIOGRAPHY

PRIMARY SOURCES

ARCHIVES, MANUSCRIPTS, AND PUBLIC DOCUMENTS

Archives Nationales (AN)

The French National Archives has several cartons of documents and newspaper clippings on the activities of militant women. Information on the right-wing Ligue patriotique des françaises can be found in carton F^7 13.215 and F^7 13.229, which also covers the Comité des femmes de la patrie française. Cartons F^7 13.086, F^7 13.266, F^7 13.349, and F^7 13.374-13.376 relate to the issue of pacifism, which attracted many French feminists in the nineteenth and early twentieth centuries. Carton F^7 13.266 also touches on the subject of woman suffrage. The report of the prefect of police on Richer's application for permission to found a journal is in carton F^7 339.

Bibliothèque Marguerite Durand (BMD)

Housed in the *mairie* of the fifth *arrondissement*, the Bibliothèque Marguerite Durand was founded in the mid-1930s as a repository for the library of its namesake. Its holdings include thousands of letters, pamphlets, newspaper clippings, handouts, and so on, catalogued under the names of individuals, titles of groups, or subject headings. These dossiers cover all of the principal and many of the minor feminist activists and organizations.

Manuscripts

Auclert, Hubertine. "Diary." Bibliothèque historique de la ville de paris. Provisional Code 4248.
Brion, Hélène, ed. "Encyclopédie feministe." 5 vols. BMD
Misme, Jane. "La Vie et la mort du féminisme." BMD
"La Vie d'action de Marguerite Durand." Dossier: Marguerite Durand. BMD

BOOKS AND PAMPHLETS

Almanach féministe 1899. Paris: Edouard Cornély, 1899.

Auclert, Hubertine. *L'Argent de la femme*. Paris: Pédone, 1904.

————. *Le Droit politique des femmes, question qui n'est pas traitée au congrès international des femmes*. Paris: Hugonis, 1878.

————. *L'Égalité sociale et politique de l'homme et de la femme*. Marseille: A. Thomas, 1879.

————. *Les Femmes arabes en Algérie*. Paris: Lamarre, 1900.

————. *Les Femmes au gouvernail*. Paris: Marcel Giard, 1923.

————. *Historique de la société le droit des femmes 1876-1880*. Paris: Robert et Buhl, 1881.

————. *Le Nom de la femme*. Paris: Société du livre à l'auteur, 1905.

————. *Le Vote des femmes*. Paris: V. Giard et E. Brière, 1908.

Audouard, Olympe. *L'Amour, le matérialiste, le spiritualiste, le complet et divin*. Paris: E. Dentu, 1880.

————. *À travers l'Amérique, le Far-West*. Paris: E. Dentu, 1869.

————. *À travers l'Amérique, North America. États-Unis. Constitution, moeurs, usages, lois, institutions, sectes religieuses*. Paris: E. Dentu, 1871.

————. *La Femme dans le mariage, la séparation et le divorce, conférence faite le 28 février 1870*. Paris: E. Dentu, 1870.

————. *Guerre aux hommes*. Paris: E. Dentu, 1866.

————. *Lettre aux députés*. Paris: E. Dentu, 1867.

————. *Le Luxe des femmes, réponse d'une femme à M. le procureur général Dupin*. Paris: E. Dentu, 1865.

————. *Le Luxe effréné des hommes, discours tenu dans un comité de femmes*. Paris: E. Dentu, 1865.

————. *M. Barbey d'Aurevilly. Réponse à ses réquisitoires contre les bas-bleus, conférence du 11 avril*. Paris: E. Dentu, 1870.

Avril de Saint-Croix, Zhenia. *Le Féminisme*. Paris: V. Giard et E. Brière, 1907.

Barbey d'Aurevilly, Jules. *Les Bas-Bleus*. Paris: Société générale de librairie catholique, 1878. Reprint. Geneva: Slatkine, 1968.

Bebel, August. *Woman Under Socialism*. 1883. Translated by Daniel de Leon from original German of the 33rd edition. New York: Schocken, 1971.

Bogelot, Isabelle. *Trente ans de solidarité 1877-1906*. Paris: Maulde, Doumenc, 1908.

Bonald, Louis Gabriel Ambroise, Vicomte de. *Démonstration philosophique du principe constitutif de la société, suivie de méditations politiques tirées de l'Évangile*. Paris: A. Le Clère, 1830.

————. *Législation primitive, considérée dans le dernier temps par les seules lumières de la raison, suivie de divers traités et discours politiques*. 4th ed. Paris: A. Le Clère, 1847.

Bridel, Louis. *La Femme et le droit*. Lausanne: G. Bridel, 1882.

————. *Homme et femme: droit français et comparé*. Paris: J.-B. Sirey, n.d.

Brion, Hélène. *La Voie féministe: les partis d'avant-garde et le féminisme*. Epons: L'Avenir social, n.d.

Buisson, Ferdinand. *Le Vote des femmes*. Paris: H. Dunod et E. Pinat, 1911.

Butler, Josephine E. *Personal Reminiscences of a Great Crusade*. London: Horace Marshall, 1896.

Cabet, Étienne. *Réalisation d'Icarie*. Paris: Prévot rue Bairlon-Villeneuve, 1846.

———. *Voyage en Icarie*. Paris: Le Populaire, 1846.

Chambon, Octave. *Le Devoir social de la femme française*. Auxerre: O. Chambon, 1902.

Compain, L.-M. *La Femme dans les organisations ouvrières*. Paris: V. Giard et E. Brière, 1910.

Congrès français et international du droit des femmes. Paris: E. Dentu, 1889.

Daubié, Julie. *La Femme pauvre au XIXe siècle*. Paris: Guillaumin, 1866.

Deraismes, Maria. *A bon chat bon rat, comédie-proverbe en un acte, en prose*. Paris: Amyot, 1861.

———. *L'Ancien devant le nouveau*. Paris: Librairie nationale, 1869.

———. *Aux femmes riches*. Paris: Chez tous les librairies, 1865.

———. *Les Droits de l'enfant*. Paris: E. Dentu, 1887.

———. *Épidémie naturaliste: Émile Zola et la science, discours prononcé au profit d'une société pour l'enseignement en 1880*. Paris: E. Dentu, 1888.

———. *Ève contre Monsieur Dumas fils*. Paris: E. Dentu, 1872.

———. *Ève dans l'humanité*. Paris: L. Sauvaitre, 1891.

———. *France et progrès*. Paris: Librairie de la Société des gens de lettres, 1873.

———. *Lettre au clergé français*. Paris: E. Dentu, 1879.

———. *Ligue populaire contre l'abus de la vivisection. Discours prononcé par Mlle. Deraismes,...à la conférence donnée la...23 septembre 1883, au Théâtre de nations*. Paris: A. Ghio, 1884.

———. *Un Neveu, s'il vous plaît, comédie en 3 actes et en prose*. Paris: Amyot, 1862.

———. *Nos principes et nos moeurs*. Paris: Michel Lévy, 1868.

———. *Oeuvres complètes de Maria Deraismes*. Edited by Anna Féresse-Deraismes. Paris: F. Alcan, 1895.

———. *Le Père coupable, comédie en 4 actes et en prose*. Paris: Amyot, 1862.

———. *Retour à ma femme, comédie en 1 acte et en prose*. Paris: Amyot, 1862.

———. *Le Théâtre de M. Sardou, conférence faite le 21 janvier 1875, la salle des capucines*. Paris: E. Dentu, 1875.

———. *Thérésa et son époque*. Paris: Librairie nouvelle, 1865.

Draigu [Léon Giraud]. *Contradictions du Code Napoléon et nécessité da la reviser*. Paris: G. Carré, 1889.

———. *Les Femmes et les libres-penseurs. Réponse à M. Benjamin Gastineau pour sa brochure "Les Femmes et les prêtres"*. Paris: Perinet, 1880.

———. *Le Roman de la femme chrétienne, étude historique avec une lettre-préface par Mlle. Hubertine Auclert*. Paris: A. Ghio, 1880.

Dumas *fils*, Alexandre. *Les Femmes qui tuent et les femmes qui votent*. Paris: Calimann Lévy, 1880.

———. *L'Homme-femme. Réponse à M. Henri d'Ideville*. Paris: M. Lévy, 1872.

———. *La Question du divorce*. Paris: C. Lévy, 1880.

———. *La Recherche de la paternité. Lettre à M. Rivet, député*. Paris: C. Lévy, 1883.

Dupanloup, Félix Antoine Philibert, Bishop of Orléans. *Les Alarmes de l'épiscopat justifiée par les faits. Lettre à un cardinal par Mgr. l'évêque d'Orléans.* Paris: C. Douniol, 1868.

Estournelles de Constant, Paul Henri Benjamin, Baron d'. *Les Femmes et la paix.* Paris: Delagrave, 1910.

Etrivières, Jehan des [Marie-Rose Astié de Valsayre]. *Les Amazones du siècle, (les gueulardes de Gambetta). Biographies de Louise Michel, Léonie Rouzade, Hubertine Auclert, Louise de Lasserre, Louise Koppe, Eugénie Cheminot, Eugénie Pierre.* 3rd ed. Paris: St. Armand (Cher), Destenay, 1882.

Exposition universelle internationale de 1889. Actes du Congrès international des oeuvres et institutions féminines. Paris: Bibliothèque des Annales économiques, Société d'éditions scientifiques, 1890.

Fallot, Tommy. *La Femme esclave.* Paris: Fischbacher, 1884.

Fourier, François Marie Charles. *Oeuvres complétes de Ch. Fourier.* 6 vols. Paris: Librairie sociétaire, 1841-1848.

———. *Théorie des quatre mouvements et des destinées générales.* 2nd ed. Paris: La Phalange, Librairie de l'école sociétaire, 1841.

Frank, Louis. *Essai sur la condition politique de la femme, étude de sociologie et de législation.* Paris: Arthur Rousseau, 1892.

Gide, Charles. *Les Prophéties de Fourier.* 2nd ed. Nîmes: Roger et Laporte, 1884.

Gide, Paul and Adhémar Esmein. *Étude sur la condition privée de la femme dans le droit ancien et moderne.* Paris: Durand et Pedone Lauriel, 1867.

Girardin, Émile de. *L'Homme et la femme: l'homme suzerain, la femme vassale. Lettre à M. A. Dumas fils.* Paris: M. Lévy, 1872.

Giraud, Léon [see also: Draigu]. *Des droits de la femme mariée sous le régime de la communauté relativement à l'aliénation de l'un de ses biens faite par le mari sans son consentement.* Paris: A. Rousseau, 1887.

———. *Des promesses du mariage, étude historique et juridique.* Paris: F. Pichon, 1888.

———. *Essai sur la condition des femmes en Europe et en Amérique.* Paris: A. Chio, 1882.

———. *Études et pamphlets. Familia.* Grenoble: Rigaudin, 1874.

———. *La Femme et la nouvelle loi sur le divorce.* Paris: G. Pedone-Lauriel, 1885.

———. *La Recherche de la paternité. Préliminaires d'un projet de loi.* Paris: G. Carré, 1890.

———. *Souvenirs du congrès pour le droit des femmes, tenu à Paris en août 1878.* Paris: A. Chio, 1879.

———. *La Vérité sur la recherche de la paternité.* Paris: F. Pichon, 1888.

Griess-Traut, V[irginie]. *Manifest des femmes contre la guerre.* Montmorency: L. Gaubert, n.d.

Guéroult, Georges. *Du rôle de la femme dans notre rénovation sociale.* Caen: A. Domin, 1891.

Guyot, Yves. *La Réglementation officielle du travail.* Paris: Guillaumin, 1894.

Héricourt, Jenny d'. *La Femme affranchie; réponse à MM. Michelet, Proudhon, É. de Girardin, A. Comte et aux autres novateurs modernes.* 2 vols. Brussels: A. Lacroix, Van Meenen, 1860.

———. *A Woman's Philosophy of Woman: or Woman Affranchised. An Answer to Michelet, Proudhon, Girardin, Legouvé, Comte, and Other Modern Innovators.* New York: Carleton, 1864.

Ideville, Henri Amédée Le Lorgne, Comte d'. *L'Homme qui tue et l'homme qui pardonne.* *Précédé d'une lettre à Alexandre Dumas fils.* Paris: E. Dentu, 1872.

Joran, Théodore. *Au coeur du féminisme.* Paris: A. Savaète, 1908.

———. *Autour du féminisme.* Paris: Bibliothèque des annales politiques et littéraires, 1906.

———. *Le Féminisme à l'heure actuelle.* Paris: V. Giard et E. Brière, 1907.

———. *Les Féministes avant le féminisme.* 2 vols. Paris: A. Savaète, 1910, 1935.

———. *Le Mensonge du féminisme.* Paris: H. Jouve, 1905.

———. *Le Suffrage des femmes.* Paris: A. Savaète, 1914.

———. *La Trouée féministe.* Paris: A. Savaète, 1909.

Lamber, Juliette [Madame Adam]. *Idées anti-proudhoniennes sur l'amour, la femme, et le mariage.* 1858. 2nd ed. Paris: E. Dentu, 1861.

———. *Mes Sentiments et nos idées avant 1870.* 6th ed. Paris: Alphonse Lemerre, 1895.

Lampérière, Anna. *Le Rôle social de la femme; devoirs, droits, éducation.* Paris: F. Alcan, 1898.

Laurent, Charles. *Les Droits de la femme. Droits politiques. Rapport par Ch. L. pour O. de Paris, Loge no. 6, le Mont Sinaï.* Paris: Mac. ˙ ., 1888.

Legouvé, Ernest. *La Femme en France au dix-neuvième siècle.* Paris: Didier, 1864.

———. *Histoire morale des femmes.* Paris: G. Sandré, 1849.

Lemonnier, Charles. *Elisa Lemonnier, fondatrice de la Société pour l'enseignement professionnel des femmes.* Saint-Germain: L. Toinon, 1866.

Léo, André [Léodile Champseix]. *The American Colony in Paris in 1867.* Boston: Loring, 1868.

———. *Un Divorce.* Rev. ed. Paris: N.p., 1869.

———. *Un Mariage scandaleux.* 2nd ed. Paris: Librairie A. Faure, 1863.

———. *Une Vieille fille.* Paris: A. Faure, 1864.

Le Play, Frédéric. *L'Organisation de la famille selon le vrai modèle signalé par l'histoire de toutes les races et de tous les temps.* Paris: Téqui, Bibliothèque de l'Oeuvre Saint-Michel, 1874. Originally published in 1871.

Leroux, Pierre. *De l'égalité, suivi d'aphorisme sur la doctrine de l'humanité.* Boussac: P. Leroux, 1848.

Levinck, Anne. *Les Femmes qui ne tuent ni ne votent.* 3rd ed. Paris: C. Marpon et E. Flammarion, 1882.

Martial, Lydie. *La Femme intégrale.* Paris: The Author, 1901.

Martin, Antoine. *De la situation politique de femmes.* Paris: L. Boyer, 1902.

Michelet, Jules. *L'Amour.* Paris: L. Hachette, 1858.

———. *La Femme.* Paris: L. Hachette, 1860.

Molay, Jean le Couteulx du. *Les Droits politiques de la femme.* Paris: V. Giard et E. Brière, 1913.

Oddo-Deflou, Jeanne, ed. *Congrès national des droits civils et du suffrage de femmes, tenu en l'Hôtel des sociétés savantes à Paris les 26, 27 et 28 juin 1908.* Autun: L'Égalité, 1910.

Oeuvres complètes de Saint-Simon et d'Enfantin, publiées par les membres du Conseil institué par Enfantin, pour l'exécution de ses dernières volontés. 42 vols. Paris: E. Dentu, 1865-1876.

Parent-Duchâtelet, Alexandre Jean-Baptiste. *De la Prostitution dans la ville de Paris*. 2 vols. 3rd ed. Paris: J.-B. Baillière, 1857.

Pelletan, Eugène. *La Femme au XIXe siècle*. Paris: Pagnerre, 1869.

Le Petit Almanach féministe illustré pour 1907. Paris: L'Union fraternelle des femmes, 1907.

Ponson, Madame M. *Le Rôle actuel de la femme. Conférence faite à la Ligue patriotique des françaises*. Bordeaux: F. Pech, 1911.

Proudhon, Pierre-Joseph. *De la justice dans la révolution et dans l'église*. 3 vols. Paris: Garnier, 1858.

————. *La Pornocratie ou les femmes dans les temps modernes*. Paris: Marpon et Flammarion, n.d.

Richer, Léon. *Alerte!* Paris: E. Dentu, 1869.

————. *Le Code des femmes*. Paris: E. Dentu, 1883.

————. *Le Divorce, project de loi précédé d'un exposé des motifs et suivi des principaux documents officiels se rattachant à la question, avec une lettre-préface par Louis Blanc*. Paris: Le Chevalier, 1873.

————. *La Femme libre*. Paris: E. Dentu, 1877.

————. *Lettres d'un libre-penseur à un curé de village, précédé d'une introduction par M. Ad. Guéroult*. 2 vols. Paris: Le Chevalier, 1868-1869.

————. *Lettres parisiennes. La politique en 1873*. Paris: Société des gens de lettres, 1874.

————. *Le Livre des femmes*. Paris: Bibliothèque démocratique, 1872.

————. *Un Mariage honteux*. Paris: E. Dentu, 1876.

————. *Propos d'un mécréant*. Paris: Panis, 1868.

————. *Le Tocsin*. Paris: Madre, 1868.

Sagnac, Ph[ilippe]. *La Législation civile de la Révolution française (1789-1804)*. Paris: Hachette, 1898.

Saumoneau, Louise. *Le Mouvement féministe socialiste*. Paris: La Femme socialiste, 1903.

Schirmacher, Kaethe. *The Modern Woman's Rights Movement*. 1905. Translated by Conrad Eckhardt. 2nd ed. New York: Macmillan, 1912.

————. *Le Travail des femmes en France*. Paris: Arthur Rousseau, 1902.

Secretan, Charles. *Les Droits de l'humanité*. Paris: F. Alcan, 1889.

Simon, Jules. *L'Ouvrière*. Paris: Hachette, 1861.

Stanton, Elizabeth Cady et al. *History of Woman Suffrage*. 6 vols. 1881-1922. Reprint. New York: Arno and The New York Times, 1969.

Thouzery, Paul. *La Femme au XIXe siècle: Ce qu'elle est. Ce qu'elle doit être*. Paris: A. Faure, 1866.

Tourmentin, J. [l'abbé Henry-Stanislas-Athanase Joseph]. *La Femme chez les Francs-maçons d'après les derniers convents du G. ˙. O. ˙.* . Paris: Comité antimaçonnique, 1902.

Transon, Abel. *Religion saint-simonienne. Affranchissement des femmes, prédication de 1er janvier 1832*. Paris: Le Globe, 1832.

Vaïsse, Jean-Louis. *Les Droits de la femme*. Paris: J. Cherbuliez, 1871.

Valette, Aline. *Oeuvre des libérées de Saint-Lazare*. Alençon: F. Guy, 1889.

Vérone, Maria. *La Femme et la loi*. Paris: Larousse, 1920.

Verrier, Dr. Eugène. *La Femme devant la science, considérée au point de vue du système cérébral, conférence faite à Paris, le 28 mai 1883, à la salle Rivoli.* Paris: Alcan-Lévy, 1883.

———. *Le Meilleur des socialismes pratiques: Le socialisme phalanstérien.* Toulouse: E. Privat, 1905.

Wattel, H. M. J., ed. *Code Napoléon.* Amsterdam: N.p, ca. 1888.

Women's Position in the Laws of the Nations. Prepared by the International Council of Women. Karlsruhe: International Council of Women, 1912.

Zévaès, Alexandre [Gustave Alexandre Bourson]. *Ombres et silhouettes: Notes, memoirs, et souvenirs.* Paris: N.p., 1928.

ARTICLES AND JOURNALS

L'Action féminine. Bulletin officiel du conseil national des femmes françaises. 1901-1914.

Adam, Madame Juliette [Juliette Lamber]. "Position of Women in France." *Review of Reviews* 15 (April 1897), 480.

L'Aurore. 3 June 1914.

L'Avenir des femmes. 1871-1879. Director: Léon Richer. Appeared as *Le Droit des femmes*, 1869-1870, 1879-1891.

La Bataille. 13 September 1885. Director: Lissagaray.

Baudrillart, Henri. "L'Agitation pour l'émancipation des femmes en Angleterre et aux États-Unis." *Revue des deux mondes* 101 (1 October 1871), 651-77.

Bonnevial, Marie. "Le Mouvement syndical féminin en France." *Revue de morale sociale* (September 1901), 257-67.

Bulletin de l'Union universelle des femmes. January 1890-August 1891. Director: Marya Chéliga.

Chéliga, Marya. "L'Évolution du féminisme." *Revue encyclopédique* (November 1896), 910-13.

La Citoyenne. 13 February 1881-16 November 1891. Founder: Hubertine Auclert. Directors: Hubertine Auclert (1881-1888) and Maria Martin (1888-1891).

Le Combat féministe. January 1913-July 1914. Director: Arria Ly.

Le Cri des femmes. Pour la paix, pour le vote politique des femmes, contre l'alcool, contre la traite des blanches. 1914. Director: Marie Dénizard.

Le Devoir. Journal of the Familistère de Guise. 1878-1906. Founder: Jean-Baptiste-André Godin.

Le Devoir des femmes françaises. April 1902-December 1913. Director: Françoise Dorive.

Le Droit des femmes. 1869-1870, 1879-1891. Director: Léon Richer. Appeared as *L'Avenir des femmes*, 1871-1879.

Les Droits de la femme. Politique, littéraire, artistique. 1900-1902.

Dronsart, Marie. "Le Mouvement féministe" *Le Correspondant* (10 October 1896), 110-37.

L'Entente. Journal féministe. April 1905-? Collaborators: Caroline Kauffmann, Odette Laguerre, Nelly Roussel, and Oddo-Deflou. Later appeared as *Organe de la Renaissance féminine.*

La Femme. 1879-1914. Founder: Mlle. C. Delpech.

La Femme contemporaine. Revue internationale des intérêts féminins. 1903-1914. Director: Jean Lagardère.

La Femme socialiste. Organe féministe socialiste. 1 March 1901-1 September 1902. Director: Elisabeth Renaud.

La Française. Journal de progrès féminin. 21 October 1906-26 December 1914. Director: Jane Misme.

La Fronde. Journal féministe. 9 December 1897-1 March 1905, July 1914. Director: Marguerite Durand.

Le Journal des femmes. Organe du mouvement féministe. December 1891-January 1911. Director: Maria Martin.

Jus Suffragii. Monthly Organ of the International Woman Suffrage Alliance. 1906-1914.

Lecoeur, Abbé. "Le Mouvement Féministe," in *Quatre conférences blanches.* Rouen: Cagniard, 1897.

Le Libérateur. Organe de la Société des amis du divorce. 17 April 1881-20 August 1881. Director: Le Commandant Épailly.

Ligue d'électeurs pour le suffrage des femmes. *Bulletin.* 1911-1914. Director: Raoul Rebour.

Ligue française pour le droit des femmes. *Bulletin.* October 1906-15 March 1915.

Le Matin. 18 December 1892, 23 March 1910.

Misme, Jane. "Les Grandes Figures du féminisme: Isabelle Bogelot, Sarah Monod, Julie Siegfried." *Minerva* (n.d.).

————. "Les Grandes Figures du féminisme: Madame Adam." *Minerva* (1 February 1931).

Nouvelle Revue internationale. 1 July 1889.

Renaud, Elisabeth. "Glimpse of the Feminist Movement in France." *Review of Reviews* 44 (September 1911), 354-56.

La Revue féministe. 5 October 1895-April 1897. Director: Clotilde Dissard.

Revue internationale. 1 June 1889.

Schmahl, Jeanne E. "Progress of the Women's Rights Movement in France." *Forum* 22 (September 1896), 79-92.

La Socialiste. 12 October 1890.

Société pour l'Amélioration du sort de la femme et la revendication de ses droits. *Bulletin.* April-June 1894-July 1910.

Tixerant, Jules. "Le Mouvement féministe sous le Second Empire." *Ligue française pour le droit des femmes. Bulletin trimestriel* (April 1911), 2-4.

Union française pour le suffrage des femmes. Association nationale affiliée de l'Alliance internationale pour le suffrage des femmes. *Bulletin.* 1911-1916.

La Vie féminine. Union littéraire, artistique et sociale. 18 March 1914-7 July 1914. Director: Valentine Thomson.

Vincent, Madame [Eliska Girard]. "Le Vote des femmes dans les élections consulaires." *La Revue féministe* (5 November 1895).

SECONDARY SOURCES

BOOKS AND THESES

Abensour, Léon. *Le Féminisme sous le regne de Louis-Philippe et en 1848.* Paris: Plon-Nourrit, 1913.

————. *La Femme et le féminisme avant la révolution.* Paris: Ernest Leroux, 1923.

————. *Histoire générale du féminisme: Des origines à nos jours.* 1921. Reprint. Geneva: Slatkine, 1979.

————. *Le Problème féministe: Un cas d'aspiration collective vers l'égalité.* Paris: Radot, 1927.

Acomb, Evelyn Martha. *The French Laic Laws (1879-1889): The First Anti-Clerical Campaign of the Third French Republic.* New York: Octagon, 1967.

Adams, George C. S. *Words and Descriptive Terms for "Woman" and "Girl" in French and Provençal and Border Dialects.* University of North Carolina Studies in the Romance Languages and Literatures, no. 11. Chapel Hill: University of North Carolina, 1949.

Albistur, Maïte and Daniel Armogathe. *Histoire du féminisme français du moyen âge à nos jours.* Paris: Éditions des femmes, 1977.

Alzon, Claude. *Femme mythifée, femme mystifiée.* Paris: Presses Universitaires de France, 1978.

Ariès, Philippe. *Centuries of Childhood: A Social History of Family Life.* Translated by Robert Baldick. New York: Vintage, 1960.

Avenel, Henri. *Histoire de la presse française depuis 1789 jusqu'à nos jours.* Paris: Ernest Flammarion, 1900.

Bardèche, Maurice. *Histoire des femmes.* 2 vols. Paris: Stocke et Maurice Bardèche, 1968.

Beales, Arthur C. F. *The History of Peace: A Short Account of the Organised Movements for International Peace.* New York: Dial Press, 1931. Reprint. New York: Garland, 1971.

Beauvoir, Simone de. *The Second Sex.* Translated by H. M. Parshley. New York: Knopf, 1952.

Bidelman, Patrick Kay. "The Feminist Movement in France: The Formative Years, 1858-1889." Ph.D. dissertation, Michigan State University, 1975.

Blaise, Suzanne. *Des Femmes de nulle part ou le préféminisme politique.* Paris: Presse-Diffusion, 1980.

Bouchardeau, Huguette. *Pas d'histoire les femmes...50 ans d'histoire des femmes: 1918-1968.* Paris: Syros, 1977.

Bouglé, C[elestin Charles Alfred]. *Chez les prophètes socialistes.* Paris: Félix Alcan, 1918.

———— and Élie Halévy, eds. *Doctrine de Saint-Simon. Exposition, première année, 1829.* Paris: Rivière, 1924.

Bouvier, Jeanne. *Les Femmes pendant la révolution, leur action politique, sociale, économique, militaire, leur courage devant l'échafaud.* Paris: E. Figuière, ca. 1931.

————. *La Lingerie et les lingères.* Paris: Octave Doin, 1928.

Boy, Magdeleine. *Les Associations internationales féminines.* Lyon: Paquet, 1936.

Brault, Éliane. *La Franc-Maçonnerie et l'émancipation des femmes.* Paris: Dervy, 1953.

Burchell, S. C. *Imperial Masquerade: The Paris of Napoleon III.* New York: Atheneum, 1971.

Camp, Wesley D. *Marriage and the Family in France Since the Revolution: An Essay in the History of Population.* New York: Bookman, 1961.

Carroll, Berenice A., ed. *Liberating Women's History: Theoretical and Critical Essays.* Chicago: University of Illinois Press, 1976.

Cassell, Joan. *A Group Called Women: Sisterhood and Symbolism in the Feminist Movement.* New York: McKay, 1977.

Chombart de Lauwe, Marie-José et al. *La Femme dans la société, son image dans différents milieux sociaux.* Paris: Centre national de la recherche scientifique, 1963.

Cipolla, Carlo M. *Literacy and Development in the West.* Baltimore: Penguin, 1969.

Clark, Francis I. *The Position of Women in Contemporary France.* London: P. S. King, 1937.

Collins, Irene. *The Government and the Newspaper Press in France 1814-1881.* London: Oxford University Press, 1959.

Corbin, Alain. *Les Filles de noce: Misère sexuelle et prostitution aux 19ᵉ et 20ᵉ siècles.* Paris: Aubier Montaigne, 1978.

Damez, Albert. *Le Libre Salaire de la femme mariée et le mouvement féministe.* Paris: Librairie nouvelle de droit et de jurisprudence, 1905.

Daric, Jean. *L'Activité professionelle des femmes en France.* Paris: Presses Universitaires de France, 1947.

Dessignolle, É[mile]. *Le Féminisme d'après la doctrine socialiste de Charles Fourier.* Lyon: A. Storck, 1903.

Duval, Fernand. *J.-B.-A. Godin et le familistère de Guise.* Paris: V. Giard et E. Brière, 1905.

Eaubonne, Françoise d'. *Histoire et actualité du féminisme.* Paris: Alain Moreau, 1971.

Edwards, Stewart, ed. *Selected Writings of Pierre-Joseph Proudhon.* Translated by Elizabeth Fraser. Garden City, N.Y.: Doubleday, 1969.

Eisenstein, Zillah R., ed. *Capitalist Patriarchy and the Case for Socialist Feminism.* New York: Monthly Review Press, 1979.

————. *The Radical Future of Liberal Feminism.* New York: Longman, 1981.

Elwitt, Sanford. *The Making of the Third Republic: Class and Politics in France, 1868-1884.* Baton Rouge: Louisiana State University Press, 1975.

Evans, Richard J. *The Feminists: Women's Emancipation Movements in Europe, America and Australasia 1840-1920.* New York: Barnes and Noble, 1977.

Ferré, Louise-Marie. *Féminisme et positivisme.* Saint-Léger-en-Yvelines: The Author, 1938.

Firestone, Shulamith. *The Dialectic of Sex: The Case for Feminist Revolution.* New York: Bantam, 1970.

Freemantle, Anne, ed. *The Papal Encylicals in Their Historical Context.* New York: Mentor-Omega, 1955.

Friedan, Betty. *The Feminine Mystique.* New York: Dell, 1963.

Gagnon, Paul A. *France Since 1789.* New York: Harper & Row, 1964.

Gennari, Geneviève. *Le Dossier de la femme.* Paris: Perrin, 1965.

Glazer-Malbin, Nona and Helen Youngelson Waehrer, eds. *Woman in a Man-Made World.* Chicago: Rand McNally, 1972.

Goland, Fernand. *Les Féministes françaises.* Paris: Francia, 1925.

Goliber, Sue Helder. "The Life and Times of Marguerite Durand." Ph.D. dissertation. Kent State University, 1975.

Gougeon, Vital. *Du vote des femmes.* Rennes: Rennaise, 1907.

Gould, Robert Freke et al. *A Library of Freemasonry.* Vol. 3. London: John C. Yorston, 1906.

Gramont, Sanche de. *The French: Portrait of a People.* New York: Putnam, 1969.

Grinberg, Suzanne. *Historique du mouvement suffragiste depuis 1848.* Paris: Henry Goulet, 1926.

Guilbert, Madeleine. *Les Femmes et l'organisation syndicale avant 1914.* Paris: Centre national de la recherche scientifique, 1966.

Guiraud, Pierre. *Sémiologie de la sexualité: Essai de glosso-analyse.* Paris: Payot, 1978.

Headings, Mildred J. *French Freemasonry Under the Third Republic.* Johns Hopkins University Studies in Historical and Political Science, vol. 66. Baltimore: Johns Hopkins Press, 1949.

Hemmings, F. W. J. *Culture and Society in France 1848-1898: Dissidents and Philistines.* New York: Charles Scribner's Sons, 1971.

Holtman, Robert B. *The Napoleonic Revolution.* New York: Lippincott, 1967.

Journet-Durca, Isabelle and Paulette Aulibé-Istin. *La Femme et ses nouveaux droits.* Paris: Albin Michel, 1975.

Keranflech-Kernezne, Simone (de Boisboissel), Comtesse de. *Madame Chenu 1861-1939.* Paris: Action sociale de la femme et le livre français, 1940.

Lacour, Léopold. *Les Origines du féminisme contemporain: Trois femmes de la Révolution: Olympe de Gouges, Théroigne de Méricourt, Rose Lacombe.* Paris: Plon, 1900.

Larnac, Jean. *Histoire de la littérature féminine en France.* Paris: Cra, 1929.

Langlois, Pamela Frances Stent. "The Feminine Press in England and France: 1875-1900." Ph.D. dissertation. University of Massachusetts, 1979.

Lefaucheux, Marie-Hélène, ed. *Women in a Changing World: The Dynamic Story of the International Council of Women Since 1888.* London: Routledge and Kegan Paul, 1966.

Lennhoff, Eugen and Oskar Posner, eds. *Internationales Freimaurerlexikon.* Austria: Verlagsanstalt, 1932.

Li Dzeh-Djen. *La Presse féministe en France de 1869 à 1914.* Paris: L. Rodstein, 1934.

Lougee, Carolyn C. *Le Paradis des Femmes: Women, Salons, and Social Stratification in Seventeenth-Century France.* Princeton: Princeton University Press, 1976.

Maitron, Jean, ed. *Dictionnaire biographique du mouvement ouvrier français.* 10 vols. Paris: Éditions Ouvrières, 1968- .

Manuel, Frank E. *The Prophets of Paris.* New York: Harper & Row, 1962.

—— and Fritzie P. Manuel, eds. *French Utopias.* New York: Free Press, 1966

Marks, Elaine and Isabelle de Courtivron, eds. *New French Feminisms: An Anthology.* Amherst: University of Massachusetts Press, 1980.

Martin, Gaston. *Manuel d'histoire de la franc-maçonnerie française.* Paris: Presses Universitaires de France, 1929.

McManners, John. *Church and State in France, 1870-1914.* New York: Harper & Row, 1972.

Miller, Michael B. *The Bon Marché: Bourgois Culture and the Department Store, 1869-1920.* Princeton: Princeton University Press, 1980.

Mitterand, Jacques. *La Politique des Franc-Maçons.* Paris: Roblot, 1973.

Monestier, Marianne. *Les Sociétés secrètes féminines.* Paris: Productions de Paris, 1963.

Moses, Claire Goldberg. *The Evolution of Feminist Thought in France, 1829-1889.* Ph.D. dissertation, George Washington University, 1978. (Forthcoming from State University of New York Press at Albany.)

Myrdal, Alva and Viola Klein. *Women's Two Roles: Home and Work*. London: Routledge and Kegan Paul, 1956.

Nelms, Brenda Flo. "The Third Republic and the Centennial of 1789." Ph.D. dissertation. University of Virginia, 1976.

Noël, Bernard. *Dictionnaire de la Commune*. Paris: Fernand Hazan, 1971.

Offen, Karen M., ed. "Women During the Third Republic." *Third Republic/Troisième République*, nos. 3-4 (1977).

————, Erna Olafson Hellerstein and Leslie Parker Hume, eds. *Victorian Women: A Documentary Account of Women's Lives in Nineteenth-Century England, France, and the United States*. Stanford: Stanford University Press, 1981.

O'Neill, William. *The Woman Movement: Feminism in the United States and England*. Chicago: Quadrangle, 1969.

Paulson, Ross Evans, *Women's Suffrage and Prohibition: A Comparative Study of Equality and Social Control*. Glenview, Ill.: Scott, Foresman, 1973.

Poirier. *L'Infériorité sociale de la femme et le féminisme*. Paris: Marchal et Billard, 1900.

Potonié-Pierre, Edmond. *Historique du mouvement pacifique*. Berne: Steiger, 1899.

Poulpiquet, Paul de. *Le Suffrage de la femme en France*. Paris: Librairie nouvelle de droit et de jurisprudence, 1912.

Prost, Antoine. *Histoire de l'enseignement en France 1800-1967*. Paris: Armand Colin, 1968.

Rabaut, Jean. *Histoire des féminismes français*. Paris: Stock, 1978.

Richardson, Lula McDowell. *The Forerunners of Feminism in French Literature of the Renaissance from Christine de Pisan to Marie de Gournay*. Johns Hopkins Studies in Romance Literatures and Languages, vol. 12. Baltimore: Johns Hopkins Press, 1929.

Ronsin, Francis. *La Grève des ventres: Propagande néo-malthusienne et baisse de la natalité en France 19ᵉ-20ᵉ siècles*. Paris: Aubier Montaigne, 1980.

Rossi, Alice S., ed. *Essays on Sex Equality, John Stuart Mill and Harriet Taylor Mill*. Chicago: University of Chicago Press, 1970.

Rowbotham, Sheila. *Women, Resistance and Revolution*. New York: Vintage, 1972.

Sanua, Louli. *Figures féminines 1909-1939*. Paris: Siboney, 1949.

Schneir, Miriam, ed. *Feminism: The Essential Historical Writings*. New York: Vintage, 1972.

Serbanesco, Gérard. *Histoire de la franc maçonnerie universelle*. 4 vols. Paris: Byblos, 1969.

Soltau, Roger Henry. *French Political Thought in the 19th Century*. New York: Russell and Russell, 1959.

Sowerwine, Charles. *Les Femmes et le socialisme*. Paris: Presses de la Fondation nationale des sciences politiques, 1978.

————. *Sisters or Citizens? Women and Socialism in France Since 1876*. Cambridge University Press, forthcoming.

————. "Women and Socialism in France 1871-1921: Socialist Women's Groups from Léonie Rouzade to Louise Saumoneau." Ph.D. dissertation, University of Wisconsin, 1973.

Stephens, Winifred. *Madame Adam (Juliette Lamber). La Grande Française. From Louis Philippe until 1917*. New York: Dutton, 1917.

————. *Women of the French Revolution*. New York: Dutton, 1922.

Sullerot, Évelyne. *Histoire de la presse féminine en France, des origines à 1848*. Paris: Armand Colin, 1966.

————. *Histoire et sociologie du travail féminin*. Paris: Gonthier, 1968.

————. *La Presse féminine*. Paris: Armand Colin, 1966.

————. *Woman, Society and Change*. Translated by Margaret Scotford Archer. New York: World University Library, 1971.

Thibert, Marguerite. *Le Féminisme dans le socialisme français de 1830 à 1850*. Paris: Marcel Giard, 1926.

Thiebaux, Charles. *Le Féminisme et les socialistes depuis Saint-Simon jusqu'à nos jours*. Paris: Arthur Rosseau, 1906.

Thomas, Edith. *Les Femmes de 1848*. Paris: Presses Universitaires de France, 1948.

————. *George Sand*. Paris: Éditions Universitaires, 1960.

————. *Louise Michel ou la Velléda de l'anarchie*. Paris: Gallimard, 1971.

————. *Pauline Roland: Socialisme et féminisme au XIXe siècle*. Paris: Rivière, 1956.

————. *The Woman Incendiaries*. Translated by James and Starr Atkinson. New York: Braziller, 1966.

Tilly, Louise A. and Joan W. Scott. *Women, Work, and Family*. New York: Holt, Rinehart and Winston, 1978.

Tixerant, Jules. *Le Féminisme à l'époque de 1848 dans l'ordre politique et dans l'ordre économique*. Paris: V. Giard et E. Brière, 1908.

Tricot, Michel. *De l'instruction publique à l'éducation permanente*. Paris: Tema, 1973.

Van de Walle, Étienne. *The Female Population of France in the Nineteenth Century: A Reconstruction of 82 Departments*. Princeton: Princeton University Press, 1974.

Villiers, Baron Marc de. *Histoire des clubs de femmes et des légions d'Amazons 1793-1848-1871*. Paris: Plon, 1910.

Weill, Georges. *Histoire du parti républicain en France (1814-1870)*. Paris: Felix Alcan, 1928.

Weston, Elisabeth Anne. "Prostitution in Paris in the Later Nineteenth Century: A Study of Political and Social Ideology." Ph.D. dissertation, State University of New York at Buffalo, 1979.

Williams, Roger L. *Henri Rochefort: Prince of the Gutter Press*. New York: Scribner's, 1966.

————. *The World of Napoleon III 1851-1870*. New York: Free Press, 1957.

Wollstonecraft, Mary. *A Vindication of the Rights of Woman with Strictures on Political and Moral Subjects*. 1792. Reprint. New York: Norton, 1967.

Wright, Gordon. *France in Modern Times*. Chicago: Rand McNally, 1960.

Yaguello, Marina. *Les Mots et les femmes: Essai d'approche socio-linguistique de la condition féminine*. Paris: Payot, 1979.

Zeldin, Theodore, *Conflicts in French Society: Anticlericalism, Education and Morals in the Nineteenth Century*. London: Allen and Unwin, 1970.

————. *France 1848-1945: Ambition and Love*. 1973. Reprint. New York: Oxford University Press, 1979.

Zylberberg-Hocquard, Marie-Hélène. *Féminisme et syndicalisme en France*. Paris: Anthropos, 1978.

————, Madeleine Guilbert and Nicole Lowit. *Travail et condition féminine (bibliographie commentée)*. Paris: Éditions de la Courtille, 1977.

ARTICLES AND PAPERS

Alcyone. "Les Femmes voteront-elles? Hubertine Auclert, la première des 'suffragistes françaises'." *La Lumière* (16 February 1933).

Arbay, Jane. "Feminism in the French Revolution." *American Historical Review* 80 (February 1975), 43-62.

Ariès, Philippe. "L'Évolution des rôles parentaux." In *Familles d'aujourd'hui*. Colloque consacré à la sociologie de la famille, Bruxelles, 17, 18 et 19 mai 1965. Brussels: L'Institut de sociologie, Université libre de Bruxelles, 1968.

Baker, Donald N. "Seven Perspectives on the Socialist Movement of the Third Republic." *Historical Reflections/Réflexions historiques* 1 (Winter 1974), 169-212.

Bell, Susan Groag. "Christine de Pizan (1364-1430): Humanism and the Problem of a Studious Woman," *Feminist Studies* 3, nos. 3/4 (Spring-Summer 1976), 173-84.

Bidelman, Patrick Kay. "Maria Deraismes, Léon Richer and the Founding of the French Feminist Movement 1866-1878," *Third Republic/Troisième République*, nos. 3-4 (1977), 20-73.

————. "The Politics of French Feminism: Léon Richer and the Ligue française pour le droit des femmes, 1882-1891," *Historical Reflections/Réflexions historiques*, 3, no. 1 (Summer 1976), 93-120.

Boxer, Marilyn J. "Socialism Faces Feminism: The Failure of Synthesis in France, 1879-1914." In *Socialist Women: European Socialist Feminism in the Nineteenth and Early Twentieth Centuries*, edited by Marilyn J. Boxer and Jean H. Quataert. New York: Elsevier, 1978.

Cromer, E. B. "Feminism in France" *Living Age* 279 (6 December 1913), 589-93.

Darrow, Margaret H. "French Noblewomen and the New Domesticity, 1750-1850." *Feminist Studies* 5, no. 1 (Spring 1979), 41-65.

Davis, Natalie Zemon. " 'Women's History' in Transition: The European Case." *Feminist Studies* 3, Nos. 3/4 (Spring-Summer 1976), 83-103.

Demos, John. "The American Family in Past Time," *American Scholar* 43 (Summer 1974), 422-46.

Elwitt, Sanford. "Social Reform and Social Order in Late Nineteenth-Century France: The Musée Social and Its Friends." *French Historical Studies* 11, no. 3 (Spring 1980), 431-51.

Evans, Richard J. "The History of European Women: A Critical Survey of Recent Research," *The Journal of Modern History* 52, no. 4 (December 1980), 656-75.

Gordon, Linda. "The Struggle for Reproductive Freedom: Three Stages of Feminism." In *Capitalist Patriarchy and the Case for Socialist Feminism*, edited by Zillah R. Eisenstein. New York: Monthly Review Press, 1979.

Hause, Steven C. "The Failure of Feminism in Provincial France, 1890-1920." Paper presented to the Western Society for French History. Eugene, Oregon. October 1980.

————. "Hubertine Auclert's Second Suffragist Career, 1893-1914: To an Unchanging Goal with Constantly Changing Tactics." Paper read to the Fourth Berkshire Conference on the History of Women, Mount Holyoke College, 24 August 1978.

————. "The Rejection of Women's Suffrage by the French Senate in November 1922: A Statistical Analysis." *Third Republic/Troisième République*, nos. 3-4 (1977), 205-37.

———— and Anne R. Kenney. "The Development of the Catholic Women's Suffrage Movement in France 1896-1922." *Catholic Historical Review* 65, no. 1 (January 1981), 11-30.

————. "The Limits of Suffragist Behavior: Legalism and Militancy in France, 1876-1922." *American Historical Review* 86, no. 4 (October 1981), 781-806.

Hufton, Olwen. "Women and the Family Economy in Eighteenth-Century France." *French Historical Studies* 9, no. 1 (Spring 1975), 1-22.

Hunt, Persis. "Feminism and Anti-Clericalism Under the Commune." *Massachusetts Review* 12 (Summer 1971), 418-31.

Juglart, Michel de. "L'Émancipation juridique de la femme en France et dans le monde." In *Histoire mondiale de la femme: Sociétés modernes et contemporaines*, under the direction of Pierre Grimal. Paris: Nouvelle Librairie de France, 1965.

Lougee, Carolyn C. "Review Essay: Modern European History." *Signs* 2, no. 3 (Spring 1977), 628-50.

McBride, Theresa. "A Woman's World: Department Stores and the Evolution of Women's Employment, 1870-1920." *French Historical Studies* 10, no. 4 (Fall 1978), 664-83.

Offen, Karen M. "The Male Feminist Phenomenon in Mid-Nineteenth Century France: The Case of Ernest Legouvé (1807-1903)." Paper presented to the Third Berkshire Conference on the History of Women. Bryn Mawr, Pennsylvania, June 1976.

————. "French Feminists Challenge the Third Republic's Public Education for Girls: The Campaign for Equal Access to the Baccalaureate, 1880-1924." Paper presented to the American Historical Association. San Francisco. December 1973.

Pope, Barbara Corrado. "Maternal Education in France, 1815-1848." *Proceedings of the Third Annual Meeting of the Western Society for French History* 3 (4-6 December 1975), 368-77.

Smith, Hilda. "Feminism and the Methodology of Women's History." In *Liberating Women's History: Theoretical and Critical Essays*, edited by Berenice A. Carroll. Chicago: University of Illinois Press, 1976.

Sowerwine, Charles. "The Organization of French Socialist Women, 1880-1914: A European Perspective for Women's Movements." *Historical Reflections/Réflexions Historiques*, no. 2 (Winter 1976), 3-24.

————. "Socialism, Feminism, and Violence: The Analysis of Madeleine Pelletier." Paper presented to the Western Society for French History. Eugene, Oregon. October 1980.

Stephens, Winifred. "Women's Suffrage in France." *Living Age*, 301 (31 May 1919), 555-60.

Thomas, Edith. "The Women of the Commune." *Massachusetts Review* 12 (Summer 1971), 409-17.

Wilkins, Wynona H. "The Paris International Feminist Congress of 1896 and Its French Antecedents." *North Dakota Quarterly* 44, no. 4 (Autumn 1975), 5-28.

INDEX

ABOUT THE AUTHOR

Patrick Kay Bidelman, a historian, has taught at seven universities in France and the United States. Most recently he held the post of Visiting Assistant Professor of History at Purdue University. His articles have appeared in such publications as *Historical Reflections* and *Third Republic*.